Y0-BVN-055

Solzhenitsyn's
Political Thought

Solzhenitsyn's Political Thought

by James F. Pontuso

University Press of Virginia

Charlottesville and London

THE UNIVERSITY PRESS OF VIRGINIA
Copyright © 1990 by the Rectors and Visitors
of the University of Virginia

First published 1990
Design by Joanna Hill

Library of Congress Cataloging-in-Publication Data

Pontuso, James F.
  Solzhenitsyn's political thought / by James F. Pontuso.
    p. cm.
  Includes bibliographical references.
  ISBN 0-8139-1283-0
  1. Solzhenitsyn, Aleksandr Isaevich, 1918– Political and social
views. I. Title
PG3488.O4Z843   1990
891.73'44—DC20   90-34241
                                                                CIP

Printed in the United States of America

To my mother who lived to see it
and
my wife who worked to pay for it.

Contents

Acknowledgments

I would like to thank most especially James W. Ceaser for his time, wise counsel, and encouragement. It would take more than one lifetime to adequately repay his generosity. Steven Rhoads offered valuable advice during the final preparation of the manuscript. Inis Claude, Jr., helped me think through many important issues during the early stages of the project. Delba Winthrop, John Dunlop, Carolyn Moscatel, Randall Strahan, John Eastby, Robert Strong, William Connelly, Clyde Lutz, Mark Rozell, Dante Germino, J. Patrick Jones, Keith Fitch, and several anonymous readers offered excellent suggestions for revisions. I would like to thank John McGuigan and Cynthia H. Foote of the University Press of Virginia for their help in bringing this book to print. The Earhart Foundation provided financial assistance for revisions of the manuscript.

Sections of this book have been published previously in a somewhat revised form.

Parts of chapters VI and VII as: "Crisis of a World Split Apart: Solzhenitsyn on the West," *The Political Science Reviewer* 16 (Fall 1986): 185–236. Reprinted with permission.

Part of chapter V as: "Solzhenitsyn on Marx: The Problem of Love of One's Own," *Teaching Political Science: Politics in Perspective* 13, no. 3

(Spring 1986): 108–19. Reprinted with permission of the Helen Dwight Reid Educational Foundation. Published by Heldref Publications, 4000 Albemarle St., N.W., Washington, D.C. 20016.

Chapter II as: "On Solzhenitsyn's Stalin," *Survey* 29, no. 2 (Summer 1985): 46–69. Reprinted with permission.

Solzhenitsyn's
Political Thought

Introduction

Solzhenitsyn and the Soviet Union

During the era of *glasnost* under Mikhail Gorbachev a joke has circulated in the Soviet Union: future Soviet historians would recall Leonid Brezhnev as the backward party official who ruled during the era of the progressive dissidents, Andre Sakharov and Alexander Solzhenitsyn. Only someone schooled in the history of the Soviet Union as it was taught by the Communist party could fully appreciate the irony of elevating the Soviet state's most vilified enemies above the rank of its longtime leader.

The changes that have occurred in the Soviet Union under Gorbachev have perplexed and fascinated observers in the West. They have introduced a new ingredient in the debate about what the Soviet Union is and will become. Certainly, the reforms must cheer the harshest critic of the Soviet state, Alexander Solzhenitsyn.

During the 1970s and early 1980s Solzhenitsyn engaged in a spirited campaign to strengthen Western opposition to the Soviet Union and to undermine the credibility of the Soviet system. Solzhenitsyn pronouncements on East-West relations were so forceful that they served to frighten or dismay many people in the West. He painted a particularly grim picture of the challenge facing Western civilization. He argued that Communism was a cancer, which lived off the corpses of its victims and which was intent on sapping the strength of its adversaries and consuming the entire world with its deadly poison. Meanwhile, he maintained, the people of the West, only half awake to the menace, sat idly by, content to amuse themselves with consumer goods, the bright and happy baubles of a materialistic culture. Many Westerners abhorred the fact that bitter medicine was called for. They were anxious about the illness, but it was an anxiety born of having to remove a piece of one's own body. For them the best solution was to ignore the whole problem.

But just how serious is the Communist threat? How accurate is Solzhenitsyn in his assessment of the dangers to our way of life posed by Communism? Solzhenitsyn's remarks concerning East-West relations need to be scrutinized in terms of the changes that have occurred in the Communist world and in light of the past actions that Communist governments have taken.

Solzhenitsyn's views on Communism are derived from firsthand experience. It was in his homeland that Communism first came to power and proceeded to carry out one of the most, if not the most, brutal social upheavals in human history. It is often said that the Soviet terror was the work of particular individuals—Stalin and his henchmen—but Marx, in whose name those individuals acted, doubted that individuals have any control over history whatsoever. Indeed, he proposed that no matter what people do, history is driven in a particular direction by its own inner laws. History, Marx argued, is moving toward a culmination in which all people will be happy.

Solzhenitsyn's books are most often set in the Soviet Union, an avowedly Marxist nation, but there is little happiness to be found in them. There is, instead, unrelenting sorrow and nearly unspeakable evil. Could something have gone wrong with Marx's prediction? If so, who has caused things to go awry?

For Solzhenitsyn the Soviet Union's "deviation" from the ideals of Marx raises theoretical and practical problems concerning the validity of that doctrine. If individuals are at fault for having perverted Marx's teaching, then it must be admitted that Marx's philosophy of history, which dismisses the importance of human action in triggering significant events, is wrong. If, on the other hand, there is something about Marxism that gives rise to violent and even malicious actions by those under its influence, then the consequences are grave indeed. It means that those who truly dedicate themselves to Marxist doctrine are likely to become rash and brutal in their dealings with others. It also means, Solzhenitsyn stresses, that the challenge which faces the West has only partly to do with Soviet arms. A more important ingredient is the power of Marx's thought. In the past seventy years, many nations have been governed by rulers claiming loyalty to Marx's principles. Although these nations have had political differences among themselves, they have all been united in allegiance to a doctrine that has a record of making people commit appalling evil; an evil that by its very nature, Solzhenitsyn claims, poses a fundamental challenge to Western ideals.

In spite of their seeming failures, the principles of Marx have found some disciples and many more intellectual adherents of various sorts in the West. This is true, Solzhenitsyn maintains, because few people have been able to perceive the full truth about Marxism; its treachery has somehow been disguised. It was given to Solzhenitsyn to announce that truth, he claims, through a number of happenstance occurrences. He found himself wrongly thrown into the human disposal system of a Marxist nation. He managed to survive an ordeal that gave him a unique perspective on Marxist justice and that developed in him a grim determination to report what he had seen. He was blessed with memory, insight, and artistic skill, all of which made it possible for him to announce to the world the events he had experienced under Soviet rule. Finally, he had the good fortune to come to world prominence, and thus be protected by world opinion, during an uncharacteristic break in the total control that the Soviet government had exercised over the arts and letters for seventy years.

Still, one is led to wonder whether Solzhenitsyn should have spoken out so forcefully on political matters. He claims to be, first and foremost, an artist and only incidentally a political commentator. He says that he is not a political scientist. Can an artist ever attain the objectivity necessary to present a thoughtful examination of politics?

In Solzhenitsyn's case the answer is yes. His conscious intent has been to depict universal, and even timeless, truths about the relationship between politics and human life. Even those who are otherwise critical of his ideas, such as Ronald Berman, agree that, "Solzhenitsyn has insisted on making his ideas of culture and politics central to his work—in fact, they are the work itself. . . . His work matters to us because it is historically persuasive, because it seems true. . . . His great strength is understanding and depiction. His work has a unique ability to portray the relation between the individual and the state."[1]

Solzhenitsyn argues that the need for this kind of art is particularly urgent today. He explains that the skepticism of the age has led many to doubt whether there are universal and timeless truths of any kind. Moral relativism has become central to the modern understanding of the world; it is a doctrine that infects both East and West. It has undermined such concepts as Truth and Goodness. These ideas, if they are accepted at all, are seen as no more than personal preferences. Of course, the reverse is also true, for the concept of evil has lost its importance as a restraint on the human will. By proclaiming that people cannot know what is right, moral relativists have made it difficult for people to resist what is evil. Although adherents of moral relativism rarely have committed crimes against humanity themselves, their doctrine has established a principle by which all manner of acts, no matter how dastardly, can be justified as matters of individual or societal prerogative.

Solzhenitsyn claims that moral relativism has not, as yet, been able to overthrow the human attachment to Beauty. The beauty of art, he says, "prevails even over a resisting heart." His hope is that although "the overly straight sprouts of Truth and Goodness have been crushed, put down, or not permitted to grow . . . perhaps the whimsical, unpredictable, and ever surprising spheres of Beauty will force their way through and soar up to that very spot, thereby fulfilling the task of all three."[2]

But how can stories about cruelty and injustice be beautiful? At first, the answer is not easy to perceive. There is much suffering recorded in the pages of Solzhenitsyn's works, and it takes a certain amount of fortitude to complete them. Yet for all the misery he chronicles, Solzhenitsyn's writings are not a harbinger of despair. Those who survived the ordeal of life under Communist rule, those who withstood the test of fire, sometimes gained an independence of spirit and a command over their lives that is inspiring to behold. Although he writes of a great social illness, his heroes point the way to recovery.

Solzhenitsyn's political comments seem more strident than his artistic endeavors. Obviously, when they were pronounced, they were intended to get people's attention. However, he claims to enjoy isolation over public debate. In the late 1980s in particular he chose to lead the solitary existence of an artist engaged in completing his life's work. Yet "withdrawing from contemporary life is no easy matter," he says, "it scorches you on all sides." He has, therefore, succumbed to the "temptation" of making public statements.[3] One perceptive young critic writes of his predicament, "Solzhenitsyn is like a classical violinist who would rather redirect our thoughts toward the higher spheres of existence through the irrefutability and beauty of art, but finds himself in the unfortunate and perhaps uncomfortable role of the trumpetist, blasting out his message of warning against the growing shadow of evil."[4] Even in his political commentaries, where he has sometimes been given to overstatement, it is fair to say that Solzhenitsyn has not shot from the hip or rushed into thoughtless remarks. All he does, he claims, is done by plan. Included in that plan is a remark that "every true path is very hard to follow."[5]

Solzhenitsyn's work presents a number of difficult problems for the interpreter. First, Solzhenitsyn is an artist, and artists oftentimes take liberties with the facts in order to present their ideas with clarity and force. The reader of artistic works (especially the historical novels of the type Solzhenitsyn writes) both gains and loses from the artist's technique. The accuracy of historical events may be altered for dramatic effect, and the reader who is unaware of the change may be led astray. On the other hand, a great artist may be able to pierce through the jumble of facts and uncover the deeper meaning of events. Strictly speaking, the artist may have altered the facts, but he has done so to convey the truth that he has apprehended from the mysterious tangle of day-to-day occurrences. Happily for Solzhenitsyn's readers in *The Gulag Archipelago* (his most "historical" book, where his most thoroughgoing attack on Marxism is found), he insists that "there are no fictitious persons nor fictitious events, . . . it all took place just as it is here described."[6]

Another problem of interpretation, perhaps a more serious one, arises because of Solzhenitsyn's treatment at the hands of the Soviet government. It is well known, as the Soviets say, that Solzhenitsyn was arrested and spent a number of years in the forced-labor camps (Gulag), that he suffered greatly during his imprisonment, and that, upon his release, he became a renowned dissident and a tenacious foe of the Soviet authorities. His readers are compelled to wonder whether his personal experiences have not biased his professional judgment as a writer. Is he so bitter that he has reported rumor and innuendo as truth? Has he fabricated stories or taken liberties with the facts as a way of throwing the worst possible light on his hated enemy, the Soviet government?

Such charges become even more serious when Solzhenitsyn's chronicle of events is compared to the more traditional histories of the Soviet Union. Although he makes no claim to the title of historian, he does insist that the dimmer picture of life under Soviet rule that he paints is more accurate than that presented by most Western scholars. In particular, they have been more measured in their criticisms of Soviet practices and less willing to endorse the more outlandish statements of Soviet oppression. For example, Solzhenitsyn has presented higher estimates of those imprisoned or executed by the Soviet government than the numbers accepted by most Western commentators. Who is correct: Solzhenitsyn or the more traditional historians?

Perhaps no fully satisfactory answer to that question is possible. However, one can make a beginning by asking: What is history? Put simply, history is a record of events that happened in the past. Our understanding of the true nature of events depends on the accuracy of the record. A historical record is composed of eyewitness recollections, either verbal or written; press reports, themselves dependent on eyewitness recollections or on the stories of reporters who happened to be on the scene; and public documents, such as laws, speeches, transcripts of trials, birth and death certificates, etc.

Solzhenitsyn maintains that compiling an accurate history of the Soviet Union using the normal sources of research has been all but impossible. First, he argues that public documents, such as those dealing with the number of people held in the camps or the average citizen's standard of living, were falsified to make conditions seem better than they were. Second, he claims that virtually everything in the Soviet Union was kept secret. It has been far more closed than even the worst non-Communist tyrannies. For most of its history, the press has been controlled; indeed, it has been run by the very same group that governs the nation. Literature has been stifled, especially works of art critical of the state. Even freedom of speech, both in public and in private, has been curtailed. Those who let their differences with government policy be known have been continually hounded and often have found themselves under arrest.

He argues that truthful eyewitness accounts have been difficult to obtain. People have been frightened of reprisals from the ever-present secret police. Furthermore, there has been a particular problem in documenting the most egregious instances of Soviet brutality. Solzhenitsyn explains that there was an unwritten law of the Gulag that held that those who have suffered the most did not live to tell their tale. For obvious reasons, a government that proclaimed itself to be the profoundest expression of human justice did not want stories of its cruelty to be aired in public; better to bury such stories where they could never be heard.[7]

Solzhenitsyn explains, moreover, that even when eyewitnesses have emerged from the Soviet grip, their stories have seemed too fantastic to be believed. He writes, "Most people in the West receive either falsified news [about the Soviet Union] or none at all. Complete information is available only to the Westerners who have spent time in Soviet prisons—and not just fifteen days but fifteen years. But when such people arrive in the West, their testimony seems so wildly improbable that no one believes them."[8]

Solzhenitsyn depends for his history of Soviet rule on what he took away from the Gulag "on the skin of [his] back," on what he learned with his "eyes and ears," and on "reports, memoirs, and letters by 227 witnesses." Further materials were provided by certain Communist party officials who, "despite their intent and against their will," inadvertently aided Solzhenitsyn in recreating events because they saw fit to commit their deeds to writing. Finally, he depends on the books of "thirty-six Soviet writers, headed by Maxim Gorky."[9]

Although Solzhenitsyn's familiarity with Soviet history is undeniable, his research has obviously not led him to survey the entire literature on that topic.[10] Yet he maintains that his record of events is less distorted than others because he actually lived in the Soviet Union, he was an inmate in the camps—the one place, he says, where Soviet citizens are truly free to speak their mind—and upon his release, he became a prominent public figure who refused to bend to the government's pressure. His reputation for implacability made it possible for him to gather information from people who might otherwise have remained silent.

Stating Solzhenitsyn's position brings us no closer to establishing the accuracy of his account. Yet three factors give credence to Solzhenitsyn's exposition. First, he is not the only dissident to expose brutality within a Communist nation. Indeed, there is a striking similarity in the testimony given by all those who have opposed their Communist rulers. Again and again witnesses have recounted horrifying tales of oppression and mass murder.[11] Although these exposés were known to Western scholars, they were thought merely to be peripheral events and not essential to comprehending the true nature of Communist nations.[12] For Solzhenitsyn and the other dissidents, however, these incidents are so widespread and commonplace that they must be considered an intrinsic element of Communist rule.

Second, Solzhenitsyn's presentation of Soviet history is so compelling and so forcefully argued that it has altered the views of many Western scholars. While Solzhenitsyn's influence has been most pronounced in France, his exposition of the Soviet terror also has come to be accepted in most Western nations by people of almost every political stripe.[13] Although this approval does little to prove the credibility of Solzhenitsyn's account, it does indicate that once the facts of Soviet life were revealed in a comprehensive way, scholars were compelled to seek new sources of information. Many in the West have come to acknowledge that the Soviet government and media, as well as its academics, have been engaged in a massive cover-up and that the cloak of secrecy hanging over Soviet life can be lifted only by turning to the dissident writings. The term *Gulag*, a word that even sounds sinister, has come to replace *concentration camp* in the popular vernacular.

Finally, during the period of *glasnost,* the Soviets themselves began to acknowledge the horrors that took place in their country. Articles were published in the Soviet press condemning the crimes of Stalin and, more importantly, implicating Lenin in the misdeeds of the past.[14] As the Communist governments of Eastern Europe have fallen, the dark secrets of how the rulers maintained power have come to light.

There is no doubt that serious students of Communism or of the Soviet Union should not take everything that Solzhenitsyn says as gospel. Yet it is fair to assume, given the constraints imposed by the rulers, that his assessment of Soviet history, relying as it does on eyewitness experience, is at least as accurate as any other. It may be, as Solzhenitsyn concedes, that he has not been able to tell the whole story, but it is just as true that no other scholar can lay greater claim to the truth. If for no other reason than that, Solzhenitsyn's exposition of Soviet history deserves serious consideration.

One final difficulty presents itself to those who wish to understand Solzhenitsyn's views. His argument does not seem to take account of the changes that took place in the Soviet Union and elsewhere in the Communist world during the leadership of Gorbachev. Solzhenitsyn has said that Communism cannot be transformed by its own rulers; it must be totally overthrown by resistance from within. Yet the reign of Gorbachev did bring about some improvements within the Soviet Union and the liberation of most of Eastern Europe. Does this mean that Solzhenitsyn's analysis of Communism is faulty? If so, what factors account for his failure to predict a loosening of the reins?

Solzhenitsyn traces the ailments of the Soviet regime to the ideology on which it rests. He argues that it was the attempt to put the ideas of Marx into practice which made all the suffering that the Soviet Union has undergone inevitable. Indeed, in his public pronouncements, he predicted that only when the Soviet leaders abandoned their commitment to Marxism could true change take place. The improvements that did occur when Gorbachev took command were, in a way, Solzhenitsyn's most prophetic judgment, for only by defecting from the dogmas of Marxism was change within the Soviet Union possible. Furthermore, Solzhenitsyn did more than any other person alive to discredit the Soviet Union, both its practices and its doctrines. His writings undermined the legitimacy of the Soviet state and thereby turned Western public opinion hostile to the Soviet system. The worldwide condemnation of the Soviet Union's policies further weakened an already fragile political and economic system, causing its leadership to take stock and to engage in some new thinking. It is possible that the very animosity that Solzhenitsyn generated against his former rulers was responsible for the leadership altering its attitudes. Thus, Solzhenitsyn may be the source of his own incorrect predictions.

Solzhenitsyn and the West

Although Solzhenitsyn's interpretation of the politics of the East has been controversial, that dispute cannot compare to the storm of protest touched off by his remarks on the West. Even his mostly sympathetic biographer notes, "where Solzhenitsyn seemed to have the power and talent to measure up to his Russian mission, in the West he appeared to be overreaching himself, and among those not swayed by his charm, authority, and charisma, a sense of disillusionment began to be perceptible."[15]

The usual charge leveled against Solzhenitsyn's views of the West holds that his Russian nationalism makes it impossible for him to grasp an open, pluralistic society. It is said that neither his former life in the Soviet Union nor his reclusive existence at his home in Vermont has prepared him for the vitality and freedom of democratic societies. Some commentators go so far as to claim that he is confused and perhaps even irresponsible in his attacks on the Western way of life. At the very least, many agree, Solzhenitsyn is guilty of ingratitude, for it was pressure from the West that kept him from a Soviet prison in the early 1970s, and it is the very freedom of the West that he so derides that allows him to express his creative insights.[16]

What puzzles critics of Solzhenitsyn the most is that he finds fault with both East and West. They seem to maintain that there are truly only two models of political organization: pluralistic societies, which leave their citizens free to decide how they should live, and authoritarian regimes—be they of the left or right—which attempt to mold people into predetermined patterns. By berating the West, his critics charge, Solzhenitsyn has placed himself in the same camp as his hated enemies, those who rule over the East.

This book argues that Solzhenitsyn's views on the West are neither inconsistent nor unappreciative. Quite the contrary, his principles derive from a deep understanding of the philosophic roots of Western culture. Moreover, Solzhenitsyn's criticism is not meant to undermine the resolve of the West, but rather to restore its highest principles and aspirations. It is exactly because Solzhenitsyn admires what is noble in Western life that he has spent so much effort in trying to warn the present-day West about its shortcomings. It is also important to note that Solzhenitsyn sees an intimate connection between the doctrines of Marx and those of the political philosophy underpinning the West—liberalism. Both doctrines, he says, grew out of a desire to satisfy the needs of the body and neglected to fulfill the requirements of the soul.

Perhaps the source of the confusion about Solzhenitsyn's thought is that his principles cannot be traced to the contemporary East, the contemporary West, or even to Russian nationalism, as is so often claimed. Rather, his views are informed by an often neglected tradition of Western thought which argues that human beings are capable of deciding right from wrong, noble from base, and just from unjust. Our capacity to reason makes such judgments possible. For example, we need not accept every form of expression, no matter how degrading, in order to protect our liberty. Instead, we can use our freedom wisely by putting laws into effect that, while not endeavoring to tyrannize over every aspect of our lives, point us in the direction of what is proper and fitting for members of a civilized society. Nor need the task of providing for our material well-being necessarily result in our throwing ourselves into an unending pursuit of wealth. Perhaps the clearest message of Solzhenitsyn's work is that the quest for freedom and security, although they are important objects in life, must be put to the service of some higher, spiritual end if life is to have meaning and importance.

CHAPTER I

A Chronicle of Terror

Scattered Incidents

During the harvest season of 1932 six collective farmers from an area called Tsarskoye Selo in the Soviet Union spent the day mowing hay. After completing their work for the collective, they went back to the fields and mowed a second time along the stubs to get a little feed for their own cows. Under the Soviet law of that time the six were arrested, tried, and convicted of banditry—stealing from the state. The sentence was carried out, and all six were shot. Commenting on the incident Solzhenitsyn writes, "Even if Stalin had killed no others, I believe he deserved to be drawn and quartered just for the lives of those six Tsarskoye Selo peasants!"[1]

If only that were all. Perhaps, if the Soviet Union had committed only this one act of cruelty it justly could have donned the mantle of leadership for progressive mankind, a role that, given its Marxist principles, it claimed for seventy years. Regrettably, Solzhenitsyn tells us, this incident is not unique in Soviet history. It is but one example of inhumanity among countless others—a mere snowflake in a blizzard of terror.

The extent of the terror can be seen in its sheer magnitude. Using the analysis of former Leningrad Professor of Statistics I. A. Kurganov, Solzhenitsyn estimates that sixty-six million people have been killed at the hand of the Soviet state.² No government, not even the widely accepted archetype of evil, Nazi Germany, has so much brutality to justify.

Numbers, of course, cannot tell the whole story. They can never convey the personal anguish of those who suffered or the arbitrariness of the state's violence. Solzhenitsyn's art brings to life the human tragedy of political terror; it puts flesh on the skeletons in the Soviet Union's past. The recounting of particular incidents is, for Solzhenitsyn, more than a simple narrative of evil. These injustices have formed his ideas; they stand as his evidence and accusation against the Soviet state and against all Communist governments. What follows is Solzhenitsyn's description of life under the heavy hand of Soviet rule.

At the height of the party purges in 1937 a district party conference met in Moscow. Presiding was the newly appointed secretary for the district party, replacing the one recently arrested. At the meeting's conclusion the customary tribute to Comrade Stalin was offered. All jumped to their feet to hail the Great Leader with "stormy applause, rising to an ovation." But after ten minutes the clapping had not ceased. Although their hands were aching, no one wanted to be the first to stop the adulation. Finally, one party member surmounted his fear and sat down; relieved, the rest quickly followed. That night the man was arrested on some trumped-up charges. He was given a ten year sentence, but during his final interrogation he was reminded: "Don't ever be the first to stop applauding!" Solzhenitsyn comments, "Now that's what Darwin's natural selection is. And that's also how to grind people down with stupidity."³

A tailor stuck his needle into a newspaper so that it would not get lost. It happened to stick in the eye of a picture of a high party official. A customer observed this: the tailor received a ten-year sentence for terrorism.⁴

Since no other paper was available, a saleswoman scribbled down a note on a piece of newspaper. Some of the writing covered a picture of Stalin. She was given ten years.⁵

A tractor driver used a pamphlet about candidates for the Supreme Soviet to fill the hole in the sole of his shoe. When the person responsible for the pamphlets noticed one missing, she found out who had it. The man was given ten years for counterrevolutionary activity.⁶

An old night watchman was sent to retrieve a bust of Stalin, but he found the statue too heavy to carry. Finally, he figured out that if he slung his belt around the bust's neck, he could barely manage to transport the load through his village. It was an open-and-shut case: ten years for terrorism.[7]

Maksimov, a fellow Solzhenitsyn met in the camps, was given eight years for praising German equipment. His criminal act arose from a speech he was asked to give to rally the troops for a winter offensive against the German invaders. Maksimov said, "We have to drive him out, the bastard, while the storms are raging, while he has no felt boots, even though we ourselves have ordinary shoes on now and then. But in the spring it's going to be worse because of his equipment."[8]

In 1950 some schoolchildren wrote and circulated the following letter, "Listen workers! Are we really living the kind of life for which our grandfathers, fathers, and brothers fought? We work—and get only a pitiful pittance in return, and they even cut down on that too. Read this and think about your life."[9] Since anyone over twelve years old could be tried as an adult, they were all given ten-year sentences.

In 1941 many of those who stayed in Moscow and armed themselves to resist the Nazi onslaught were arrested once the danger had passed. For their courage they were denounced as enemy sympathizers who had waited for the Germans to arrive. Their accusers were none other than the party and government officials who had fled in panic.[10]

During and after World War II any Soviet soldiers captured by the Germans were considered spies against their homeland. Upon their liberation they were moved from the harsh life of Nazi concentration camps to the somewhat harsher life of Soviet forced-labor camps.[11]

All of these incidents occurred during the Stalinist era, a time well known for its cruelty and injustice. Yet Solzhenitsyn takes great pains to point out that although the terror reached its zenith under Stalin, he did not institute the machinery of state-sponsored violence, nor did his death bring an end to political oppression.

For example, in 1922 Tanya Khodkevich was arrested because she wrote these lines to her children, "You can pray freely. But just so long as God alone can hear." The Soviet tribunal before which she was tried acknowledged her right to self-expression; after all, the revolution had liberated people. Nonetheless, it sentenced her to ten years hard labor for sharing the verses with her children. Evidently, the judge's rationale was that one could voice one's deeply held religious beliefs, but not so that anyone could hear—especially one's children.[12]

In the same year a trial was held for the metropolitan of the Russian Orthodox church. There was nothing unusual in this, given the sentiment of the party, as presented at the trial by People's Commissariat of Justice Krasikov. He explained, "The whole church [is] a subversive organization. Properly speaking, the entire church ought to be put in prison." The proceedings were not a model of judicial impartiality. The defense attorney was continually threatened with arrest for pointing out that, "There are no proofs of guilt. There are no facts. There is not even an indictment."[13] Despite what seemed to be convincing arguments in his favor, the church leader was convicted. The defense attorney only escaped imprisonment by allowing his gold watch to be expropriated. A witness for the defense was not so lucky. Professor Yegorov was summarily arrested after he had given evidence supporting the metropolitan. Not all was lost, however; Yegorov, well aware of Soviet jurisprudence, had packed a bag.

From the beginning days of the revolution in 1918 and for most of the period of Lenin's rule, the Cheka, Soviet security police, shot more than one thousand people per month. These officially documented executions do not include those nameless thousands who, with Lenin's approval, were sunk on barges.[14]

In 1962, during the reign of Khrushchev, the entire town of Novocherkassk rose up in a general strike to protest simultaneous, but unrelated, economic directives that lowered piecework rates at the same time they increased food prices, resulting in a 30 percent drop in the workers' standard of living. After some street demonstrations in front of party headquarters, soldiers fired on the protesters until "puddles of blood were . . . formed in the depressions of the pavements."[15] Still the people of Novocherkassk did not surrender. All evening they stayed in the streets demanding to see the member of the Central Committee, Mikoyan, who had arrived on the scene. Finally, an audience was granted to a group of workers, where it was decided that those responsible for the shootings would be punished and that the local party organization would be investigated.

The next day Mikoyan was on the radio announcing that peace had been restored. The agents provocateurs and enemies of the state who had begun the disruption and who had fired into the crowd were now safely in custody, he assured the listeners. In reality, the authorities had arrested all the workers who had met with the local party committee. The dead and wounded simply disappeared, and, so that no one would protest, their families were deported to Siberia. None of these events was ever reported in the Soviet or Western media.[16]

These incidents have been reported to give the flavor of Solzhenitsyn's life and times. One could go on with such tales for volumes, as Solzhenitsyn does, but that too would reveal only the tip of the iceberg. What of those who are still too frightened to divulge their stories? What of those who suffered the worst? The dead can tell no tales. A fuller understanding of Soviet terror requires a broader view. Solzhenitsyn's account of life in the gristmill of socialist justice provides an insight into the nature of the Soviet regime.[17]

Soviet Law

Solzhenitsyn's research has led him to believe that during the Russian Revolution the Cheka was given almost unlimited authority to thwart the enemies of the newly established socialist state. In many ways it was a unique institution, since it combined the powers of investigation, arrest, interrogation, trial, and execution of sentence. It is not surprising that a harsh and uncompromising force was necessary to secure order, peace, and, of course, a Bolshevik victory during the turbulence of the revolution and the violence of the civil war. Certainly Lenin did not hesitate to call for such measures as would secure his ends. Solzhenitsyn quotes the following letter that Lenin wrote to the head of the Cheka:

> I am sending you an outline . . . of the Criminal Code. . . . The basic concept . . . is . . . openly to set forth . . . the motivation . . . and the justification for terror, its necessity, its limits.
> The court must not exclude terror. It would be self-deception or deceit to promise this, and in order to . . . legalize it . . . it is necessary to formulate it as broadly as possible, for only revolutionary righteousness and revolutionary conscience will provide the conditions for applying it more or less broadly in practice.[18]

As is the case in many violent upheavals, the Bolshevik terror did not cease once the revolution had been secured. Quite the contrary, Solzhenitsyn argues, once the civil war had ended the Cheka was ordered to intensify its repression of the bourgeoisie. The violence was not undertaken to quell civil unrest, but grew out of an ideological commitment to overturn the order of society. The revolutionaries saw their enemies among the middle class, those who would normally be considered law-abiding citizens. Lenin announced that a common, unifying purpose of the new revolutionary order was "to purge the Russian land of all kinds of harmful insects." The insects were, of course, those born to the wrong families, i.e., "class enemies." This group also included "workers malingering at their work" and "saboteurs who call themselves intellectuals."[19]

Looking back now it seems as if the new government was bent on smashing the will of its own citizens—if need be, by destroying millions of people. Wave after wave were arrested and punished under various pretexts. No summary could be complete. It would not begin to tell of the numberless groups of people rounded up: the "wreckers," the "centers," the counterrevolutionaries. Nor does it tell of the millions incarcerated for individual reasons. Since the Cheka (later to be universally known by it various acronyms MGB-NKVD-KGB) has always conducted its business in absolute secrecy, it is impossible to know what prompted it to go after one person, while leaving another alone.[20]

In addition to those who found themselves members of an outlawed group or those who expressed any doubt whatsoever about the infallibility of Soviet rule, Solzhenitsyn reports that many people were arrested because someone denounced them. The practice was universally accepted by the police (the Organs as they called themselves) as sufficient grounds for arrest and usually conviction. In reality, Solzhenitsyn explains, squealing on others to the Organs, an act invariably carried out in secret, often was done for personal gain, to obtain the position of a higher-up or as a way of keeping oneself out of trouble. The arrested were rarely confronted by their accusers. They were simply picked up by the Organs and tortured into confessing some imaginary crimes. Often they were made to implicate others in their "plot," as the circle of those in jail widened.

What is most surprising about the practices of Soviet justice, according to Solzhenitsyn—who bases his claim on extensive conversations with his fellow prisoners during his incarceration and after his release—is that almost all of those arrested were innocent, not only of any crime, but of any political activity whatsoever. Despite the severity of Communist rule, he holds that very few people actively contemplated its overthrow and even fewer took steps to that end. There were differences among the ruling group, of course, but this would account for only hundreds—at most thousands—of the millions made to suffer. Certainly, he speculates, such a phenomenon is unique in human history; millions of a nation's own citizens put in camps or shot for no apparent reason.[21]

To say that people were apprehended for no reason may seem an extreme statement. Solzhenitsyn presents the following examples. One woman went into NKVD headquarters to ask what to do with the unweaned infant of a neighbor who had just been taken into custody. She waited for two hours, whereupon she was thrown into a cell and later given a sentence. Solzhenitsyn presumes that the NKVD had not met its quota and needed a body. A judge was arrested after a judicial proceeding in which he opposed the sentence proposed by the state prosecutor. One fellow ran afoul of the law by claiming that highways in the United States were paved. Some engineers were jailed as wreckers—a term employed to place blame on evildoers for the failed economy—who took an "anti-Soviet" line concerning the physical properties of metals.[22] Enough.

Along with the usual humiliation of arrest, prisoners faced a grueling interrogation at the hands of the Organs. Most perplexing about the ordeal was that the interrogators did not really want to uncover the truth. The actual purpose of interrogation, Solzhenitsyn explains, was to wrench a confession from the accused so as to justify the anonymous denunciation. Prisoners were also coaxed into implicating others so that the Organs could fabricate new cases, thereby justifying their own power and privilege.

How were confessions obtained? Solzhenitsyn reports that a variety of ingenious methods were used. They ranged from trying to persuade ("You are going to get a prison term anyway, so why not make it easy on yourself?") to screaming threats, confusing prisoners by night interrogations, playing on family affections, tickling, extinguishing lit cigarettes on the skin, employing bright lights or loud noises, beating people, stuffing them into boxes, throwing them into latrine pits, forcing prisoners to stand still or kneel or sit on backless benches for days, denying them sleep, food, and water, leaving them in cells infested with lice or insects, squeezing off their fingernails, bridling them by binding their hands and feet together behind their backs, or breaking their backs.[23]

Solzhenitsyn calls interrogation the evil of the Middle Ages magnified by science. Many brave people did not survive the ordeal because they would not implicate their friends or family. By refusing to submit, such people gained nothing in this life, except perhaps their personal integrity. They perished alone, their strength of character unacknowledged, except as a minor annoyance to their interrogators; their gallantry unrewarded by the honor it deserved. Solzhenitsyn explains that the interrogation was the first great divider of souls. The weak and the average yielded and were more likely to be spared, while the best people were singled out for destruction by their acts of resistance. Yet he does not condemn those who made confessions. Faced with the well-fed energy of the Organs, it is little wonder that most could not withstand the secret police's onslaught. Those who have never found themselves in an utterly hopeless situation, he reminds his readers, should not cast stones at those who have.[24]

Since in most cases interrogation resulted in a confession, the outcome of the trial was predetermined. Yet there were other reasons why those standing before socialist judges had little chance of receiving a fair hearing, Solzhenitsyn explains. First, most courts were closed and their proceedings kept secret; thus, they could be conducted in any manner the state saw fit. Second, there was no separation between the investigative and the judicial organs of government (nor generally between the executive and the judicial departments of government). Nicholai Krylenko, once chief prosecutor for the Soviet Union before his own downfall at the hands of Stalin, explained that the All-Russian Central Executive Committee "pardons and punishes at its own discretion without any limitation whatever," which, he concluded, "shows the superiority of our system over the false theory of separation of powers." Yakov Sverdlov, the committee's chairman, added, "It is very good that the legislative and executive powers are not divided by a thick wall as they are in the West. All problems can be decided quickly." For example, Solzhenitsyn explains that a judge could change a ruling—over the telephone if need be, and invariably to give a tougher sentence—six months to ten years after the original decision had been handed down.[25]

Third, socialist law was not fixed. It could be changed from case to case according to the circumstances. Solzhenitsyn again quotes Krylenko, "Don't tell me our criminal courts ought to act exclusively on the basis of existing written norms. We live in the process of Revolution. . . . We are creating a new law and a new ethical code. . . . No matter how much is said here about the eternal law of truth, etc., we know . . . how dearly these have cost us." The purpose of judicial proceedings was not to discover the truth or to insure that justice be done, but to further the political aims of the government. Hence, Krylenko commented that Soviet tribunals were "at one and the same time both the creator of the law . . . and a political weapon."[26]

The political weapon of socialist justice could be effective only if a new sort of guilt or innocence were introduced into the courtroom. Krylenko reasoned, "A tribunal is an organ of the class struggle of the workers directed against their enemies [and must act] from the point of view of the interests of the revolution, . . . having in mind the most desirable results for the masses. . . . No matter what the individual qualities [of the defendant], only one method of evaluating him is to be applied: evaluation from the point of view of class expediency."[27]

Solzhenitsyn points out that defendants, finding themselves "inexpedient," had virtually no chance of proving their innocence. Again he quotes Krylenko, who explained that if "this expediency should require that the avenging sword should fall on the head of the defendants, then no . . . verbal arguments can help." Guilt could even be applied to the offenses that a person *might* commit. As Krylenko put it, "We protect ourselves not only against the past but also against the future."[28] As we shall see in a later chapter, Solzhenitsyn traces the tyrannical nature of socialist justice to Marxist roots. According to Marx, as history changes, so do notions of right and wrong, and of just and unjust. The concept of justice may recur, but its content varies according to the ruling group that defines it. The only true permanence in history is that change does occur and that it will eventually bring the socialist era into being. Whatever aids in that endeavor is just; whatever hinders it is unjust. Marxism provides an excuse for doing whatever one wants and calling it lawful.[29]

Fourth, even when there were laws protecting those on trial or in prison, no one paid attention to them. Solzhenitsyn tells of many instances in which both captive and captor alike were surprised when confronted with an actual Soviet statute.[30]

Finally, the law was all-inclusive; it covered every possible human activity, even thought. "In truth," Solzhenitsyn writes, "there is no step, thought, action, or lack of action under heaven which could not be punished by the heavy hand" of Soviet law.[31]

The absolute character of Soviet law originated in the sweeping Article 58 of the Criminal Code. Drafted by Lenin as a way of making any form of opposition illegal, the code was adopted in 1926. Once the draft had hardened into law, citizens could be imprisoned under Article 58 for:

"Anti-Soviet Agitation, Counter-Revolutionary Activity, Counter-Revolutionary Trotskyite Activity, Suspicion of Espionage, Contacts Leading to Suspicion of Espionage, Counter-Revolutionary Thought, Dissemination of Anti-Soviet Sentiments, Socially Dangerous Element, Criminal Activity [unspecified], Member of a Family (of a person convicted under one of the foregoing categories)."[32]

As if the parameters of Article 58 were not broad enough, the authorities insisted on giving its statutes the widest possible interpretation. For example, Solzhenitsyn points out that people actually did not have to commit a crime to be prosecuted, they only had to intend the commission of an offense. As Krylenko said, whether the deed "was carried out or not has no essential significance." The effect of the law was to make intent identical with action, causing Solzhenitsyn to remark, "Whether a man whispered to his wife in bed that it would be a good thing to overthrow the Soviet government or whether he engaged in propaganda during an election or threw a bomb, it was all one and the same! And the punishment was identical!!!"[33]

Life on the Inside

Needless to say, most people who stood before Soviet courts found themselves in prison. Solzhenitsyn distinguishes those in prison according to their offenses. There were the politicals, usually convicted under one of the provisions of Article 58, and the thieves, incarcerated for the crimes punished by every society, i.e., murder, theft, robbery, etc. The sentence given to thieves varied according to the crime, as it did for politicals during the early years of the revolution. However, by the mid-1920s the term for politicals was increased and made a standard length, eight to ten years (usually ten) of forced labor. When the death penalty was abolished after World War II, the standard sentence was made twenty-five years.[34]

Of the number who received the supreme measure, as a shot in the back of the head was called, only rumor survives. Solzhenitsyn estimates that between 1 and 1.7 million people were disposed of in this way. He reports that the NKVD men who were swept into prison in the downfall of state security chief Yezhov boasted that .5 million had been killed in 1937–38 alone.[35]

After receiving their sentence, the vast majority of prisoners were sent

to toil in what the party called corrective labor camps and what Solzhenitsyn calls, in a play on words, destructive labor camps. He argues that
since Marx contends that man is constituted by labor, it is little wonder
that the state turned to labor as a way of disposing of its outcasts. The
rationale was to reform—or to reforge, in Soviet parlance—the wayward
through physical labor. As the party tightened its control over the population, the forced-labor camps, the Gulag, quickly grew. Solzhenitsyn estimates that at their peak, the camps held perhaps one-fifth of the Soviet
population. Everyone in the nation was affected, since virtually all had
family or friends serving a sentence. Vast islands of prisoners cropped up
in even the harshest and remotest regions of the Soviet Union, until, as
Solzhenitsyn suggests, the inhabitants of the Gulag, united by the cruelty
of their overlords, became a nation of slaves within their own country.[36]

Great convoys of prisoners lumbered between the many camps, deliv-
ering the convicted to serve their sentences. Prisoners were often stacked
hundreds to a railroad car so that they were unable to move, or even to
relieve themselves. Without proper food, ventilation, or sanitation, many
did not survive the ordeal.[37] When the rigorous journey was at its end,
zeks, the name given Soviet prisoners, reached their final destination, the
forced-labor camps. A major theme of Solzhenitsyn's work is an account
of the nature of these camps and a recollection of their history. He relates the story of the first camp on Soloveysky Island in the White Sea,
and explains how that experiment spread, cancerlike, until its evil encompassed the entire nation. In fact, he maintains that the Gulag was,
and continued to be for seventy years, an integral part of the Soviet
system.[38]

Conditions in the camps, he reports, were unbelievably harsh. Only
those jobs that no one else would perform were given to the zeks. They
were expected to labor at the most physically exhausting tasks without
the necessary means of survival. Their daily ration of food consisted of
soup or gruel and fourteen ounces of wet black bread. Even this meager
portion could be cut if zeks did not complete their work norm. They were
rarely issued the proper attire to protect themselves against inclement
weather. Some zeks were even forced to work in the bitter cold of Siberia
wearing the same clothes in which they had been arrested the previous
summer. Knowledgeable zeks never gave up their heavy coats and winter
boots, even on the hottest days. They knew that clothing which wore out
or was lost might not be replaced and that Arctic winters without such

apparel were lethal. Zeks lived in cold, insect-infested barracks that, for security reasons, cramped many prisoners together. They labored without the proper equipment. But, of course, this was the point. Since the nation could not afford to build factories that produced labor-saving devices, it turned to labor-intensive methods of building the economy. In theory the trade-off does not seem so bad, but to the zeks who, among other things, were made to dig vast canals out of the frozen tundra, using only picks and shovels, the exchange was a less than satisfactory one. The life of the zeks, says Solzhenitsyn, "Consists of work, work, work; of starvation, cold, and cunning. This work, for those who are unable to push others out of the way and set themselves up in a soft spot, is that self-same general work which raises socialism up out of the earth, and drives us down into the earth." [39]

In order to build socialism, zeks mined gold in regions above the Arctic Circle (the bitter cold froze most of them to death), toiled in copper mines (the dust was lethal within a year), cut and hauled timber by hand out of the vast Russian forest (the exertion needed to meet the work norms on which food was rationed killed most people), and labored at other miserable and dangerous jobs that the authorities threw at them. Marx may have reasoned that labor had made the species human, but Solzhenitsyn concludes that the labor which zeks were made to perform made most of them into corpses. [40]

Not only did zeks have to contend with backbreaking labor and a harsh environment, man-made cruelty served to make their lives even more miserable. First, explains Solzhenitsyn, they were organized into work brigades. Ostensibly, the brigades were a way of showing socialist solidarity among the workers. In reality, they were a means of coercion, since the entire brigade was given a work norm, that, if not reached, resulted in the group receiving short rations. Needless to say, such an organization created enormous social pressure on every individual to meet the quota. [41]

Second, the work norms were set so inhumanly high that the extra rations awarded if the goal was met did not compensate the worker for the energy expended: a method intended to drive the always-hungry prisoners to toil by dangling food in front of them. The goal was to extract the maximum amount of labor at the minimum cost (except in human lives, of course). Under such conditions people were reduced to the lowest level of humanity, acting purely on the basis of their hunger. Solzhenitsyn explains:

> Your mind is absorbed in vain calculations which for the present cut you off from the heavens—and tomorrow are worth nothing. You *hate* labor—it is your principal enemy. You hate companions—rivals in life and death. You are reduced to a frazzle by intense *envy* and alarm lest somewhere behind your back others are right now dividing up that bread which could be yours, that somewhere on the other side of the wall a tiny potato is being ladled out of the pot which could have ended up in your bowl.[42]

Third, the guards were given complete power over prisoners. They could and sometimes did shoot zeks for fun or when an individual chanced to step out of a marching line. They were never punished for their actions. Beatings and torture were common. Already dehumanized by their training, guards looked on the prisoners shuffling before them in pitiful lines as some sort of diseased animals. All this was planned, reasons Solzhenitsyn. The goal was to leave zeks with no wills of their own and to make their every action, no matter how minute, dependent on the guards. Racked by hunger and terrorized by their wardens, zeks had little choice but to obey.[43]

Fourth, there were informers (stool pigeons, Solzhenitsyn calls them) everywhere. Every action, lack of action, or conversation that might even vaguely present a threat to the authorities was reported to them by informers. The zeks' lives were made all the more abject by the danger they faced in making the slightest whisper of a complaint. Every moment of their existence, they had to be watchful that someone was not spying on them. As for the stool pigeons, their lives were no less miserable, perhaps, but they received extra rations for their secret dispatches.[44]

Fifth, trustees, who performed the easiest and most desirable jobs in the camps, stole from their fellow prisoners. For example, Solzhenitsyn explains that zeks assigned to kitchen duty ate food allotted for the whole camp. Since there was rarely enough food to go around and since a short ration meant certain death for those working at hard labor, the good fortune of the trustees rested on the corpses of their campmates.

Trustees got their favored positions by performing some service for the guards. Stool pigeons traded information, women exchanged sex, and the thieves bartered anything they could pillage from the packages sent by the families of the hapless politicals.[45]

Finally, as if everything else were not enough, the political prisoners were victimized by the thieves. Bands of thieves, joined together by the rules of their criminal code, continually badgered and bullied the unorganized politicals, frightening them into handing over their meager possessions. Both in and out of prison, thieves preyed upon innocent and law-abiding people, whose virtue and honesty they disdained as gullible foolishness. The thieves' code consisted of little more than debauchery and the satisfaction of immediate physical desires—thus, Solzhenitsyn comments, it reduced them to the level of beasts. Evidently they had passed that threshold of evil beyond which reform of the soul becomes all but impossible; and, he implies, people without souls are not truly human.[46]

These hardened criminals came to play a special role in the camps, one that, Solzhenitsyn argues, reveals something important about the character of Marxism. It is true, of course, that thieves were a social nuisance and had to be incarcerated, but it is also true that a life of crime was often excused and sometimes even fostered by the Soviet authorities. After all, the Progressive Doctrine, as Solzhenitsyn ironically calls Marxism-Leninism, claimed that human beings are not responsible for their actions. Instead, economic conditions give rise to aberrant behavior. Thus, criminality among the thieves did not indicate a lack of character on their part, but showed, once again, the corrupting influence of bourgeois society. Once the levers of oppression were removed, so the theory went, crime would vanish. In fact, the thieves were considered social allies of the revolution, since they too were enemies of private property. Stalin, who once robbed banks, fondly dismissed the thieves' behavior as redistribution of wealth, an additional form of class struggle.

Given the ideological tolerance toward the thieves, Solzhenitsyn argues, it is little wonder that prison authorities formed an alliance with them to crush the true enemies of the revolution, political prisoners. With the concurrence of the guards, thieves terrorized politicals, keeping them divided and distraught, and, not incidentally, lessening the possibility of resistance against the established order. Thieves were allowed to become informal power brokers within the camps. They held the best jobs and used their positions to further the interests of their band (a sort of criminal patronage system).

In the topsy-turvy world of the Gulag, real criminals were thought of more highly than honest, upright people, interned for some fabricated offense or for having the wrong social origins. Solzhenitsyn maintains that this inversion in the normal order of society is symptomatic of Marxist egalitarianism. The thieves were accepted by the party because they were part of the lower class. Their alliance with the progressive forces of history depended on the condition of their being lower. But, Solzhenitsyn wonders, was their place in the social hierarchy not the result of their own behavior? Did not their creed dismiss any thought of the future in a perpetual quest for instant gratification? Did not this lack of what once was called virtue and is now called forethought make it impossible for them to rise in social rank, as an honest, hardworking person might? Solzhenitsyn contends that by celebrating the lower, Marxism actually rewarded profligacy and vice at the same time it punished virtue.

He goes on to suggest an even more insidious comparison between thievery and Marxism. Both, he says, depend on a kind of redistribution. There is, however, little nobility in this urge to expropriate. It is spurred on by the low passion of envy; an envy turned against the success and talent of others.[47]

According to Solzhenitsyn the Progressive Doctrine misunderstood the intransigence of the thieves, and as a result, a strange thing occurred. The thieves were not reformed by their experience in the collective labor camps; rather, their hardened credo became the prevailing ethos of the Gulag. The guards learned from the rapacity of the thieves to use their position to take all they could. And what else could the politicals do but accept this egocentric way of life, merely as a means of survival?

An even more shameful result of the leveling of humanity, Solzhenitsyn insists, is that the criminal creed spread outward from the camps, finally engulfing the whole of Soviet society. After all, the thieves' sentences were comparatively light, and on more than one occasion Stalin saw fit to issue them a blanket pardon. Hardened criminals—some of them, in contradiction to the progressive principle that human beings are products of their environment, born after the revolution—were turned loose to prey on an unsuspecting populace. When they were caught again, their punishments were just as slack. And there for all to see was an example of how crime paid. If a society coddles and even praises its criminals while millions of innocent people are thrown in jail, then the lesson learned is the one taught by the thieves.[48]

Both nature and man seemed to conspire against the political zeks. Forced into slavery by the masters of a new age, stripped of all human dignity and personal initiative, they found their lives almost unendurable. Critically harsh conditions forced the zeks to face the deepest dilemma of their lives. Should they gain a little something for themselves by squealing on their fellow inmates, or by selling out to become a whore of the guards, or by stealing food intended for the mouths of others? In the Gulag the choice was starkly clear: survival or conscience. Solzhenitsyn writes, "Survive! At any price! This is a great fork of camp life. From this point the roads go to the right and to the left. One of them will rise and the other will descend. If you go to the right—you lose your life, and if you go to the left—you lose your conscience."[49]

The majority, of course, chose to save their own skins. Yet not all did. Many people of strong character and high morals silently carried their virtue with them to the grave. Some even survived the Gulag without compromising, gaining a spiritual strength unimaginable to the outside world. The courage of those who failed to be corrupted by the camps raises another question concerning Marxist principles. Solzhenitsyn wonders if the environment actually is decisive in forming character. Life in the camps, he says, shows that Marx is wrong. Human beings can act independently of the economic structure, even if it is an economy of slave labor. Quoting M. A. Voichenko with approval, Solzhenitsyn writes, " 'In camp, existence did not determine consciousness, but just the opposite: consciousness and steadfast faith in the human essence decided whether you became an animal or remained a human being.' "[50]

Solzhenitsyn estimates that perhaps one-fifth, or even as few as one-eighth of the camp veterans ever lived to see release. Yet even the end of term did not bring a return to normal life. Many of those who were not slapped with another term were cast, in perpetuity, into internal exile—some in the very region where they had served as prisoners. Treated as pariahs, often they could find work only in the brigades that they had so recently left. They led marginal lives until the Khrushchev period, when the majority of Stalin's slaves returned home.[51]

Yet even in the mainstream of Soviet life, zeks could rarely be free from the memory of the camps. For most, the experience had shattered their health and broken their spirit. Not only did they have to contend with all the psychological problems associated with a long and bitter captivity, but they were confronted with a culture now permeated with the camp ethos. Solzhenitsyn explains:

> Everything of the most infectious nature in the Archipelago—in human relations, morals, views, and language—in compliance with the universal law of osmosis in plant and animal tissue . . . dispersed through the entire country. While the government attempted . . . to re-educate the prisoners through slogans, . . . the prisoners more swiftly re-educated the entire country. . . . The thieves' philosophy, which initially had conquered the Archipelago, easily swept further and captured the All-Union ideological market, a wasteland without a stronger ideology. The camp tenacity, its cruelty in human relations, its insensitivity over the heart, its hostility to any kind of conscientious work— all this . . . made a deep impression on all freedom.[52]

Life on the Outside

What sort of life did the Soviet Union provide for those lucky enough to remain in freedom? To begin with, Solzhenitsyn maintains, even on the outside the long arm of the Gulag reached out and touched every Soviet citizen. Since nearly everyone had a friend or relative on the inside, all realized that they too could disappear into the camps; and fear hung like a pall over Soviet society.[53]

The Gulag was not the only form of terror that the party inflicted on the Russian people, of course. Solzhenitsyn points out that, among other crimes, it also: dispersed the Constituent Assembly; capitulated to the Germans in World War I; introduced punishment and execution without trial; crushed workers' strikes; plundered the countryside to such an extent that peasants revolted, and when this happened it crushed the peasants in the bloodiest manner possible; smashed the Church; introduced the first concentration camps; introduced the use of hostages—the Organs seized, not the fugitive, but rather a member of his family or simply someone at random, and threatened to shoot him; deceived the workers by its false decrees on such things as land, peace, and freedom of the press; exterminated all other parties; carried out genocide of the peasantry—fifteen million peasants were shipped off to their deaths; introduced serfdom, the so-called internal passport system; and created a famine, causing six million persons to die in the Ukraine between 1932 and 1933.[54]

To round the picture out, he explains that the Soviet government stifled Russian culture, suppressed Russian literature, engaged in a senseless military buildup that impoverished the nation, and instituted the most elaborate secret police force in history, the primary aim of which was to spy on its own people.[55]

Solzhenitsyn argues that it is difficult to imagine a system of government which would have a more devastating effect on the people. He then goes on to explicate the ingredients of Soviet rule that gave the regime its totalitarian character.

1. People were in constant fear. Everyone knew of the midnight arrests, the disappearances of neighbors or fellow workers; they had heard of the executions and seen reports of the show trials. Some were so frightened that they were actually relieved to be arrested. They all understood that the wrong word or gesture could send them into the abyss.

Yet arrest was not the only threat. There were also "purges, inspections, the completion of security questionnaires, . . . dismissal from work, deprivation of residence permit, expulsion or exile."[56]

2. Average Soviet citizens were in a position of servitude. Their fate was in the hands of the authorities who held the power of life and death over them. There was not even a place to complain. The least criticism could be taken as disloyalty and result in a trip to the camps. Nor was there a place to run. The internal passport system insured that people stayed where they were; where they could be watched.

3. The society was permeated with secrecy and mistrust. Secret denunciations were universally accepted by the Organs as grounds for arrest and conviction. People rarely came face to face with their accusers. Everyone was suspect, everyone was on guard. Such an atmosphere made candor impossible. Open and sincere conversations were rarely heard.

4. The population was ignorant of what was going on around it. Not only did the party keep almost everything secret, but fear made even the simplest communication between people difficult. Solzhenitsyn explains, "Hiding things from each other, and not trusting each other, we ourselves helped implement that absolute secrecy, absolute misin-

formation, among us which was the cause of causes of everything that took place—including both millions of arrests and the mass approval of them also."[57]

5. Squealing (as Solzhenitsyn calls informing) was developed to an extraordinary extent. Solzhenitsyn speculates that perhaps one in four or five city dwellers in the Soviet Union had been recruited by the secret police. He speculates that an important reason for enlisting so many people—even though most of their information was of little consequence—was to establish the impression that the Organs were everywhere, always watchful.

6. Betrayal became a way of life. People became so terrified that they did nothing when neighbors and friends mysteriously disappeared. As in a plague, people avoided the families of the arrested. Not a finger was lifted in protest because to do so could bring a prison term of one's own. Betrayal was so widespread that public denunciations came into vogue. It was not uncommon to hear in some public meeting or read in some Soviet newspaper, "I, the undersigned, from such and such a date, renounce my father and mother as enemies of the people."[58]

7. People became corrupt. Success came to those who, imitating party officials, used any means to achieve their goals. Soviet citizens came to believe that advancement depended less on ability and achievement than on brutality and cunning. Denunciation of one's superiors became a particularly attractive method of moving up the ladder of success.

8. The lie became a form of existence. Arrest, upheaval, brutality, shortages, inefficiency, and starvation were the way of life in the Soviet Union, but one could never speak of these things. Rather, one had to applaud the leadership—its every deed, every word. When something went wrong the party claimed that it was the fault of some malevolent conspiracy, recruited by the West and intent on destroying socialism. A surrealistic atmosphere gripped the nation. Normal people had to contend daily with reportage of the type taken from *Pravda*, 28 May 1938: "Heightening our revolutionary vigilance, we will help our glorious intelligence service, headed by the true Leninist, the Stalinist People's Commissar Nikolai Ivanovich Yezhov, to purge our higher educational institutions as well as our country of the remnants of the Trotskyite-Bukharinite and other counterrevolutionary trash."[59]

Solzhenitsyn insists that the lie was not merely a mischief; rather, it permeated the manner in which people spoke and even thought. "There exists a collection of ready-made phrases, of labels, a selection of ready-made lies. . . . And not one single speech . . . nor one single book . . . can exist without the use of these primary cliches. In the most scientific of texts it is required that someone's false authority or false priority be upheld somewhere, and someone be cursed for telling the truth; without this lie even an academic work cannot see the light of day." [60]

9. The whole system rewarded cruelty. It spread downward. The brutal were rewarded with advancement; the more reticent were passed over, replaced, or even purged. How could it be otherwise? Class warfare was praised and cruelty instilled, while pity, kindness, and mercy were ridiculed. Given the pervasive ethic of class hatred, it is little wonder that many lost sight of the difference between good and bad.

10. Soviet citizens adopted a slave psychology. Most feared loss of their jobs, their families, their freedom, and, of course, their lives. They knew there was always something more that the state could take from them, something to make their lives more miserable. And what could they do? The state totally controlled the media. It spewed forth a constant barrage of propaganda, aimed at instilling the ideas of socialist superiority while casting Western nations as warmongers on the verge of attacking the Soviet Union. So tight was the state's grip on the flow of information that even history could be changed—and was, any number of times, to accommodate shifts in the leadership. No news of the armed peasant uprisings ever appeared in *Izvestia* nor was the truth of the workers' strikes ever printed in *Pravda*.[61]

Public opinion could not counteract the state's high-handed measures. Any opposition that might have formed—for instance, in the church, among workers, or in non-Communist parties—was thoroughly crushed. For any who did speak out, arrest was sure and swift. A perverse natural selection occurred in which the brave perished and the weak survived. Furthermore, Russians did not have a strong tradition of involvement in national government, although Solzhenitsyn maintains that there was a history of participation at the local level. As in any society, most people were naturally lawful and did what they were told. (Even after arrest the most common response was to believe that it was all a mistake that would be straightened out in the morning.) What experience the Russian people did have in public affairs was embodied in their cultural tradition. But to the Progressive Doctrine local culture was not progressive, thus it was systematically destroyed, to be replaced by sterile party jargon. In fact, Solzhenitsyn complains, the attack on the indigenous culture has been so complete that the language itself has degenerated.[62]

Despite all the extenuating circumstances—the terrible strength of the Progressive Doctrine and its incalculable brutality—one should not suppose that Solzhenitsyn excuses the Russian people for having become slaves. Quite the contrary, he accuses them of a loss of "civil valor." Expressing his own frustration at having been part of the mob carried into servitude, he writes: "We didn't love freedom enough. And even more— we had no awareness of the real situation. We spent ourselves in one unrestrained outburst in 1917, and then we hurried to submit. We submitted with pleasure! . . . We purely and simply deserved everything that happened afterward."[63]

CHAPTER II

Solzhenitsyn's Stalin

Solzhenitsyn's massive indictment of the Soviet Union raises one question before all others: Why? The question has been asked so many times in so many ways that it now seems trite. Why were millions of innocent people rounded up, forced to work themselves to death, shot or sunk on barges? Can all this be explained by the "cult of personality"—a Soviet euphemism, one suspects, for calling Stalin a madman? Was it necessary, as others have reasoned, to prepare the Soviet Union for war? Was it, as the philosopher Maurice Merleau-Ponty argued, but later retracted, the price paid for rapid industrialization?[1] Perhaps there is an even deeper meaning to it all. If Marx's determinism is correct, History may have demanded that the gruesome game be played out.

In looking for the causes of the Soviet terror, it is appropriate to begin with the most obvious target—Stalin.

Some Explanations of the Terror

It is ironic, Solzhenitsyn muses, that the man whose name was reverently on the lips of half the population of the world as the Great Leader of Socialism should now be blamed for having led the Progressive Movement down the false path of tyranny. Yet today the former Great Leader of Progressive Mankind is cast as the scapegoat on whose head Progressive Mankind places many of the evils of the movement.

At one time, of course, adherents of the Progressive Movement defended Stalin's every action. They put forth a variety of rationalizations, some serious, some frivolous, for his excesses.[2] Solzhenitsyn's appraisal of those explanations provides a fuller understanding of the roots of the Soviet Terror.

First, it has been argued, by Merleau-Ponty for one, that because all the great world powers stood against Communism, the Soviet Union had to be more intolerant of divergent opinions than did its enemies, the states in the West. Faced with a continual threat to its political life, the Soviet government had no option but to enforce strict discipline. In short, foreign policy considerations were the source of the Great Terror.

Solzhenitsyn's analysis of the Stalinist era shows that this argument has little validity. A government does not make loyal subjects of its people, he contends, by terrorizing them. The opposite is likely to occur, and did, at the outbreak of World War II. Many Soviet citizens, especially in the Ukraine, welcomed the German invaders as liberators. These hapless Russians, unable to swallow the mindless propaganda fed to them by their government, simply could not believe that what had been the most advanced people in Europe had suddenly turned into barbarians. Not until the SS began to spread its own terror, Solzhenitsyn reports, did the Russian people decide that their own devil was better than a foreign one.[3]

Of course, it might be that Stalin believed he could terrorize people into becoming active participants in the "defense of socialism," as Stalin's measures were called by the party. Such a policy may be reduced to the idea that one should hurt one's friends so that they may hurt one's enemies. All governments do this to a certain extent; they compel people to serve in the military and forbid them to desert. Yet the Soviet rulers went far beyond this limited form of compulsion. A rational person could have expected that the policy of terror would make its victims resentful. Is it not reasonable to assume that a citizen might look upon a foreign invader as a friend when his own government has become his worst enemy?

Still, Solzhenitsyn's reasoning is not conclusive as regards Stalin's motivation; Stalin might have believed that starving people to death, torturing them, and sending them away to death camps would encourage a feeling of esprit de corps. Solzhenitsyn's argument does emphasize that Stalin was a tyrant, gone mad with his own power. More important for

Solzhenitsyn, as we shall see, Stalin dedicated himself to a policy of terror as the result of his adherence to Marxist ideology. In any case, Stalin's behavior is difficult to explain in terms of Soviet "encirclement" by threatening foreign nations.

A second thesis put forward in defense of Stalin holds that he was preparing the nation for war. The Great Friend of the Soldiers' prescience led him to rid the nation of its soft elements, while putting the strong in key positions.[4] Solzhenitsyn, who can lay a certain claim to being a military historian (*August 1914*), argues that this idea cannot be supported. He shows that Stalin was totally unprepared for Hitler's attack and for the war that followed; Stalin was fooled by Hitler.[5] Solzhenitsyn claims that in order to show Hitler its peaceful aims, Stalin's government "did everything it could to lose the war: destroyed lines of fortification; dismantled tanks and artillery; removed effective generals; and forbade armies to resist."[6] He even accuses Stalin of treason. He explains: "Treason does not necessarily involve selling out for money. It can include ignorance and carelessness in preparations for war, confusion and cowardice at its very start, the meaningless sacrifice of armies and corps solely for the sake of saving one's own marshal's uniform. Indeed, what more bitter treason is there on the part of a Supreme Commander in Chief?"[7]

A third explanation for the terror holds that Stalin's hand was forced by real differences within the party's leadership and by the threat that elements hostile to socialism would seize on any weakness to overthrow the government. In order to maintain stability, Stalin had to keep the warring factions in check. Hence, the terror was necessary to save the regime, and through it, socialism.

There is good cause for saying that the Soviet government could not have survived without the use of terror, Solzhenitsyn agrees, but he argues there is little cause for believing that differences within the party existed or that an organized opposition stood in the wings, ready to seize power. Even if one takes into account Kirov's murder and the party purges that followed, the overwhelming majority of those arrested before 1937 had little or nothing to do with politics. Most were ordinary people trying to cope with their daily lives. Casting them as a political opposition, hungry for power, overlooks the facts. History has been misrepresented, Solzhenitsyn maintains, because the party members who lived through the ordeal were people of letters and could write of their suffering. They encouraged the myth that the terror included only party members and that they alone took the brunt of Stalin's excesses. A far greater number of ordinary people suffered, but fewer of them wrote. Solzhenitsyn points out that there were no real differences within the party. Communist leaders, except for Trotsky, applauded everything Stalin did, right up to the time they were thrown into the meat grinder themselves. He writes:

> the majority of those in power, up to the very moment of their own arrest, were pitiless in arresting others, obediently destroying their peers in accordance with those same instructions and handed over to retribution any friend or comrade-in-arms of yesterday. And all the big Bolsheviks, who now wear martyrs' halos, managed to be the executioners of other Bolsheviks (not even taking into account how *all of them* in the first place had been the executioners of non-Communists).[8]

Undoubtedly there were differences of opinion on specific policies, the pace of industrialization for example, and there was the inevitable scramble for advancement and power. Yet Solzhenitsyn maintains that on all the important matters the party was remarkably united. All agreed that industrialization had to advance and that the position of the party had to be unchallenged. There were no cries of indignation from loyal Communists when other parties were eliminated, when civil liberties were ignored, and when the kulaks were exterminated.

To make his point, Solzhenitsyn chronicles the attitude of party members who found themselves citizens of the Gulag. Almost to a person they separated themselves from the the other prisoners whom they considered, in accordance with the propaganda, enemies of socialism. Generally, they displayed the same contempt and haughty indifference toward the camp community as they had before their incarceration toward the general population. They accepted without question the necessity of the Gulag; they only objected to their own mistaken arrest. Under conditions that might have shaken the faith of Abraham, they refused to disavow their earthly saint, Stalin.[9] There were, perhaps, a few who showed independence of spirit, but not many.[10] The true cost of party discipline was the loss of an individual point of view. All their beliefs, everything they had worked for, rested on loyalty to the party. Where else could they turn for guidance but to the party? And the party demanded that they grovel.[11]

The only true resistance to Stalin's rule, at least in the camps, came from the Trotskyites. They staged a long and difficult hunger strike to gain better conditions for political prisoners, especially themselves. Solzhenitsyn writes of them: "They conducted a regular underground struggle in the late twenties, deploying all their experience as former revolutionaries, except that the GPU arrayed against them was not as stupid as the Tsarist Okhrana. I do not know whether they were prepared for the total annihilation which Stalin had allotted them, or whether they still thought that it would all end with jokes and reconciliations. In any case, they were heroic people." [12]

Despite their best efforts, the Trotskyites failed to bring about better conditions in the Gulag. In truth, Solzhenitsyn concludes, they had little chance of succeeding against the formidable adversaries they confronted. If they did not jump every time the Great Leader lifted his finger, the rest of the party did, and in the end, that is why they were beaten.

But where were all the great revolutionaries who had so staunchly withstood the tsar's jails? Many Communists who had served terms under the old regime were unprepared for the brutality of the new order. Solzhenitsyn argues that few socialists had ever been tortured by the tsar's agents, nor were any threatened by the tsar's prison guards, who had themselves turned against their government. For those engaged in hunger strikes or in some form of passive resistance, the sentence, if convicted, was an added three months. The same offense under Communist rule brought immediate execution. In fact, the number of people receiving the death penalty under tsarism was minuscule when compared to those shot after the revolution. Hard labor was a pleasure outing compared to the Gulag. Prisoners could even write if they so desired. Lenin published two of his most important books while in prison and exile—he refused to do manual labor, and he was not punished for his refusal. Solzhenitsyn, who had no choice but to toil as a bricklayer, had to memorize everything he was later to put on paper.

There can be little doubt, Solzhenitsyn claims, that conditions for prisoners under tsarism were far superior to those under the historically more advanced stage of Communism. First, he explains, although Russia was not a democracy prior to 1917, its rulers were influenced by public opinion. For the most part, people were allowed to speak their minds, and, to a lesser extent, to write freely. This had an enormous effect on what the government could do. Second, the tsars of Russia, autocrats though they were, did not understand their power to be unlimited. They were restrained by a moral code passed down to them by generations of fellow Christians. They were prohibited from doing what Marxist ethics allowed. God knows, they probably would have loved to shoot a few revolutionaries, but their moral compunctions acted as a brake on their ruthlessness.

Solzhenitsyn tells the story of Tsar Alexander II, who put himself in prison for a few hours in order to discover what those he had sentenced were experiencing. Three hours is not much, but can anyone suppose that Stalin—or Lenin, for that matter—ever tried to feel such empathy for his fellows, for his political enemies?[13]

When Communists were released from prison and rehabilitated, they did not protest the brutal treatment that their fellow countrymen were enduring, nor did they object to the insane policies that had led to so many being imprisoned. They went right back to their old jobs and carried them out with the same ruthless vigor as before, all the while extolling the virtues of the Best Friend of the Prison Guards.

Another formulation used to explain the Stalinist era maintains that it was all a throwback to earlier times. Russian culture and history, so the argument goes, have conspired to give Russians a defective character, one that allows them to become easy fodder for tyrants. Such prestigious scholars as Richard Pipes and Robert C. Tucker[14] have concluded that Stalinism was a betrayal of Marxism-Leninism and a reversion to tsarism.

Partly in response to the theses of Pipes and Tucker and partly in response to other American scholars and statesmen, such as George Kennan, Averell Harriman, and Henry Kissinger, Solzhenitsyn set down his thoughts in an essay first published in *Foreign Affairs* entitled "How Misconceptions about Russia Are a Threat to America." There he states that the comparison between Stalin and even the worst tsars is misleading. "What model," he asks, "could Stalin have seen in the former tsarist Russia?":

> camps there were none; the very concept was unknown. Long stays in prison were very few in number, and hence political prisoners—with the exception of terrorist extremists, but including all Bolsheviks—were sent off to exile, where they were well fed and cared for at the expense of the state, where no one forced them to work, and whence any one who wished could flee abroad without difficulty. . . . the [total] number . . . of prisoners . . . [was] less than one ten-thousand [that] of [the]

> Gulag. All criminal investigations were conducted in strict com-
> pliance with established law, all trials were open and defendants
> were legally represented. The total number of secret police
> operatives . . . was less than presently available to the KGB of
> the Ryazan district alone. . . . In the army there was no secret
> intelligence . . . whatsoever . . . since Nicholas II considered
> [such] activity an insult to his army. To this we may add the
> absence of special border troops and fortified frontiers, and the
> complete freedom to emigrate.[15]

Much of what historians now think about Russia before 1917, Solzhenitsyn claims, has been influenced by Soviet scholarship. In truth old Russia could boast:

> of a flourishing manufacturing industry, rapid growth, and a
> flexible, decentralized economy; its inhabitants were not con-
> strained in their choice of economic activities. . . . the material
> well-being of peasants was at a level that has never been reached
> under the Soviet regime. Newspapers were free from prelimi-
> nary political censorship. . . . there was complete cultural free-
> dom, the intelligentsia was not restricted in its activity, religion
> and philosophical views of every shade were tolerated, and in-
> stitutions of higher education enjoyed inviolable autonomy.[16]

The image of Russia as a backward and evil nation, he continues, was
carried to the West by émigrés who were themselves revolutionaries and
who had an interest in undermining support for the tsar. Their aim was
to convince the West, which was in the midst of its own social revolution,
that the old regime was covered with blood. Surely they were successful,
comments Solzhenitsyn, for the outrage they produced against the tsar
has not been matched by a similar indignation against the reign of the
Soviet rulers.[17]

No, Stalin was not a throwback to old Russia. He was no modern-day
tsar whose Russian nationalism[18] so blinded him that he instinctively
oppressed his own people. That idea, claims Solzhenitsyn, was fabricated
by the European Left as a means of salvaging something of their socialist
ideals once the truth about Stalin became known. Stalin had little connection to the past or to Russian nationalism—except during World War
II, when his people's love of country saved him from military defeat. Solzhenitsyn explains: "only by some evil figment of the imagination could
Stalin be called a 'Russian nationalist'—this of the man who extermi-

nated fifteen million of the best Russian peasants, who broke the back of the Russian peasantry, and thereby Russia herself, and who sacrificed the lives of more than thirty million people in the Second World War, which he waged without regard for less profligate means of warfare, without grudging the lives of the people."[19]

Portrait of Stalin

One view of Stalin that Solzhenitsyn does accept is that, at least in part, the Georgian was a tyrant in the traditional sense of the term, i.e., a man who ruled in his own interest. He grants that his description of Stalin derives from speculation rather than personal knowledge.[20] Yet, as one commentator has written, "there is probably no portrait of the dictator which is especially superior to this one."[21] In his novel *The First Circle*, Solzhenitsyn uses the device of an internal dialogue to present the ruler's ideas and motivations. The reader is given to believe that he is privy to Stalin's innermost thoughts and feelings.[22] Allaback objects that such a method "rarely works with historical personages." It is as if "Stalin is squatting in Solzhenitsyn's hand."[23] Yet it is testament to Solzhenitsyn's artistry that the method does seem to work for most who read Solzhenitsyn's portrayal; it is a thoughtful examination of why tyrants act as they do. The reader should be warned, however, that Solzhenitsyn's depiction of Stalin is a fictional one. The importance of the characterization rests more on the attempt to understand the motivations of a dictator than it does on the historical accuracy of the facts.

Stalin is presented as a man who has not entered public life exclusively for altruistic reasons. He has used his position to satisfy his desire for female companionship, good wine, and good food, his greatest pleasure.[24] At least he once loved these things before old age overtook him and nature denied him their charms. Along with a physical decline, boredom has crept into his life, creating that deep languor known only to those whose every wish is immediately fulfilled.[25]

Stalin trusts only those subordinates who, like him, are self-seeking. He does "not understand the motives . . . of people committed to staying poor, like Bukharin." He even allows Soviet soldiers to plunder Germany at war's end; a decision based on "what he himself would have felt had he been a soldier."[26]

Whether Stalin's physical appetites ever actually waned can only be surmised. Yet Solzhenitsyn's portrayal is meant to convey a subtle warning to all the pleasure seekers of this world. He instructs them, as Epicurus—whose ideas figure prominently in *The First Circle*—once did, that delights of the body are fleeting at best and that even people who have the fullest opportunity to satisfy their every desire may find enjoyment slipping from their grasp and their lives empty of meaning.

If Stalin has lost some of his sensual desires, his love of praise has certainly not diminished. He enjoys the fact that his name, "filled the world's newspapers, was uttered by thousands of announcers in hundreds of languages, cried out by speakers at the beginning and end of speeches, sung by the tender young voices of Pioneers, and proclaimed by bishops." [27]

But what is the meaning of the cult of personality? Solzhenitsyn suggests that as with most people of great political ambition, Stalin wants to be remembered for his deeds. He hopes his biography—which, he is comforted to know, is selling in the millions—will perpetuate his achievements.

> The elemental, honest words of this book acted on the human heart with serene inevitability. His strategic genius. His wise foresight. His powerful will. His iron will. From 1918 on he had for all practical purposes become Lenin's deputy. (Yes, yes, that was the way it had been.) The Commander of the Revolution found at the front a rout, confusion; Stalin's instructions were the basis for Frunze's plan of operations. (True, true.) It was our great good fortune that in the difficult days of the Great War of the Fatherland we were led by a wise and experienced leader— the Great Stalin. (Indeed, the people were fortunate.) All know the crushing might of Stalin's logic, the crystal clarity of his mind. (Without false modesty, it was all true.) His love of the people. His sensitivity to others. His surprising modesty. (Modesty—yes, that was very true).

He is also proud of his literary achievement, since he knows "his every word straightway belonged to history." [28]

True, the Greatest of Greats had attained many honors in his life, but he wondered whether he should not aspire to one more. After all, "there was nothing bad with the word 'emperor.' It simply meant 'commander,' 'chief.' " [29]

However, there is a price he must pay for his great accomplishments;

he is set off from the ordinary people. When one reaches his level, who is left as an equal? He worries that "there was no one to ask advice from; he alone on earth was a true philosopher. If only someone like Kant were still alive, or Spinoza, even though he was bourgeois. . . . Should he phone Beria? But Beria didn't understand anything at all." [30]

The problem confronting Stalin in his quest to be respected, loved, and even glorified is that he does not come by praise honestly. Indeed, he terrorizes people in order to obtain it. His desire for honor derives, not from the noble sentiment of magnanimity,[31] but from the stronger passion of envy; a fact over which Abakumov muses before entering his chief's office:

> But he knew his Boss. One must never work full force for Stalin, never go all out. He did not tolerate the flat failure to carry out his orders, but he hated thoroughly successful performance because he saw in it a diminution of his own uniqueness. No one but himself must be able to do anything flawlessly. So even when he seemed to be straining in harness, Abakumov was pulling at half-strength—and so was everyone else.
>
> Just as King Midas turned everything to gold, Stalin turned everything to mediocrity.[32]

Stalin is especially mindful of all the bearded men who laughed at him in the hectic year of 1917. None of them would ever mock him again. They could no longer say anything to diminish his glory. Even the founder's work had to reflect this. It had been changed, twice. (Stalin had Lenin's works rewritten so that Stalin's role in the revolution would be more significant.)[33]

Solzhenitsyn's derisive account of the cult of personality makes the serious point that Stalin is caught in a trap of his own making. His insecurities force him to seek the praise of others. Yet those same anxieties make him fearful of what people would say if they were free to speak their minds. He demands that others tell him what he wants to hear, yet there remains in his mind a nagging doubt: all the cheers ring hollow. Perhaps even the dim recognition has arisen that the respect he so deeply covets can only be given by free people, but is easily mouthed by slaves. Underneath the bizarre histrionics that all but deified Stalin during his reign, Solzhenitsyn perceives a man desperately trying to gain in quantity what he could never achieve in quality.[34]

An even more dangerous passion that Solzhenitsyn's Stalin exhibits is not a wholly ignoble one. As is the case with many ambitious people, Stalin wants the world to dance to his inner tune, but not simply because he loves to wield power. The world, after all, is a very untidy place. People continually disagree with one another on just about everything. They are always pulling at cross purposes. Often their squabbles become violent and cruel. Stalin's experience has taught him that "the people themselves swarmed with shortcomings."[35] He wants to cure humanity of its maladies; a feat he can accomplish only by making everyone follow a single lead. In this endeavor Stalin can legitimately claim that he has been more successful than any other person in history. Solzhenitsyn writes, "There had been many other remarkable edicts. However, he still found one weak spot in the whole architectonic system, and gradually an important new edict was ripening in his mind. He had everything nailed down for good, all motion stopped, all outlets plugged, all 200 million knew their place—only the collective farm youths were escaping."[36] Of course, he has even greater plans in mind. "How would that sound, Emperor of the Planet? Emperor of the Earth!"

Even for the Greatest of the Greats, however, things had never worked out quite correctly. There "were always people who interfered," for example, Tito, who "was apparently a British spy." "When one had been removed, someone else always turned up to take his place."[37]

What makes Stalin's grandiose designs particularly virulent is the addition of ideology. Tyrants of old believed that they could bring their countries to heel, but they never had so many zealous followers who believed it with them. They were intoxicated by their own self importance, but in reality they stood alone. They did not have a philosophy of History that made their every act infallible. Marxist ideology compounds the natural megalomania of tyrants because it justifies all they do.

Solzhenitsyn's glimpse into Stalin's life presents two other traits usually associated with tyrannical rule: cruelty and cunning. From an exchange between Stalin and Abakumov in *The First Circle*, the reader learns that:

> Stalin was terrifying because one mistake in his presence could be that one mistake in life which would set off an explosion, irreversible in effect. Stalin was terrifying because he did not listen to excuses, made no accusations; his yellow tiger eyes simply brightened balefully, his lower lids closed up a bit—and there, inside him, sentence had been passed, and the condemned

man didn't know: he left in peace, was arrested that night, and
shot by morning.

The silence and that squint of the lower lids were the worst of
all. If Stalin threw something heavy or sharp at you, if he
stamped on your foot, spat on you, or blew a burning coal from
his pipe in your face, that anger was not the ultimate anger, that
anger passed. If Stalin was crude and cursed, even using the
worst profanity, Abakumov rejoiced: it meant that the Boss still
hoped to straighten him out and go on working with him.[38]

Furthermore, Stalin's cruelty has spread downward, engulfing the entire
society. Just as one real Stalin rules the nation, so, many little Stalins
govern its parts.[39]

A tyrant is not in power long if he lacks cunning. Stalin has shrewdly
destroyed all those who might have challenged his supremacy. They were
"choked, shot, ground into manure in the camps, poisoned, burned,
killed in automobile accidents or by their own hands."[40]

Solzhenitsyn reports as a fact in *The Gulag Archipelago* that a key
attribute of Stalin's success was his ability to manipulate people. "Therein
lay his dark and special talent, his main psychological bent and his life's
achievement: to see people's weaknesses on the lowest plane of being."[41]
He maneuvered the members of the Politburo into signing the death war-
rants of their fallen colleagues. They all knew they were sending innocent
people to their graves, but fearing reprisals, they went along. One by one
their own turns came, but they had no grounds for defense. What could
they plead, innocent? Those who defend lawlessness, after all, should not
be surprised when lawlessness overwhelms them.[42] Solzhenitsyn's Stalin
seems to have learned a lesson taught by Machiavelli. He knows the "ancient key to popularity: first to encourage the executioners and then, in
good time, to repudiate their immoderate zeal. He had done this many
times and always successfully."[43]

No picture of a tyrant would be complete without examining the driving force of his life: fear. Stalin's fear borders on paranoia. It had all
begun in 1937, at "the twentieth anniversary of the Revolution, when
there was so much reinterpretation of history."

> He had decided to look over the museum exhibits to be sure
> they hadn't got something wrong. In one of the halls . . . he had
> seen as he entered two large portraits high on the opposite wall.

> The faces of Zhelyabov and Perovskaya were open, fearless, and
> they cried out to all who entered: "Kill the tyrant!"
> Stalin, struck by their twin stares as by two shots, drew back,
> wheezed, coughed. His finger shook, pointing at the portraits.
> They were removed immediately. . . . From that very day, Sta-
> lin had ordered shelters and apartments to be built for him in
> various places. He lost his taste for dense city surroundings, and
> settled in this house in the suburbs, this low-ceilinged night of-
> fice near the duty room of his personal guard.
> And the more people's lives he took, the more he was op-
> pressed by constant terror for his own.[44]

Only the uncovering of plots by the secret police can quell Stalin's fore-
boding. No effort is spared unearthing "terrorism" aimed at "his price-
less person." But what if no conspiracies exist? The secret police must
show its vigilance; thus it fabricates intrigues. The dissatisfied must be
put under arrest, the unhappy kept under control. But since knowledge
of so much unrest strikes greater fear into the tyrant's heart, malcontents
must be thwarted before their plans "reach the stage of actual preparation." Abakumov reassures his chief, "We catch them at the moment of
inception, of intention."[45] In the deadly game Abakumov plays with the
Boss, he must convince the aging despot that his apprehensions are not
merely cowardice (yes, conspiracies do exist), without frightening him
completely (we work tirelessly to expose them). No head of state security
can ever accomplish such a feat.

Solzhenitsyn's scathing attack on the tyrannical life concludes with a
not-so-subtle warning to would-be tyrants. Their lives could become as
miserable as did Stalin's just before his death: "Growing old like a dog.
An old age without friends. An old age without love. An old age without
faith. An old age without desire."[46]

Stalin and Marxism-Leninism

Solzhenitsyn accepts the fact that Stalin's peculiar personality played a
part in the terror, but he rejects the idea that the "cult of personality"
was the sole, or even the most important, reason why Stalin acted as he
did. After all, Stalin had a justification for the massive upheaval of society
that he orchestrated. The one most often cited is that Russia's suffering
was necessary to bring about rapid industrialization.

Perhaps the clearest expression of the rapid industrialization doctrine is found in Arthur Koestler's novel *Darkness at Noon*. Koestler argues that before the revolution Russia was a backward, almost feudal society. The people, primitive in their folkways, were ill-prepared to adopt the advances of the industrial age. In order to modernize such a country, the fabric of society had to be ripped apart and rebuilt anew. Not only did the economy have to be overhauled, but the psychological makeup of the people had to be transformed. Peasants, the vast majority of the population, needed to learn the mores of the technological era.

Proponents of this view argue that such a massive change entails hardship. Yet, measured against the suffering of, say, the English peasants of the seventeenth century, who were forced off their land and into factories by market capitalism, the Russian peasants fared no worse. The real difference had to do with time. What took a century in Great Britain was accomplished during the first five-year plan in the Soviet Union. In any case, the argument concludes, Russian society, including the peasantry, was better off, materially and otherwise, after the transformation occurred.[47]

Solzhenitsyn accepts that the goal of industrialization motivated Stalin to act, but he maintains that the Soviet leader could have pursued this policy in a far more humane manner. Instead, Stalin promoted the ideologically correct, but totally inefficient, method of forced collectivization. To accomplish his ends the kulaks had to be destroyed. Party propaganda explained that they were rich, fat peasants who had more land than they could use and who exploited others into cultivating it. They were "bloodsuckers" on the socialist community and it was the duty of the Great Leader to eliminate them.[48]

But is there not another way of looking at these people? It is not impossible to see them as industrious, skilled farmers, who, when given the opportunity to improve themselves, did just that. If some gained a measure of success greater than others, that did not necessarily make them mercenary, it only meant that they were good at what they did. Once again, the practical effect of Marxist equality was to punish the virtue of hard work and to reward the unproductive and the unprepared.[49]

Those peasants not forced into the camps were made to join the kolkhoz, the communal farms. The "community" of the kolkhoz was not built on the traditional communal life of the village. Instead, people were more or less thrown together, their former lives wrenched from them. In

the name of progress, they were given internal passports that made it all
but impossible for them to leave their place of work. When in the dark
days before socialism people were tied to the land, the political and economic system was called serfdom. Living on a kolkhoz was probably less
attractive than traditional serfdom, since conditions were not ameliorated by a rich local and religious culture, extending back generations in
time. At least there was one noticeable improvement: serfdom was given
a different name.[50]

Industrialization was not solely the burden of the peasants, of course.
The entire society was made to bear its weight. Solzhenitsyn does not
give the typical explanation of how industrialization was accomplished—
the party seized excess capital from the population and used it to under-
write industrial projects. Rather, he argues that the real contribution of
the population was its sweat, or in this case blood, equity. Was there a
way Russia could have developed into a modern industrial economy at
the pace the party had in mind without the use of forced labor? From a
certain perspective the camps were an ideal solution to an almost intractable problem. They could provide a ready source of labor with little
monetary cost and an absolute minimum outlay of resources. (An econo-
mist would tell us that there were few opportunity costs.) Work was obtained by a method learned from the Eskimos. A fish on a pole was held
out in front of a running dog team. Continually driven by hunger, the
zeks were compelled to labor in return for their meager ration of food.[51]

There was an even more important reason behind the creation of the
camps, Solzhenitsyn reports. Dirty, distasteful, and backbreaking labor
could be extracted from workers without the enormous additional expense of providing them with a social infrastructure. He explains:

> The reason why the camps proved economically profitable
> had been foreseen as far back as Thomas More, the great-grand-
> father of socialism, in his *Utopia*. The labor of the zeks was
> needed for degrading and particularly heavy work, which no
> one under socialism would perform. For work in remote and
> primitive localities where it would not be possible to construct
> housing, schools, hospitals, and stores for many years to come.
> For work with pick and spade—in the flowering of the twentieth
> century. For erection of the great construction projects of so-
> cialism, when economic means for them did not yet exist.[52]

Gulag economics did have its costs, however. Solzhenitsyn appraises
the price tag of the Belomar (White Sea) Canal at a quarter of a million

lives. A pet project of Stalin, the canal was built mostly by hand in such haste that it was made too shallow to transport any but the lightest ships. In effect, a quarter million prisoner-laborers' lives were lost for nothing.[53] The zeks built useful things too.[54] Indeed, they succeeded in building a socialist economy, or at least they were instrumental in industrializing Russia for their Communist masters. In doing so, Solzhenitsyn insists, they showed that the camps were the main prop of the regime.[55] After all, if rapid industrialization was necessary to fulfill the principles of the party and the slave labor of the Gulag built the greater part of that industry, what other conclusion is possible?

Granting, as Solzhenitsyn does, that the terror was a useful device to bring about modernization, one is led to raise further questions: Why was modernization needed at all? More precisely, why was industrialization so dear to Stalin that it had to be accomplished immediately? The answer to this question, Solzhenitsyn suggests, cannot be found by looking solely at Stalin's personal motives of self-aggrandizement. Rather, the answer lies in the ideology that put so much stress on economic development.

In almost all the policies he adopted, Stalin was guided by the ideas of Marxism-Leninism. His actions rarely deviated from tenets of that doctrine. Solzhenitsyn states: "We must justifiably wonder whether 'Stalinism' is in fact a distinctive phenomenon. Did it ever exist: Stalin himself never tried to establish any distinctive doctrine . . . nor any distinctive political system of his own. All Stalin's present-day admirers . . . insist that he was a faithful Leninist and never in any matter of consequence diverged from Lenin."[56]

There was one important point of departure that Stalin made from the Progressive Doctrine. As Solzhenitsyn's portrait makes clear, Stalin was a tyrant and, seeking personal aggrandizement, he raised his own importance by lowering that of the party. "Stalin did perhaps manifestly depart from Lenin in one respect (though he was only following the general law of revolutions): in the ruthless treatment of his own party, which began in 1924 and rose to a climax in 1935. Can this be the decisive difference, the distinguishing mark which tells our present-day progressive historians that 'Stalinism' belongs in the exclusive list of anti-human ideologies, whereas its maternal ideology does not?"[57] Despite this one difference Solzhenitsyn concludes that: "close study of modern history shows that there never was any such thing as Stalinism (either as a doctrine, or as a path of national life, or as a state system), and official circles in our country, as well as the Chinese [Maoist] leaders, have every right to insist on this. Stalin was a very consistent and faithful—if also very untalented—heir to the spirit of Lenin's teaching."[58]

Finally, Solzhenitsyn maintains, no serious adherent of the Progressive Doctrine can subscribe to the idea that "Stalinism" was an independent variable that prompted historical change or that all the faults of the Soviet government can be traced to the cult of personality. There are two reasons for this. First, if Stalin is to blame for the terror, then it must be admitted that human volition directs history. To grant that a single individual, even a dictator, has such freedom of choice, would undermine the principle of historical necessity, the core of Marx's argument. Second, if Stalin engineered the modernization that took place in the Soviet Union, then it was he, and not the law of economic development, who is responsible for the movement of history. In either case, Marx's theory of history is wrong, and socialism is neither inevitable nor, for that matter, choiceworthy.

If a serious Marxist adopts the concept of "Stalinism," Solzhenitsyn reasons, he is logically driven to give up the theoretical underpinnings of Marxism. Yet the alternative is surely no more attractive. To embrace Marx's historical determinism, one is compelled to admit that History's plan was at work in all the evil deeds, in all the suffering, in all the terror. It was all necessary and happened just the way it was supposed to in order to bring about a higher stage of economic development.[59]

We can sum up Solzhenitsyn's position as follows: He blames some of the terror on the peculiar personality of Stalin and on the wily Georgian's quest for personal aggrandizement. Yet, as we shall see in what follows, Stalin gained justification for his actions from the historical precedents set down during the reign of Lenin. And, in the most important respect, Stalin was led to behave as he did because he was a follower of the principles of Marx.

CHAPTER III

Solzhenitsyn's Lenin

ccording to Solzhenitsyn the causes of the terror cannot
be understood adequately by examining its excesses; a
fuller account is possible only by studying its ideological
roots, by looking at the contribution of Lenin. It is to
Solzhenitsyn's Lenin that we must now turn.

Lenin's Rise to Power

Lenin is usually portrayed as the long-suffering revolutionary whose prescience, determination, and tactical genius allowed him to consolidate the
disparate elements of the Russian Revolution into a spectacular Bolshevik victory. Solzhenitsyn does not share fully in this view of his former
hero. In fact, his controversial depiction of the great revolutionary differs
markedly from almost every other one written. He claims that the true
history of Lenin has been "carefully concealed" and that actual events
"have received little attention." [1] His own characterization rests on "forty
years" of "working on the image of Lenin." Over those years, he "gath-
ered every grain of information . . . every detail" of Lenin's life so as "to
recreate him alive, as he was." [2]

To begin with, according to Solzhenitsyn, Lenin was not long-suffering.
He lived the petit bourgeois existence of an émigré. He did not work,

except in the sense of laboring for the revolution, choosing instead to live by the good graces of his family and on the contributions given to the party, often by guilt-ridden industrialists. Even his arrest and exile were not terribly burdensome. His sentence was light—mere exile.[3] He was not forced to work, and, with his mother's help, he was able to "afford a balanced diet." The solitude gave him the opportunity to write two political tracts.[4]

Nor was Lenin particularly prescient. Solzhenitsyn maintains that he was surprised when World War I broke out and even more astonished when the rebellion began in his own country.[5]

No one can doubt Lenin's persistence, nor the fact that he was a good tactician.[6] Solzhenitsyn even claims to have imitated his onetime idol during his own struggles with the Soviet authorities.[7] Yet the author of *Lenin in Zurich* does not subscribe to the theory that Lenin's abilities were crucial in initiating the Revolution. Indeed, by 1914, on the eve of the war, he claims Lenin was fighting indecisive battles against Swiss socialists for the leadership of the international socialist movement. Solzhenitsyn explains that at times, "fewer than a score, mostly those who evaded the draft" came to Lenin's meetings. His organization in Switzerland consisted of eight people. Once a meeting was called at which Lenin was to read a report, and no one at all showed up to listen. To make matters worse, the revolutionary fervor in Lenin's own country had cooled. After 1905 the party had "shriveled to nothing"; the workers had "swarmed . . . into legal bodies." Trade unions had "sapped the underground of its vitality."[8]

Given his insignificant influence on world events, it is little wonder that Lenin greeted the war with such favor. Publicly he paid lip service to the socialist line opposing all wars, but in reality he knew that a major conflict presented socialists with a remarkable opportunity to advance their cause. His banner was to convert the war into a civil war.[9]

When one thinks of the Russian Revolution, the usual image that comes to mind is of Lenin and the Bolsheviks being swept into power on the heels of a popular revolution. In reality, Solzhenitsyn argues, the revolution was begun without any positive ideals or goals. It was not fought *for* anything, but against the catastrophic losses incurred by Russia during the war. Millions of Russian soldiers died needlessly, he asserts, because "Nicholas II prolonged [a] senseless war with Wilhelm instead of saving his country by concluding a separate peace (like Sadat today

[1978])."[10] Despite the terrible strain on his nation, the tsar felt honor-bound to uphold his commitment to Russia's allies. Solzhenitsyn explains, "Nicholas II, in fact, lost his throne because he was too loyal to England and France, too loyal to that senseless war of which Russia had not the slightest need; he allowed himself to be drawn into that atmosphere of militarist madness which reigned in liberal circles at the time. And these liberal circles were anxious to get their Western allies out of trouble at the expense of the lives of Russian peasants—they were afraid of getting a low rating from the Allies."[11]

The tsar's momentous decision to pursue the war might not have been so costly, Solzhenitsyn reasons, if Russia had been better prepared for combat. But during the years of relative peace, the officer corps had become heavy with careerists who understood the bureaucratic road to promotion, but who were singularly unfit to lead men into battle. Unlike their German counterparts, Russia's military leaders had not schooled themselves in the latest tactics and strategy of warfare. When conflict came, they were consistently outmaneuvered.

Along with the ineptitude of its military leadership, Solzhenitsyn holds that Russia's defeat was the result of technological backwardness. The reader of *August 1914,* Solzhenitsyn's account of General Samsonov's disastrous rout—a cataclysm from which the nation never recovered—is tempted to say that the tsar's forces lost the war before the first shot was fired. They lost because Nicholas would not, or could not, given the character of the economy, compete in the European arms race.[12] When his troops engaged in modern warfare without the means to fight such a war, they were slaughtered. To end the useless massacre, they rebelled and in doing so initiated an even worse calamity.[13] Comparing Solzhenitsyn's *August 1914* to General Golovin's *The Russian Campaign of 1914,* one commentator sums up Russia's weaknesses in its first decisive engagement as follows:

> Both authors stress the blunder made by the Russian military command at the conference table with France before the war: Acceptance of a commitment to begin an offensive on the 15th day of mobilization. Both criticize the decision to conduct offensive operations simultaneously on two fronts. Both convey a dismal impression of military leadership where seniority and favoritism stifled talent and initiative. Both complain of general unpreparedness, of technical inadequacies that compounded

> problems of transport, communication and supply. Both point
> to the difficulties faced . . . by [commanders] compelled to carry
> out plans they disapproved with staffs they had not chosen.[14]

A second widely accepted reason for the Bolshevik rise to power was the aid given to its leaders by the German high command. Solzhenitsyn maintains that the assistance was far more extensive than Lenin's renowned train ride through Germany under the watchful eye of the German army. Solzhenitsyn argues that the Bolsheviks were supported financially and given indirect access to the Germans by the shadowy figure of Alexander Parvus (an alias for Alexander Helphand). Along with Trotsky, Parvus had taken a leading role in the 1905 revolt in Russia.[15] By 1914, he had become an enormously wealthy German citizen, as well as an agent of the German high command. True, Lenin resisted Parvus's more outlandish schemes, partly out of "socialist honor" and partly because he feared the forceful Parvus might emerge as the leader of the revolution.[16] Yet (as Solzhenitsyn documents) on the theory that an enemy of my enemy is my friend, the Germans sent aid to Russian radicals and, because of Parvus, much of the subsidy found its way into Bolshevik hands.[17]

A less immediate, although perhaps more significant, reason the Bolsheviks so easily gained power, Solzhenitsyn reasons, was that the old regime had lost its credibility. The tsar had fallen into disfavor as the result of the 1905 massacre in St. Petersburg. After the revolt of that year had been put down, the tsar never regained the wide approval he had once enjoyed. As his personal popularity slipped, so did the legitimacy of his government. "The youth of well-to-do families" took to disobeying the laws, Solzhenitsyn explains, and "began to consider a prison term an honor."[18] Yet few of those engaged in revolutionary activities were ever caught, and even fewer actually went to prison. The most common punishment was internal exile, from which revolutionaries easily escaped to Europe or even back to their own homes. With the sanctions behind the laws lost, or at least seriously undermined, confidence in the regime slipped even lower.

For Solzhenitsyn, Tsar Nicholas was far less an oppressor than popular history has made him out to be. Usually he is depicted as a ruthless, authoritarian monarch so intent on keeping power that he would employ any means, even the dreaded secret police, to gain his end. Solzhenitsyn claims that this distorted picture of the Russian autocrat was carried to the West by intellectuals, who, although they were fleeing from Bolshevik violence, felt they had a score to settle with the tsar. Rather than being ruthless, Solzhenitsyn concludes, the tsar's government, for the most part, was inept.[19]

The decline of the Orthodox church further eroded public confidence in the old regime. The church had given a justification for the social order and had provided a spiritual basis on which the inequalities within Russian society could be accepted. Its message had lifted believers beyond the cares of improving their lot in this life. Its teachings had made them more concerned with the salvation of their souls than with the satisfaction of their bodies. People dedicated to such ideals are notoriously bad revolutionaries. However, "on the eve of the revolution," Solzhenitsyn writes, "the Church . . . was utterly decrepit and demoralized."[20] With their religious faith shaken, many Russians turned to politics and to revolution in the belief that social transformation would change their lives for the better.

If the spiritual basis of tsarism had withered, its intellectual support was almost nil. In his essay on the relationship between the intelligentsia (both prerevolutionary and postrevolutionary) and society, translated as the "Smatterers," Solzhenitsyn contends that almost the entire prerevolutionary educated class deliberately set out to undermine the stability of their society. He defends this thesis by first attempting to define the intelligentsia. He quotes a witticism of G. Fedotov that they were a group of people "united by the idealism of their aims and the unsoundness of their ideals." In a more serious vein he cites Vladimir I. Dal, the author of a Russian dictionary and Solzhenitsyn's authority on many terms, who defined the intelligentsia as "the educated, intellectually developed part of the population" but who added that "we have no word [for] moral education," for that which "educates both mind and heart."[21]

Although the old intelligentsia embodied many virtues, according to Solzhenitsyn, it was led to "revolutionary humanism" by its belief in the possibility for "immediate reform" of society.[22] It disdained moderation and fanatically sought to remake the world according to abstract notions of egalitarian justice. Leftist ideas became particularly popular among the intelligentsia because in them was found the hope of becoming part of "the Great Natural Order," a quest necessitated by the intelligentsia's all but obligatory atheism.[23] Indeed, leftism and atheism were closely allied. Christianity, which had given the traditional explanation of the purpose of life, directed people not to expend their energies on social reform, but to dedicate themselves to personal salvation. These ideas were anathema to the left because they led people to supinely accept the edicts of any government, no matter how backward, as long as it allowed them to practice Christian beliefs. Reacting to this passivity, the left abandoned religion entirely; social reform became the purpose of human existence.

In its rush to transform the world, Solzhenitsyn explains, the intelligentsia lost sight of the limits of political reform. With little or no knowledge of Russian history or tradition, it deified the people, blamed all their faults on the state, and proclaimed that under a new order their sorrows would vanish. With no experience in public affairs whatever, it insisted that abstract notions of right could be applied directly to society, replacing age-old customs and institutions. Perhaps most importantly, it allowed its "love of egalitarian justice, the social good and material well-being of the people" to paralyze its "love and interest in the truth."[24] It is ironic, comments Solzhenitsyn, that members of the intellectual class should throw themselves into a movement whose collective nature denied their individual creativity. In doing so, he asks, were not intellectuals relinquishing the very thing that gave their lives meaning?[25]

He even considers Tolstoy's later writings, which certainly were not irreligious, responsible for bringing about the revolution. Although Tolstoy's ideas about the virtues of the simple life, nonresistance to evil, and the universal brotherhood of mankind were never put into practice, Solzhenitsyn argues that they helped mold more than one generation's notions about ethics and politics.

Stated briefly, Tolstoy held, first, that human beings do not and cannot control history, and, second, that love towards one's fellows is the best hope for the salvation of humanity. The two propositions are connected, for if one cannot control history, one need not worry about the consequences of one's actions; there is no reason to be prudent. Events will take their course, no matter what; thus one has a right and an obligation to obey the love commandment and not take actions against other human beings, even to resist their evil deeds.[26]

However, if, as Solzhenitsyn suggests, human beings can affect history, then the love commandment is politically foolish. It results in the acquiescence of the moral, who accept the love commandment, to the rule of the evil, who brutally reject it. Allowing evil to have its way surely cannot be the goal of moral principles. Hence, prudent opposition to evil cannot be abandoned.[27]

Solzhenitsyn allows that Tolstoy's views have a certain abstract nobility. But in practice they resulted in: a sanguine acceptance of one's fate, which may have encouraged some in high military circles not to prepare adequately for war; an unduly high expectation, bordering on perfectionism, of what could be achieved in civil society; and a self-interested abuse of pacifist ideals in order to avoid military service, i.e., cowardice.[28] Clearly, he concludes, it is imprudent to propose ideas that could bring about defeat in war, with all the dire consequences that entails. Nor is it always wise to proclaim moral virtues that can easily be turned into a justification for saving one's own skin.[29]

The broadest reason Solzhenitsyn offers for the downfall of tsarism is that history seems to be moving towards greater and greater forms of equality and away from those associations resting on a complex social hierarchy. The autocracy and class structures of the old regime depended for their stability on certain beliefs about the individual's relationship to society and the human race's place in the whole of the created universe. For various reasons (some of which will be discussed later) those beliefs had been largely discredited by 1917, and replaced by a burning passion for equality. Tsarism, born of an aristocratic age, was no match for the new ideas and was easily swept aside. Indeed, Solzhenitsyn wonders whether any social structure, except one supported by force, can withstand the impulse towards equality. All depend on some form of hierarchy; thus, all are criticized for their inequity. Certainly Lenin was aware of the temper of his times; he always attacked his political adversaries from the left.[30]

What has just been said about the victory of the idea of equality seems, at first glance, to contradict Solzhenitsyn's position on the possibility of the human race controlling history. After all, how much choice can there be if history is rushing ever onward in a particular direction? On this point, Solzhenitsyn's views are very similar to those of Tocqueville and very unlike those of Marx.[31] For both Solzhenitsyn and Tocqueville, the movement of history towards greater forms of social equality has been inexorable. Yet for both, the real issue is what form that equality will take in the future. Will people be free and equal, or will they become equally slaves? Will equality provide the opportunity for human excellence to develop, or will it smother talent and ambition, reducing humanity to its lowest common level? In spite of the movement of history (one is tempted to say, because of the movement of history) mankind is faced with a choice. Depending on what decision is made, both Solzhenitsyn and Tocqueville make clear, either liberty or servitude will reign.[32]

For Solzhenitsyn, one of the most important reasons the Bolsheviks were able to seize power was the ineffectiveness of all the moderate political parties. These parties were controlled by the intelligentsia. When these people had finally succeeded in shaking the old order enough to make it collapse, they were totally unprepared to take charge. Their ideals were impractical, their reforms were unworkable, and, most importantly, their notions about how to govern were naive. He writes of their inexperience:

> the intelligentsia proved incapable of taking action, quailed, and was lost in confusion; its party leaders readily abdicated the power and leadership which had seemed so desirable from a distance; and power, like a ball of fire, was tossed from hand to hand until it came into hands which caught it and were sufficiently hardened to withstand its white heat (they also, incidentally, belonged to the intelligentsia, but a special part of it). The intelligentsia had succeeded in rocking Russia with a cosmic explosion, but was unable to handle the debris.[33]

He is especially caustic in blaming Russian liberals for their indecisiveness during the provisional government.[34] They were far better at criticizing than at ruling. He complains:

> These were the same liberal statesmen who, for years, went on protesting that they were worthy to represent Russia, that they were wonderfully clever, that they knew everything there was to know about how to guide Russia, and that, of course, they were far superior to the Tsarist ministers. In fact, they turned out to be a collection of spineless mediocrities, who let things slide rapidly into Bolshevism.[35]

He even goes so far as to argue that there never truly was an October revolution in which liberals let "power slip from their hands"; rather, "they were never able to seize power in the first place." The February revolution "was going nowhere except into anarchy" and it "fell unaided." Russian liberals could not maintain their ascendant position either because they did not understand or because they could not undertake the harsh necessities of political life.[36]

In the face of this attack on liberal principles, one could retort that liberals have a healthy aversion to wielding power. Their understanding of the relationship between the state and its citizens is one of limits. Had the provisional government been serious about consolidating its position and bringing order to a vast empire in a virtual state of chaos, it would have had to employ stern measures—measures even beyond those once used by the tsar. Despite the dire consequences of inaction, liberals simply drew back from making that choice.

Moreover, the critic of Solzhenitsyn might say that if Russian liberals were mediocre, it is because those who hold liberal principles distrust high ambition. Extraordinary character and democratic government, not to mention party politics, are rarely compatible. Hence, the type of person (if any such existed at that time) who might have led Russia from tumult to stability would likely have been excluded from obtaining high office. By comparison, the United States has been fortunate. After all, historians might be writing today about the mediocrity and weakness of American politicians (if any such country by that name existed) had not America's two greatest leaders, Washington and Lincoln, held power, by happy coincidences, during its two greatest crises. As the leader of the continental army, Washington could easily have abused his power and authority. Lincoln was elected president by the fewest popular votes of any chief executive in American history.[37]

Solzhenitsyn might respond to this criticism by saying that if liberals were unprepared to undertake the sometimes agonizing steps needed to govern, then why were they so intent on overthrowing the tsar? Was not a period of slow but steady accommodation better than a chaotic upheaval?[38]

In the end, leadership passed to people who were not reticent about using power. Solzhenitsyn contends that Lenin and the Bolsheviks succeeded, in part, because they were more ruthless than all their opponents. They defended their use of terror as a legitimate means of securing compliance. Lenin is said by Solzhenitsyn to have based his actions on Marat's bloody dictum: "Man has a right to wrest from his fellow man not only superfluous possessions but bare necessities. So as not to perish himself, he has a right to cut his neighbor's throat and devour his still quivering body." He is also said to have learned from the Paris Commune that compromise with other parties and classes was impossible. Only by "shooting hostile classes wholesale" could the proletarian victory be gained.[39] Even after power had been gained, Lenin insisted that the party "must not exclude terror" as a tool for maintaining its position.[40]

Solzhenitsyn holds that the Bolsheviks' only claim to rule was their willingness to use superior force. They had virtually no popular support within the nation. Their views never had been widely accepted. Only elements within the intelligentsia embraced them. In his continuing effort to revise our understanding of Russian history, Solzhenitsyn argues: "The whole February Revolution was the work of two capital cities; the entire peasant country, the entire active army, only learned with bewilderment about the revolution after it happened. . . . the Civil War is quite incorrectly assumed to have been between Reds and Whites, whereas, in reality, the most important thing was the popular opposition to the Reds in the years 1918 to 1922—a war in which, according to modern reckoning, 12 million people were lost"[41] After considering Solzhenitsyn's account, one is tempted to ask: who fought for the Reds? But whether or not this controversial interpretation is valid, it is certainly beyond doubt that the Bolsheviks had few compunctions about seizing and holding power.

One last explanation, a very unscientific one, is given for the Bolshevik rise to preeminence: they were lucky. Fate seemed to favor them in a number of cases—all too many for Solzhenitsyn. He mentions, for example, the battle of Sivash Bay where the winds caused the shallow water to recede, giving the Bolshevik army an open attack route that it used to triumph in the engagement. The outcome of this battle is recognized to have affected decisively the course of the civil war.[42]

Portrait of Lenin

Solzhenitsyn portrays Lenin as a man of great strengths and even greater weaknesses. Lenin's strengths included a passionate commitment to his cause, bordering on an obsession. In *Lenin in Zurich*, Solzhenitsyn's fictitious account of one period in Lenin's life, from which all of what follows in this section is derived, the leading Bolshevik is pictured as becoming "ill" if "a single . . . hour" was wasted away from his work. "Everything . . . in his life—food, drink, clothes, house and home—had not been for him; indeed, he had wanted nothing of all this except as a means of keeping himself going for the sake of the cause." Even when luxuries were readily available, Lenin had a "deep antipathy" toward them. For him "there had to be discipline" in everything, especially if one wanted to "build up" the "powerful drive" necessary to inspire a revolution.[43]

It was to Lenin's credit, Solzhenitsyn concedes, that he could convey his own sense of urgency to others. He "open-heartedly lavished all his fervor" on his comrades "so that each one felt himself to be the most important person in the world." In order to further socialist aims, he treated "every youngster as his equal, with perfect seriousness," and never begrudged "the effort spent on conversation with the young, wearing them down with questions, questions, questions, until he could slip a noose on them."[44]

Lenin had a great ability to enlist others into his cause, and, Solzhenitsyn claims, he had an even greater ability to use others for his cause. For instance, he was aided by his family, particularly his wife and mother. The former provided him with a stable and orderly homelife, so that all his energy could be spent on his work, and the latter "helped him out of family funds." Oftentimes he persuaded his friends to do his bidding for him. They would carry on the bitter factional struggles that took place at almost every socialist meeting, allowing Lenin to remain above party infighting. Despite his well publicized differences with other socialists, he persuaded them to provide him aid, including financial support. He was not ashamed to seek the help of the capitalist arm of oppression, the police, when he felt threatened. Nor was he averse to enjoying the civilized and comfortable libraries of Switzerland, despite it being no more than a "lackey's republic" and an "imperialist state." He even accepted money shelled out "in a fit of businessman benevolence."[45]

One knack that Lenin used with great success was his ability to manipulate others. In particular, Solzhenitsyn explains, he understood how to play on the sympathies and antipathies of liberals. He is described as having turned a "youth-day" antiwar rally into a prosocialist march, and as having engineered an antitsarist campaign, centered on the liberal press's animosity toward autocracy. Not only did he intend for Russia to be "shaken by destructive propaganda" from within, he also wished it to be "besieged by a hostile world press." He mounted an attack on the old regime in socialist newspapers throughout Europe, foreseeing that the "excitement of Tsar baiting" would "spread to the liberals . . . the dominant section of the press throughout the world," and might even "win public opinion in the United States." [46]

Solzhenitsyn's admiration for the strengths of Lenin's tactics has been stated earlier. Lenin sensed when to act, when to seize the crucial moment between "'no longer' and 'not yet.'" [47] Of course, he was famous for splitting the party and splitting it again until those left were a dedicated and disciplined group willing to employ any means necessary to achieve victory.

While Lenin's idea of a small, strongly motivated party was undoubtedly an asset in the scramble to gain power, Solzhenitsyn contends that it must be considered a weakness from the perspective of Marxist egalitarian principles. Indeed, he represents Lenin as an elitist who in both his private and professional life "was careful to assert his superiority." Despite claiming the equality of rights, for example, he never treated his "womenfolk" as peers, expecting them instead to sit "quietly in their seats" and "not to fidget" too much. He considered himself superior to all his socialist colleagues and thought some of them so foolish that "equality with" them "was unthinkable." [48]

While working feverishly to bring about a revolution on their behalf, Lenin never put much trust in the masses. He considered them, especially the peasants, "ignorant rabble," who could be convinced of nothing except through the use of slogans and propaganda. He was always alert to the need for translating his arguments into "Marxist vernacular." [49]

Lenin also had serious reservations about majority rule. He preferred to undermine the moderate stance that normally forms within any coalition by holding up strict socialist ideals. He always attacked from the left, which, ironically, led him to favor a resolute minority over a placid majority. This was especially true in times of social upheaval, when he reasoned that a tiny group of provocateurs could halt the normal workings of society. When tempers were high, even a single shrill voice could bring about a riot.

According to Solzhenitsyn, one of Lenin's more obvious faults was his love of personal success. He is depicted as longing for the revolution partly from an ideological commitment and partly out of the hope that he would lead the movement. His soaring ambition blinded him to the effects of his own self-interest. For example, when the party took care of his needs and even provided him with an occasional extravagance, he is portrayed as having masked his delight in personal gratification. He rationalized that a "professional revolutionary should be relieved of the need to worry about his livelihood." He even considered his good health a weapon of the revolutionary struggle and insisted that "party funds . . . be used for its maintenance" and for "excellent doctors." When the party expropriated some funds (the Tiflis affair) in 1908, he was not averse to buying concert tickets, having a holiday in Nice, traveling, taking cabs, living in a hotel, or renting a Paris apartment for a thousand francs.[50]

These minor indiscretions do not belie the fact that, for the most part, the leader of the revolution lived austerely, limiting his material comfort in order to further his cause. But did he deny himself out of a true commitment to socialist ideals, or was his moderation part of the public image essential to becoming the leader of the socialist movement? Stated differently: Did Lenin's quest for high honor and renown turn him away from the petty concern for material well-being? Solzhenitsyn infers that ambition was at least as important as ideological purity in taming Lenin's avarice.[51]

By presenting this point, Solzhenitsyn makes his readers consider whether others could attain Lenin's level of asceticism. After all, not everyone is Lenin. How can those less devoted to the cause of social transformation and less driven to deny those pleasures that tempted even Lenin hope to live up to his rigorous standards of self-denial? If they cannot (and Lenin's theory of a conspiratorial party seems to concede that fact), then do not the principles of a socialist revolution, which demand that one subordinate one's own interests and desires for the sake of the interests and desires of all humanity, run counter to the desires and aspirations of the majority of mankind? Does such a movement not ask more than most people are willing to sacrifice? Does it not violate nature itself?[52]

Lenin's zeal for his movement also led him to forswear other important aspects of life. Solzhenitsyn hints that he mistook the laws of revolutionary struggle for the laws of life in general, causing him to miss certain experiences that broaden awareness and give depth to understanding. For example, he is depicted as having no true friends. At various times, others were close to him, but as situations changed so too did those relationships. He did require comrades to further his aims, but as each crisis passed so did his need for associates. "An hour later they were already receding, and he would soon clean forget who they were and why he had needed them." With the possible exception of his lover, Inessa Armand, "all men and women Lenin had ever met in his life he had valued only if, and as long as, they were useful to the cause."[53]

In fact, Lenin is said to have consciously cut himself off from humanity. A bitter experience with Plekhanov early in his career and interminable factional squabbles thereafter had taught him never to "believe anyone" and never to "let sentiment tinge his dealings with others." He developed a siege mentality, saw enemies at every turn, and took offense at the smallest slight. He made decisions about people solely on the basis of their party loyalty, so much so, in fact, that he was a poor judge of character. He had full confidence in Malinovsky, who made professions of ideological orthodoxy, but who, it turned out later in a much celebrated incident, was an agent of the tsar's secret police.[54]

In seeming contradiction to the ideal—from each according to his ability—Lenin is not described as a generous person. He is shown excluding one particularly famished émigré from his dinner table. He is even said to have scolded his wife for feeding the destitute fellow breakfast and admonished her that if he were given nothing he would soon stop coming.[55]

Lenin's disdain toward others extended to his scholarship. It upset him to talk to anyone who strenuously opposed his views, and therefore he mostly avoided the divergent Russian émigré community. When he did converse with others, it was not an open and free discussion where partners exchange ideas in order to deepen their own understanding, as in the traditional conception of dialectics, but resembled instead "a teacher confronting his class: the whole class may disagree, but the teacher is right just the same." Because of his isolation, he had no one on whom to test his ideas. He fabricated his own reality, regardless of the facts confronting him. When writing, "he had all his findings clearly in mind long before he had" finished a work. At times "his foresight . . . became so acute that he knew remarkably early, before he sat down to write, what his conclusions would be."[56]

One cannot help but be struck by the irony of the great hero of a movement dedicated to the community of the human species being led astray by his separation from other people. What is even more tragic, according to Solzhenitsyn, is that Lenin failed to perceive or comprehend crucial aspects of everyday life because he so fully committed himself to the abstract, theoretical tenets of Marx. For example, at one point Lenin is shown planning the reform of Swiss society. Although his general ideal was equality of condition, he seemed to pull his specific proposals for change out of thin air. How much land each family was to be allowed, how much each should be taxed, and who could become a citizen were decisions Lenin made arbitrarily. The deadly serious point behind Solzhenitsyn's ironic characterization is that Lenin became the ruler of one of the largest nations on earth without any previous practical experience in public affairs. Is it any wonder that chaos ensued? [57]

The intellectual amaurosis that afflicted Lenin because of his dedication to Marxism manifested itself in a variety of other ways.

Solzhenitsyn explains, for instance, that "all opposition exasperated" Lenin, especially on theoretical questions, "where it implied a claim to his leadership." He spent much of his adult life engaged in factional strife in order to assert his title to supremacy, thinking it naive "that all Marxists stood for the same things, and could work in harmony." [58] One can only wonder why these fervent differences of opinion did not tell Lenin something. How was the prophecy about the state withering away ever to come true if even socialists could not agree among themselves? They held fairly similar beliefs and, except on questions of means and leadership, had pretty much the same interests. But what of those differences of opinion that arise when interests clash? How could all be united in a Communist society without some sort of referee—that is, a state—to ameliorate the naturally divergent sentiments so commonly a part of human social life? For Solzhenitsyn, Lenin gives no hint of an answer because he was completely oblivious to the questions.

It is well documented in Lenin's own writing that his adherence to Marxist theory led him to make false predictions. As Solzhenitsyn points out, *Imperialism: The Highest Stage of Capitalism* contends that the revolution could begin only in advanced industrial nations. Even Switzerland, a country renowned for its political stability and social harmony, he held to be ripe for civil strife. [59]

Solzhenitsyn forces his readers to face an even more important difficulty. Why should Lenin have favored a revolution in Switzerland at all? Why did he wish to overturn a popularly elected government in which the masses fully participated and from which they enjoyed almost complete civic freedom? It is not as if the Swiss had to make a choice between hunger and freedom, as is often said to be the case in developing nations today. Switzerland was a land of plenty; everyone had enough to eat—too much for Lenin's tastes. Luxuries were available to all, although admittedly in varying degrees. Even property, which Lenin wanted to confiscate, was held by the vast majority of Swiss. Furthermore, despite its traditional requirement that a citizen militia be maintained, Switzerland followed the openly avowed socialist line, denouncing World War I and refusing to enter it. Why would Lenin transform a people's culture and mores when it was exactly those long-standing practices that had allowed the Swiss to so prosper? [60]

At one point in Solzhenitsyn's portrait, Lenin is depicted telling a member of Lenin's Zurich group that he should "educate himself." Despite his socialist leanings the fellow just could not grasp the need for a revolution in his homeland. But what was Lenin really asking? Should this person have immersed himself in Marxist literature so that he would dismiss the virtues of Switzerland? In a sense Lenin's "education" had led him to deny the evidence of his own senses. So intent was he on creating a perfect world fashioned after an, as yet, unseen ideal, that he was incapable of recognizing even the most decent society. Lenin saw politics in global terms, it is true; hence, a worldwide revolution was necessary to sweep away the evils of capitalism. Yet this very dedication to universal upheaval, Solzhenitsyn claims, hindered Lenin from appreciating the particular, i.e., Switzerland. Solzhenitsyn makes the point masterfully, as only an artist can. He writes about Lenin:

> He rolled along, a short stocky figure, scarcely troubling to avoid those in his path. There, close by, was the city library. He could go there, but he had journals and books for today's work on call at the cantonal. He hurried fast as he could along the loathsome bourgeois embankment, where the smell of delicatessen and pastry wafted from doorways to tickle jaded appetites, where shopkeepers had performed miracles of ingenuity to offer their customers a twenty-first version of sausage and a hundred and first variety of *pàtisserie*. Windows full of chocolates, smokers' supplies, dinner services, clocks, antiques flashed by. . . . It was difficult on this smart embankment to imagine a mob with axes and firebrands someday smashing all the plate glass to smithereens.
> But—it must be done! [61]

Lenin also failed to acknowledge the fairness of bourgeois society as a whole. Many of his socialist comrades entered business and became rich, ostensibly to aid the cause. Despite this, Lenin refused to grant the justice inherent in equality of opportunity. But, if even socialists could become successful, was not the road open to all?

Solzhenitsyn presents Lenin as having been so wrapped up in the revolutionary struggle that he overlooked important signs in his personal life that might have led him to question the veracity of his ideals. This was particularly true of his relationship with Inessa Armand. To a dedicated Marxist, Solzhenitsyn explains—applying Marx's ideas literally—human interactions are supposed to be governed by economics and by the laws of class analysis. But Lenin's feelings towards his mistress escaped the net of Marxian causality. It seems that eros, one of the most potent human motivations, has little or nothing to do with the productive forces of society.[62]

For Solzhenitsyn, one of Lenin's most grievous faults was his hatred of his own country. Lenin was jubilant when war broke out. He considered it a gift of history, since dislocation and misery, so endemic to armed conflict, are the breeding ground of rebellion. He needed his people to suffer, for their torment was his road to success. Only by going through agony would they come to see the wisdom of his principles.

More than that, he wanted Russia to lose the war. He knew that defeat would disgrace those in power and sound the death knell of tsarism. Given his stand, he was, in all but name, a German sympathizer. He is said to have admired German efficiency and weapons, while despising Russian perseverance that supinely accepted the most horrible losses in defense of the nation. He is depicted as having followed the war closely, heartened by fresh news of Russian catastrophes and frustrated by the steadfast endurance of Russian peasants.[63]

He would just as soon have had Russians turn their bayonets against their fellow countrymen if that aided the socialist cause. Solzhenitsyn makes his readers ponder the costs of such a policy. What of all those who suffered and died so that the Bolsheviks could triumph? Were they not part of that humanity that Lenin's doctrine was so intent on saving?[64]

It is true that committed socialists could not be patriots; they had to be "anti-patriots," since their principles went beyond the borders of any one nation and encompassed all mankind. In Solzhenitsyn's view, however, Lenin's internationalism was little more than a manifestation of a loathing toward his homeland, its people and culture. He is said to have considered Russia a "slovenly, slapdash, eternally drunk country"; his only tie to his homeland was his interest in ruling it.[65] Similar to the Russian aristocracy, he found his native tongue inferior and used it only as a necessary expedient.

Solzhenitsyn compels his readers to reexamine the high ideals of socialist internationalism. For these ideals to succeed, it seems the long-standing bonds that tie a nation and its people together must be torn asunder. Therefore, one is obliged to ask whether such ideals do not violate an ancient rule of political life. Lenin, at least, was driven to hurt his countrymen, those who would normally be considered his friends, and to help his nation's foes in war, those who, in the traditional view, would have been his enemies.

For Solzhenitsyn, who considers nations "the wealth of mankind" that harbor "a unique facet of God's design," the disappearance of "nations would impoverish us not less than if all men should become alike." [66]

Lenin's Ideas in Action

What happened when Lenin was able to put his ideas into practice? The first thing he discovered was that people's behavior did not fit the mold of his theory. When this occurred, he was faced with a choice. He might have abandoned his abstractions, or he could have forced the recalcitrant into conforming to his ideals. Except for a time during the N.E.P. (New Economic Policy), Solzhenitsyn maintains that Lenin chose the latter course; his understanding of Marxism had given him a tyrant's heart.[67]

Indeed, according to Solzhenitsyn, Lenin's success at seizing and holding power rested on a lesson he had learned from the Paris Commune. Lenin reasoned that the French workers' revolt of 1871 had failed because the progressive forces did not destroy their enemies en masse. To win future revolutions, he concluded, the proletariat could not compromise or bargain; it had to annihilate its opponents.

To secure a socialist victory, Lenin justified and supported the use of terror. Terror is the random use of violence, undertaken as a means of frightening a population into compliance. Therefore, it should not seem at all strange that Solzhenitsyn holds Lenin accountable for the bizarre and merciless events chronicled in chapter one, above.[68] It is true, no doubt, that Stalin put his imprint on the scale of the terror—he arrested one hundred to find the two guilty—but the principle was the same. It was Lenin who instituted the arbitrary use of violence against his own people, and it was his example that Stalin followed.[69]

Furthermore, after he came to power, "Lenin never dropped violence and terror as fundamental methods of his program." It was he, not Stalin, who took land away from the peasants in 1922; who deceived the workers by not letting them manage the factories; who used the military to subdue peasant uprisings; who all but totally destroyed the nobility, the clergy, and the merchant classes; who forced trade unions to become tools of the state; who set the Soviet Union on the road to collectivization and superindustrialization; and who instituted a system of government that ruled without the restraint of law.[70]

He was also responsible for creating an atmosphere of hatred and intolerance in his country. It was Lenin who called the non-proletariat "insects," to be crushed. Because he was a dictator, his attitudes became public policy. A prime example of this occurred, according to Solzhenitsyn, in Lenin's dealings with the intelligentsia. In a letter to Maxim Gorky, who was attempting to intercede for some of his imprisoned friends, Lenin expressed his thoughts about the intelligentsia. "In actual fact they are not [the nation's] brains, but shit." Elsewhere, he explained that the "pious" educated classes were "slovenly" and that they had never been true allies of the workers' cause.[71]

Inevitably, Solzhenitsyn explains, Lenin's subordinates adopted his attitudes. For example, in 1920 a group of the intelligentsia who attempted to steer a middle ground between the various schools of thought within Russian society was brought to trial in the case of the Tactical Center. These people, among them Tolstoy's daughter, were not charged with having formed an opposition—joining any independent organization was held to be a serious offense, for groups might challenge the party's total control—but rather with having undertaken to familiarize themselves with one another's views (they were talking to each other). Nikolai Krylenko, chief Soviet prosecutor, argued during the trial that "even if the defendants . . . did not lift a finger" to oppose the government, "nevertheless . . . even a conversation over teacups as to the kind of system that should replace the Soviet system . . . is counterrevolutionary. . . . [Not] only is any kind of action against [the Soviet state] a crime . . . but the fact of inaction is also criminal."[72]

The intent behind the Bolsheviks' attack on the intelligentsia is clear, Solzhenitsyn claims. It was not that intellectuals actually took part in activities opposed to the party; quite the contrary, most supported its goals. It was just that they were a potential source of resistance because of the independence of their thoughts. They could not so easily be bundled up and controlled. As Krylenko makes clear, "this social group" speculated about things other than the workers' state, and thus it had "outlived its time." Members of the Tactical Center received a three-year sentence; subsequently, the term for being a Russian humanist was stiffened.

Although Krylenko is quoted here, clearly Lenin knew and approved of what was going on. He was not one to sit idly by while important matters passed him unnoticed. Later, when Stalin all but extinguished the prerevolutionary intelligentsia, was he doing any more than carrying out Lenin's plans for the disposal of "social refuse?"[73] Lenin rid his society of "social refuse" by establishing the forced-labor camps, first at the Solovetsky Islands and then throughout the country. So began the Gulag Archipelago with its millions of tragic stories, of which Solzhenitsyn professes to have uncovered only a fragment.

Again the same question forces itself to the surface: Why did Lenin do it? Again Solzhenitsyn insists that the question can only be answered by going deeper. "The whole trouble," he writes, "lies at the roots of this doctrine [Marxism]; this doctrine could not bear other fruits than those it actually bore."[74]

Solzhenitsyn's assertion obviously raises some serious issues. After all, it cannot be denied that Lenin changed Marx's teaching. The revolution was supposed to take place in an advanced industrial nation and not in a relatively backward one, such as Russia. As Marx foresaw it, the actual revolt would be a mass uprising in which impoverished workers, the vast majority of the human race, would expropriate the riches of a few remaining overbloated capitalists. One need not read very far in Lenin's writings to discover that he rejected a mass movement in favor of a disciplined and conspiratorial group that would act as the vanguard of the proletariat.

Solzhenitsyn does not disagree with this view. He acknowledges that the revolution occurred "too soon" to be in accord with Marx's analysis and that extraordinary measures were needed to modernize Russia's economy. He even attests to the fact that Lenin made a unique contribution to Marxist doctrine. He explains: "Lenin did indeed develop Marxism, but primarily along the lines of ideological intolerance. If you read Lenin, you will be astonished at how much hatred there was in him for the least deviation, whenever some view differed from his even by a hair's breadth. Lenin also developed Marxism in the direction of inhumanity."[75]

If Lenin changed Marxism, how can Marxist doctrine be blamed for Lenin's political activities? Solzhenitsyn responds that it was not that Lenin went astray by restating Marx's principles, rather it was adherence to those precepts that made his intolerance, callousness, and elitism inevitable. In other words, he holds that Marx's philosophy is such a misrepresentation of the realities of human life that those under its influence are propelled into making tragic errors. If, as he argues, Communism developed exactly as should have been expected, given its premises, then Marx can be held responsible for the deeds of both Lenin and Stalin.

Conclusion

To sum up, Solzhenitsyn claims that the Bolshevik rise to power was far from a popular uprising. It was partly the result of weaknesses within the ruling class, whose way of life had been undermined by the "progressive" ideas of the Enlightenment. The Bolshevik success was due also to their greater willingness to employ violence as a means of securing power. Indeed, they were willing to do almost anything, even cede a vast stretch of Russian territory to the enemy, in order to gain ascendancy.

Solzhenitsyn attempts to show that the ruthlessness of the Bolsheviks in acquiring power set the tone for the way they governed once they were in command. They were heartless in pursuing their policies; they showed little sympathy for the Russian people or for their way of life; and they set in motion a lawless system of government, which, while it never rivaled Stalin's in the extent of its horrors, did not differ from Stalin's in its basic principles.

In placing blame for the foundations of this brutal regime, once again Solzhenitsyn finds more than one culprit. Lenin was partly the cause. His single-minded pursuit of success and his narrow partisan perspective helped set the tone for the tyrannical government that the Bolsheviks established. Yet there was also an element in the ferocity of Bolshevik rule that Solzhenitsyn blames on Marx's ideas. This controversial assertion can be considered only after we have reached a fuller understanding of Solzhenitsyn's treatment of Marx.

Solzhenitsyn on Marx

The writings of Solzhenitsyn are most often taken to be a historical indictment of the Soviet Union. In that regard they have had an enormous influence. They have further discredited the legitimacy of Soviet rule amongst their readers in the East; they have generally hardened public opinion in the West by clearly revealing the totalitarian character of the Soviet government; and they have played an important role in undermining Euro-Communism.[1]

Along with their importance as a history of Soviet deeds, Solzhenitsyn's writings have another, more comprehensive intention. It is the thesis of this chapter that Solzhenitsyn's works make a theoretical attack on Marx's philosophy. To say that Solzhenitsyn criticizes Marx is (in a dialectic way) both an understatement and an overstatement. Nowhere in his writings does he systematically lay down his differences with Marx, nor can the full measure of his objections be found by looking solely to one of his works. There is no treatise contra Marx, probably because Solzhenitsyn does not write treatises. Wherever one looks in Solzhenitsyn's works, however, there is a criticism of some aspect of Marx's ideas. This chapter shall discuss Solzhenitsyn's attack on Marx's views concerning: the prediction of future trends, revolution, class analysis, the primacy of economics, history, human nature, labor, property, family relations, philosophy, atheism, and the aims of socialism—freedom, equality, and community. It is tempting to say that Solzhenitsyn wishes to undermine every important aspect of Marx's doctrine.[2]

Before beginning a discussion of Solzhenitsyn's arguments against Marx, it is appropriate to acknowledge that a great controversy rages over what Marx's philosophy means. Should it be interpreted to signify that the movement of history inexorably determines human fate, or is its purpose to indicate a trend in historical development that individuals may or may not accept in deciding their future? The literature on Marx is so extensive and contradictory that one knowledgeable commentator seems to have thrown up his hands in despair at discovering the one, true Marx. Raymond Aron writes, "The philosophy of Marx, precisely because of its intrinsic ambiguity, . . . has always lent itself to many interpretations, some of which are more convincing, . . . but all of which, strictly speaking, are tolerable."[3]

Because of the complexity of Marx's thought, it is with some trepidation that an interpretation of his work, especially one so brief, is put forward. Yet in order to understand Solzhenitsyn's criticism of Marx, it is necessary to present a capsulization of Marx's major ideas. There seem to be two broad schools of thought concerning Marx. The older interpretation, what we shall call here the mechanistic view, holds that according to Marx human life is determined by the economic structure of society. This is so because the most primary activity of human existence is labor—the labor necessary to secure one's livelihood. Since the earliest stages of human development, the fruits of labor have not been shared equally among those who toil. The division of labor, the means by which tasks are most efficiently accomplished, has had the consequence of creating social distinctions, which harden into social classes. Those at the top of the social hierarchy reap greater benefits from the economic arrangement than do those at the bottom, so much so in fact, that the lower classes of the capitalist era are compelled to work for subsistence wages.

Marx goes beyond this analysis of social inequality, of course. He reacts to Hegel's notion that the seemingly random events of history do have a comprehensible meaning and order. He agrees with Hegel that each historical era has governing principles on the basis of which individuals within that era justify their actions. He also agrees that these fundamental beliefs vary from historical era to historical era, but that finally there will be a time—an absolute moment—when the meaning of the movement of history and the relation among historical eras will become apparent. Marx's great contribution to philosophy is his insight that the driving force behind historical change is not the unfolding of the Idea, as Hegel had maintained, but the struggle between social classes over the fruits of labor. Hegel, too, had reasoned that there was an ongoing conflict between master and slave, but he had held this dispute to be primarily a war of ideas, of consciousness. Marx, on the other hand, maintains that the ideas expressed by a particular class are merely a way of defending its economic power and social position. Indeed, ideas and consciousness are manifestations of the economic arrangement. They reflect the way in which the economic structure is organized to produce the goods and services necessary for life. Thus, the predominant ideas tend to justify the way of life of the ruling group, e.g., the hierarchical ethos of feudalism favored the aristocratic class, while the values inherent in a free-market system favor the capitalists.

According to Marx each social system is transformed by its own inner contradictions; it falls of its own weight. For instance, it is the competitive nature of the free market that dooms capitalism. In order to keep up with their rivals and not be run out of business, corporations are compelled to produce goods more quickly and efficiently and at the same time to lower the cost of production. To accomplish these twin goals the owners must introduce ever-more complex machines and simultaneously reduce the wages paid to workers. As a result, the workers, numerically the largest class, become alienated from their labor and, indeed, their very existence. They are made to work at mindlessly tedious jobs, the result of assembly line techniques and advanced machinery, for subsistence wages, the absolute minimum expenditure needed to keep them alive as functioning units of production. All fulfillment is lost in such labor since the worker has control over neither the finished product nor the means by which those products are created.

Only after a time do the fatal flaws of capitalism become apparent. Capitalism's very efficiency causes its downfall. It produces such a glut of material goods that consumption falls behind production, resulting in massive layoffs and eventually economic collapse. During these boom and bust cycles a few large businesses swallow up all the rest. The inequity of a system in which the owners enjoy all the luxuries of life but do not labor and the workers labor but live in poverty becomes so apparent that the workers finally seize the means of production and transform the social arrangement so that all share equally in its bounty.

The dispute between the two interpretations of Marx, as we shall see below, arises over whether Marx believed this process of historical change to be inevitable, thereby negating human freedom, or whether he held the rise of capitalism to be a historical trend, the worst excesses of which could be overcome by human action. The mechanistic Marxists seem to insist that human fate is determined independently of human will, in short, that existence determines essence. The humanistic adherents of Marx claim that nowhere in Marx's philosophy is human fate predetermined by uncontrollable economic forces; rather, once liberated from capitalist ideology, the human will can play a role in shaping the future society. Thus, essence determines existence.[4]

The primary reason for the reevaluation of Marx's thought—which gave rise to the new interpretation of his ideas—was the publication of his early writings. A number of major intellectual figures, including Sartre, Merleau-Ponty, Fromm, Marcuse, and Avineri, have brought to light new facets of his philosophy. Focusing on the goals of liberation, equality, and community that Marx deemed essential to a worthwhile human existence, these thinkers claim that Marx was never a crude materialist and that his work is an open-ended philosophic dialogue. Marx's later writings—*Capital,* for example—which attempt to "prove" the laws of historical change, are, for a variety of reasons, discounted by these scholars. For example, Avineri contends that the mechanistic tone of Marx's later works was due primarily to Engels's oversimplification. To the end of his days, Avineri insists, Marx was humanistic and democratic.[5]

Solzhenitsyn criticizes both the humanistic and mechanistic versions of Marxism, although he reserves his greatest antipathy for the latter, in part because the mechanistic view of Marx predominates in the Soviet Union and in every other nation where Communists have come to rule. He explains, "Communism is as crude an attempt to explain society and the individual as if a surgeon were to perform his delicate operation with a meat ax. All that is subtle in human psychology and in the structure of society (which is even more complex), all this is reduced to crude economic processes. This whole created being—man—is reduced to matter."[6] As for the claim that Marx is a humanist, a position found primarily in the West, Solzhenitsyn finds it too fantastic to be believed. As will be shown below, he reasons that even when the most humanistic of Marx's goals are pursued, unintended consequences follow; Marxism makes its adherents overlook the hard facts of political life, opening the way to injustice and incompetence.[7]

There is also an important sense in which it does not matter to Solzhenitsyn which interpretation of Marx is the more accurate. In his own way he applies the biblical injunction "by their fruits shall you know them" to Marxism, with unpleasant results for its author. Yet his authority for a practical criticism of theory does not rest solely on religion. It was Marx himself, in the Preface to *A Contribution to the Critique of Political Economy*, who insisted that societies be judged by what they are and not by what they pretend to be.[8]

A word of caution must be added before proceeding to Solzhenitsyn's critique of Marx. It would be unfair and philosophically incorrect to maintain that if Marx says one thing and the Soviet experience shows that something else has occurred, then Marx's proposition is inaccurate. Indeed, since the Soviet Union has never claimed to have attained the final stage of Communism, which Marx foresaw would eliminate human conflict and injustice, no empirical observations made in that nation can serve as a refutation of Marx. Yet Solzhenitsyn does criticize Marx on the basis of observable evidence. Solzhenitsyn's method in this regard is to relate stories or episodes in the life of his nation that test Marx's ideas in practice. He recounts the experiences of actual people in real situations when confronted with Marxian social experimentation. What happened, for example, when Marx's ideas concerning property, family, and equality were applied to practical affairs? How did people react? What were the consequences?

Such a method does have serious flaws, of course. There is no strict scientific basis, mathematical correlation, or repeatable experiment that will prove that Solzhenitsyn's evidence necessarily leads to his conclusions. Yet Solzhenitsyn's stories and anecdotes are worthy of serious consideration, nonetheless. They convey, or at least are meant to convey, the normal human reaction to the practical application of Marx's proposals. Each episode may have involved only a limited number of people, but the response was shared by millions, if not most, Russians. Indeed, the reactions are so widespread and similar, one must conclude that Solzhenitsyn holds them to be universal. Thus, Solzhenitsyn's critique of Marx's philosophy proceeds by testing that theory against the dictates of human nature.

The Problem of Prediction

Following the lead of Hegel, Marx claims to have understood the movement of history. On the basis of that knowledge Marx makes predictions about the character of future historical epochs. For example, Marx foresaw that capitalism would bring misery and poverty to the workers who toiled to produce its wealth. Solzhenitsyn points out that almost nothing that Marx predicted has actually come true.

To begin with a crucial fact, the free-market system has not impoverished the workers. Communist societies have never produced "as much food, clothing and leisure" as people in the West enjoy under capitalism, Solzhenitsyn comments. Moreover, the economic well-being of the West has not depended on colonialism (one of Lenin's additions to Marx). Only after Europe shed its colonies, Solzhenitsyn claims, was it able to achieve its post-World War II economic miracle.[9] Marx also was wrong in predicting that revolutions would begin in the most advanced industrial countries.[10] The reverse occurred. As in Russia, revolutions have taken place in relatively underdeveloped nations, where the working class was small.

Marx's most inaccurate prediction, argues Solzhenitsyn, is "the picture of how the world would rapidly be overtaken by revolution and how states would soon wither away." He continues, "such a view is sheer delusion, sheer ignorance of human nature," and points out that it is precisely in those nations which claim a Marxist paternity where the state is most powerful. He questions Marx's contention that the rise of socialism would herald the decline of war. The Soviet invasion of Budapest and of Prague, the occupation of Eastern Europe and the Baltics, and the Sino-Soviet border clashes belie the peaceful intention of Communist governments. Whether or not Marx was correct in his prognostications would be of little importance if those predictions were not the basis for calling people to revolt. Since they "have failed to predict a single event," is it not justified to call the whole of Marx's teaching into question? Solzhenitsyn reasons that "Only the cupidity of some, the blindness of others, and the craving for faith on the part of still others" would allow such a "bankrupt doctrine," with such an abysmal record for accuracy, still to have adherents.[11]

Revolution

At Marx's graveside eulogy Engels paid his friend what he considered a high honor by calling him "before all else a revolutionist."[12] Certainly no political philosopher has a greater claim to the title. At various times he called for "smashing" the machine of the state and "breaking up" the old society. He wrote of "hand to hand combat" in which "the people must be taught to be terrified of themselves." Well aware of what a revolution entails, he quoted, with approval, from George Sand's novel *Jean Ziska,* "Combat or death: bloody struggle or extinction. It is thus that the question is inexorably put." Even after the revolution, Marx foresaw that to succeed the proletariat would need to adopt "measures of *force*" and that nonproletariat classes "must be forcibly removed or transformed, and the process of their transformation must be forcibly accelerated."[13]

Solzhenitsyn's research has led him to believe that "if you read Marx attentively you will there find Leninist formulations and tactics already completely outlined, with repeated calls for terror, violence and the forceful seizure of power." Elsewhere, he quotes from Marx's writings to make his point, "'Reforms are a sign of weakness. . . . The movement for reform in England was an error. . . . Democracy is more terrible than monarchy or aristocracy. . . . Political freedom is false freedom, worse than the worst form of slavery. . . . Given universal suffrage, revolution hasn't got a chance. . . . After coming to power—terror. . . . they will begin to regard us as monsters—but we don't give a damn.'"[14]

Solzhenitsyn is not naive about the importance of revolutions in shaping history. He understands that to search into the origins of most political societies is to discover "revolutions and seizures of power."[15] He even acknowledges Machiavelli's point that the "puritanical air" at the first stages of social upheavals can induce a sense of virtue.[16] However, as a means of counteracting the rebellious fervor instilled by Marxism, he informs us of the human costs of bloody insurrections. He claims that in the present state of the world little good can be said for violent revolution. He even hesitates in calling for its use against the most extreme forms of tyranny—in the Soviet Union, for example.[17]

First, he maintains that a bloody uprising is likely to ruin the economy of a nation for many years. Even if the regime that comes to power is better than the one it replaced, still it would face the very difficult task of rebuilding a shattered industrial base. Thus, whatever political advantages might be gained by overturning the old order are likely to be offset by the suffering created in an economic crisis. Second, those most likely to lead a revolution are usually unfit to govern the nation afterward. How, he wonders, can the leaders of a revolution put aside their grenades and machine guns and become compassionate rulers? Internecine war rarely produces magnanimous victors. Third, even if revolutionary commanders are not ruthless people, they usually have little or no experience in the art of governing. Hence, force replaces statesmanship. Perhaps more importantly, revolutionaries often lack the technical know-how necessary to make the economy work. They may even be hostile to technicians, for the expertise of such people is likely to have put them in high-paying and important posts under the old regime.[18]

One disturbing consequence of revolution is that it unleashes all the human passions. Even beyond the bitterness produced between warring factions, there is a great deal of lawlessness, such as assault, murder, theft, etc., created when the rules of the old society are suspended and the new ones have yet to take their place. At such times, too, racial or national hostilities are easily exacerbated. Such disturbances are not fatal to a new administration, Solzhenitsyn reasons, but they are bothersome and take an enormous effort to bring under control. An added cost of revolution to an already burdened economy is the support of a large police force.[19]

In social revolution the organs of repression must also be used to strip the old ruling class of its privilege. It is an "old, old ironical story," Solzhenitsyn muses, that rebels who liberate jails are forced to set up some of their own. It is to be expected that defenders of the old order will suffer in the wake of a social transformation; as Lenin was fond of saying, omelets cannot be made without breaking some eggs. By bringing up the point, however, Solzhenitsyn asks his readers to think more deeply about the nature of revolution. First, the act of suppression implies that revolutions actually are not fought for the universality of mankind, as Marx claimed. Usually one group wants to take away what another group has. Furthermore, no sooner does a new ruling group come to power than it demands special privilege to accompany its new status. Solzhenitsyn relates that during the camp uprisings, of which he was a part, some of the leadership and many of the hit men (those who killed stoolies) demanded extra rations even though it meant their fellow prisoners went hungry. In the end one ruling class just replaces another.[20]

What sort of people are likely to enforce the rules of the new state? What sort of people will rise to the top in a society where violence and brutality reign? Obviously, Solzhenitsyn reasons, people with harsh and brutal personalities are just what a new regime needs. The new leadership is likely to rely on people for whom the goals of the revolution mean very little. They are more interested in personal rewards and pleasures, one of which could be the enjoyment of seeing others suffer.[21]

Furthermore, Solzhenitsyn states that according to "a universal law," all "vast and bloody revolutions . . . invariably devour their own creators." He does not explain, however, why this universal law is binding. Perhaps, one might speculate, it is because passions run so high. Or it could be, as his treatment of Stalin suggests, that dedication to ideology is so strong during a revolution that personal differences between leaders are transformed into matters of high principle that can be resolved only by one side extinguishing the other.[22]

Marxist uprisings are particularly pernicious, he asserts, because they have as one of their aims the destruction of the old culture.[23] But when the old ways are gone, what is to take their place? Reminiscent of Edmund Burke, Solzhenitsyn believes that culture takes centuries to construct. The trials and errors of many generations leave a legacy of wisdom in the traditions and customs. Culture civilizes people, teaching them right from wrong, noble from base, true from false. It provides ways of coping with the natural rhythm of life—birth, marriage, aging, and death. At its highest, culture exemplifies the peak of human activity. The arts, philosophy, and literature reflect man's endeavor to capture the elusive essence of beauty and truth.

Marx would have us sweep all this "muck" aside and create a new culture ex nihilo. Solzhenitsyn argues that the labor of generations is nearly impossible to replace. In fact, when tradition is destroyed, a vacuum is created into which flows the coarsest kind of human thinking. Chapter 1 of this book showed how easily the thieves' philosophy spread from the camps to Soviet society. The destruction of culture does not mean that man's creative talent will be unleashed, Solzhenitsyn concludes. Rather, it is far more likely to result in the degeneration of morals and manners to the lowest level of common humanity.[24]

Class Analysis

One of the worst aspects of Marxism, Solzhenitsyn complains, is its faulty understanding of society and the division of classes. According to Marx, human suffering, at least in the modern age, originates in the bourgeois way of life, in capitalism. The "absolute general law of capitalist accumulation 'establishes' the irreconcilability of class antagonism," he writes. At one end of the division are riches and opulence; at the other, poverty and degradation. To reach this conclusion, Marx begins with the premise that man's most fundamental activity, providing for his physical needs, influences all that happens thereafter. He writes, "life involves above all eating and drinking, shelter, clothing. . . . This is the first historical act . . . which must be fulfilled . . . today as well as a thousand years ago." From this premise Marx insists that the way in which people gain their livelihood affects whatever else they do. In a real sense, he claims that people are what they produce and the way they produce it. He argues, "The way in which a man produces his food, . . . his mode of production, . . . is . . . a definite way of expressing . . . life. As individuals express their life, so they are. What they are, therefore, coincides with what they produce and how they produce. The nature of individuals thus depends on the material conditions which determine their production." Naturally, it follows that if people are conditioned by circumstances external to themselves, their opinions and actions will be shaped by those circumstances. He writes of people that, "their personality is conditioned and determined by very definite class relationships. . . . A nobleman, for instance, will always remain a nobleman and a commoner always a commoner, . . . a quality inseparable from his individuality." To follow this argument to its logical conclusion is to discern that class antagonisms cannot be ameliorated. Once it is admitted that the basis of human opinion, hence motivation, lies in the structure of society and outside the control of human beings acting as independent agents, then the only possible way to resolve differences between people is to abolish those things (classes) that make them different. It is as if a person meeting a member of a different class were encountering an alien being. The class structure makes their life experiences utterly different from one another, and since this experience is the basis of their opinions and ideas, these too are utterly incompatible. People from different classes cannot compromise because they share no common ground on which compromise can be based. As Marx formulates it, there cannot be "an equilibrium between . . . forces. . . . contradictions . . . must be overthrown."[25]

Solzhenitsyn objects to this analysis on a number of grounds. First, he reminds us that by denigrating compromise Marx made his followers into self-righteous zealots. They saw no need to temper their judgments and, in fact, held that any agreement with other classes was illegitimate. They were left with no alternative but to tear their opponents to pieces.

Second, the class theory proclaims that people are evil, not on the basis of anything they have done—undermining the socialist regime, for instance—but on the basis of their social standing at birth. Individual innocence or guilt has little place under such a principle; the state is empowered to suppress "socially dangerous" elements on the basis of their "class origin." Chekist (member of the secret police) M. I. Latsis made this perfectly clear, "'In the interrogation do not seek evidence and proof that the person accused acted . . . against Soviet power. The first question should be: What is his class, what is his origin, what is his education and upbringing?' "[26]

When Marx called for the suppression of the bourgeoisie, perhaps he meant no more than to have the class structure overturned. Solzhenitsyn brings home the stark reality that in practice the abstract idea of transforming class relations translates itself into the "annihilation" of "concrete two-legged individual[s] possessing hair, eyes, a mouth, a neck and shoulders."[27]

He bitterly mocks Marx's notion that class origin is the single constituent of human motivation. If that were true, he argues in a satirical chapter of *Gulag II* entitled, "Zeks as a Nation," the prison population would constitute not only a distinct class within Soviet society, but it should be considered a different nation. Its citizens have a unique mode of production—slave labor—a separate language, a common history, and their own set of customs. Since they have no control over the means of production and do not share in the fruits of their labor, they have, given Marxist dialectics, a historical mission to overthrow their oppressors, the Communist state.[28]

For Solzhenitsyn class background is only one of the elements that make up the human personality. People have far more things in common (for example, culture) than can be discovered by looking at their status in a social hierarchy. Since they share a capacity for speech and reason, human beings are able to resolve their differences through deliberation. Moreover, they are open to "spiritual conversion." Even in the absence of a universal revolution they can rise above the narrow interests of class or party and act for the common good.[29] Finally, he argues that the very concept of rigid class stratification is inaccurate. Classes are fluid; their composition continually changes as people move up and down the social ladder.[30]

Primacy of Economics

Marx's most famous contribution to the history of thought is his teaching that man's social activity originates in economics. It follows that politics is derivative of economics, the state being a mechanism by which the ruling class holds its superior position. The ruling class's oppression may not be overt, however. The many may even choose the government under which they live, since they accept the ruling ideology of that particular historical epoch. Moreover, the ruling class is not necessarily cynical. Its members would most likely believe that the government is just and that the social hierarchy is ordained by nature or God. Only after the productive forces change do the stark inequities of a social or political system become apparent. Whatever form the regime takes, it does little to influence the underlying productive forces that dominate and control human life. Marx provides the following example, "Property, etc., in short, the entire contents of law and state is the same in North America and in Prussia, with few modifications. In North America the republic is a mere form of the state as monarchy is here. The content of the state remains outside these constitutions. . . . the material state is not political."[31]

If the problems confronting people are economic, Marx reasons, then the solutions too must be economic. Reform can occur only when the productive forces are changed. Furthermore, when the means of production finally fall into the hands of the proletariat (when everyone owns everything), the political arrangement will not matter. The cause of oppression will have disappeared so that the mechanism of oppression, the state, will wither away. One commentator writes, "Man, from being a dwarf will become a giant, and the new man will have no need of the institutions that served as fetters in his prehistory." [32]

The antidote to such idealism, Solzhenitsyn counsels, is the reign of Stalin. There is little doubt that Marx would have been appalled by Stalin's despotism; he specifically rejects the "cult of personality." Yet Solzhenitsyn wonders at the utility of a doctrine that makes no provision for governing, institutes no checks against tyranny, and lays down no limitations on the exercise of power. For example, he comments that in the Soviet Union, "the legislative, executive and judicial authorities [are] at the mercy of a telephone call from the one and only, self-appointed authority." In comparison to Western countries the protection of natural rights under "advanced Soviet jurisprudence [is] barbaric." "In our country," he complains, "everything is permissible." [33]

In this instance he is criticizing Marx, not for what he said, but for what he did not say. By presenting no scheme for arranging political life and by refusing to consider man's natural ambition, Marx committed a sin of omission. He left the countries that have accepted his principles completely unprepared for the political squabbles and contests for power and influence that are inevitable in social life. Ignorance of the true springs of human action may not be sufficient cause to blame Marx for the ascent of Stalin, but surely it can be considered a necessary cause. Or is it better to say that by providing no political check on ambition, Marx allowed Stalin (and all the other Communist dictators) to happen?

Marx did not think it necessary to formulate an institutional arrangement for his future society, however. He preferred democracy, but one unencumbered by the fetters of past democratic institutions. He foresaw the universal, free, and spontaneous association of all individuals. Putting aside for the moment the practicality of such a goal, one might ask how Marx's ideals could come into being. After the revolution he insisted that a transitional form of the state would be required. It would be a unified centralized administration resting, in the short run at least, on the "revolutionary dictatorship of the proletariat." [34] But would not some have to be more equal than others during the period of transition? Or did Marx really believe that all the workers would suddenly begin to think and act alike?

In the real world no revolution can succeed without leadership. Once in command, Solzhenitsyn contends, human beings, even the vanguard of the proletariat, are confronted by the temptations of power. Power is intoxicating, he explains; those who possess it come to have a certain aura about them. They are feared and respected by others, and are likely to expect greater privilege to go along with their higher rank. Most often they become proud of their distinction, since, as he puts it, pride "grows in the heart like lard on a pig." Once gained, power is very difficult to relinquish; people tend to cling to it in order to protect their privileges. Who wants to be demoted back to the masses?[35]

Marx had expected the love of honor, privilege, distinction, and power to disappear once private property was abolished. But Solzhenitsyn shows that human nature is not that easily transformed. Economic arrangements may change, but people's desires and passions remain. Indeed, nowhere has the grab for power been more evident than in socialist countries, proving once again that certain traits are synonymous with human life and not intrinsic to a particular mode of production.[36]

There is an even greater danger in the exercise of power. Solzhenitsyn contends that lurking within the human soul is a desire to lord it over others, to make them completely dependent on one's will, to watch them suffer. This dark tendency emerges when a person gains total control over the life of another. Using the example of the camps, he shows how the guards—the Dog Service, he calls them—were utterly corrupted by the complete power they wielded over the prisoners. They quickly became arrogant, smug, lascivious, greedy, and cruel. They used the zeks as slaves and concubines. They stole the prisoners' meager belongings and used the prisoners' suffering to entertain themselves. He writes, "Human nature, if it changes at all, changes not much faster than the geographic face of the earth. And the very same sensations of curiosity, relish, and sizing up which slave-traders felt at the slave-girl markets twenty-five centuries ago . . . possessed the Gulag bigwigs." Could such creatures really be "the heirs of a universal human culture?" Solzhenitsyn muses.[37]

Marx's disregard for the importance of politics led him to misunderstand one of the most elemental of human desires. When one ruling class is overthrown, the leaders of the revolution are bound to take its place. Privilege is rarely abolished, it is merely passed from one elite to another. "The prohibition of all privilege," Solzhenitsyn explains in response to a proposal by Andrei Sakharov, "is . . . a mere cry from the heart, and not a practical task. . . . In Russia such prohibitions, reinforced by powder and shot, have been known in the past, but privilege popped up again as soon as there was a change of bosses." By way of eliminating inequality, the revolution in Russia did little more than exchange an avaricious bourgeoisie for an even more avaricious bureaucracy.[38]

History

Just exactly how Marx thought history moved, and whether he believed it was activated by a causal chain initiated by human production, is a matter of debate. What is clear, however, is that Marx left the impression that history was moving inexorably toward its culmination in the proletarian revolution and the Communist epoch. Indeed, there is a great deal of evidence to support such an interpretation. Marx begins by asserting that man is primarily a producer, since he must produce to survive. As man creates his means of subsistence, so he establishes the rest of his social life. All is contingent on the mode of production used to maintain his physical well-being. Man is capable of changing history, but not in the way one would usually think, i.e., by a conscious act of will. Rather "by . . . acting on the external world, and changing it, he at the same time changes his own nature." This interpretation resolves two seemingly contradictory statements by Marx: "circumstances make men just as much as men make circumstances," and "Are men free to choose this or that form of society for themselves? By no means. Assume a particular state of development in the productive forces of man and you get a particular form of commerce and consumption . . . and a corresponding organization of the family, of orders, of classes, in a word, a corresponding civil society." As the economic arrangements change, so does the nature of society, as Marx expresses in his oft-quoted remark: "The hand-mill gives you society with the feudal lord; the steam-mill, society with the industrial capitalist." Thus, the history of mankind can be understood only by investigating the material forces that lie behind and move events.[39]

Marx's reflections on historical change led to the conclusion that notions of morality and rights alter from one era to another in line with the reorganization of productive forces. He states, "the class that is the ruling material power of society is at the same time its ruling intellectual power. . . . The ruling ideas are nothing more than the ideal expression of the dominant material relationships grasped as ideas. . . . The dominant idea . . . is expressed as an "'eternal law.'" He further rejects the proposition that people are endowed with natural rights. It is exactly those rights that the bourgeoisie claim are natural, he contends, that have tied the masses to the slavery of wage-labor.[40]

It is a matter of some controversy whether Marx agreed with Engels's assertion that *all* morality is variable according to its time and place in history. Engels's formulation, written before Marx's death and claiming his authority, is as follows, "We therefore reject every attempt to impose on us any moral dogma whatsoever as an eternal, ultimate and forever immutable ethical law. . . . We maintain on the contrary that all moral theories have been hitherto the product . . . of economic conditions of society obtaining at the time."[41]

Solzhenitsyn points out that all four of these propositions—history moves inevitably towards a workers' state, individuals do not control history, human beings are endowed with no intrinsic rights, and morality is variable—have been accepted as the correct Marxist-Leninist doctrine wherever revolutionary Communists have come to power. The consequence of this teaching has been to anoint party decisions with the infallibility of historical inevitability. Hence, party authority has become absolute.

In practice Marx's ideas allow party leaders to adopt any position whatever if they feel it may be conducive to the success of the movement. (Recall, for example, what Krylenko said on the expediency of Soviet criminal proceedings.) Taking full advantage of the latitude it enjoys, the party, on more than one occasion, has found it useful to ally itself with and even to aid some of the more reactionary forces of history. In the search for the most opportune course, party chiefs, in line with Marxist principles, have given little thought to the "fetters" of past morality and ethics. After all, if traditional morality and ethics are merely the discredited remnants of an antiquated mode of production, is it not correct that Communist leaders should adopt new, proletarian norms of behavior? As it turns out, Solzhenitsyn contends that the new standards are nothing more than the expression of the leader's unrestrained individual will, or, as was once said about Stalin, his "iron will."[42]

While the practical results of Marx's teaching was to liberate party leaders from moral limits, it has had the opposite effect on the vast majority of the party rank and file. In their case, choice has been riveted to the absolute will of history as it expresses itself through party decisions.

For example, Solzhenitsyn recalls that party loyalists never opposed Stalin. His commands were enthusiastically obeyed, his excesses were blamed on someone else—usually a puppet of the reactionary forces of history. Even when party members were themselves arrested, they refused to resist, complaining only of the "mistake" that had led to their personal misfortune. They did not evidence a will of their own, accepting in all things the current party line. Taking his cue from Arthur Koestler, Solzhenitsyn holds that loyalists could not object to anything the party did. To do so would cast doubt on the inevitable victory of socialism. Their entire life's work would have meant nothing.[43]

The willingness of party members to do whatever their leaders asked of them has resulted in the rulers having almost unlimited power. Perhaps this, more than any other fact, accounts for the totalitarian nature of Communist societies. Old-style despots may have had the most grandiose schemes in mind, but they could count on only a few diehard supporters, and whomever else they could buy, to carry them out. Communist tyrants have enjoyed the vigorous support of people who are convinced of the rightness of their cause and who do not ask questions about the ethics of their actions. Unlimited power in the hands of unrestrained will, it seems, is the consequence of Marx's teaching about history.

Not only does Solzhenitsyn criticize Marx for the effects of his philosophy of history, but he doubts whether those ideas have much validity. For example, if Marx was right, then no changes would have occurred in party policy after Stalin's death. In contradiction to the progressive laws of economics, however, under Khrushchev the government did change, if only for a short while. With Beria's fall it loosened its grip just a bit. The worst excesses of the terror ended, and the number of people interned was reduced. Is this not proof, Solzhenitsyn asks, that individual human beings, for reasons having little to do with the productive forces, can control the movement of history? Had Marx anywhere suggested that individual leaders would have such leeway? What else is the "personality cult" but an admission that persons can and do have an influence over events?[44]

Solzhenitsyn makes the point with an almost vindictive glee. He explains that the Stalinists who were in the Gulag did nothing to oppose their beloved leader. They accepted their fate and Stalin's brutality as ordained by sacred history. Later, when the "cult of personality" was exposed—that is, the party line changed—they were disgraced for not having resisted Stalin. A just fate, Solzhenitsyn suggests, for those who decide to genuflect before the vagaries of history.[45]

He makes the point in another way. If everything in society changes along with the mode of production, why does not language change? Since language does not change radically at each turn of history, perhaps the human capacity for speech—hence, reason—is independent of changes in the economic structure, a conclusion that casts doubt on Marx's theory of historical development.

Solzhenitsyn recognizes, of course, that language can be modified. In fact, he holds that one of the most calamitous effects of Soviet rule has been the degradation of the Russian language. The abolition of private property seems to have had little to do with this change, however. Rather, it was the awkward and mediocre mind of Stalin, along with the incessant sloganeering of the party, that invaded even the highest regions of expression and poisoned a language rich in tradition and subtlety. Again, it appears that individuals have taken a leading role in the creation of history.[46]

Human Nature

In his analysis of human nature Marx begins with a rudimentary, yet most important, fact: people must provide for their physical well-being. The distinguishing characteristic of the human species is its capacity to fulfill its needs through the activity of conscious production. In an effort to make life better and easier for themselves, people discover new ways of doing things; they create new modes of production. In transforming the economic structure, they also change the superstructure. Ideas about "morality, religion, metaphysics and all the rest of ideology" are modified, for these things are not "independent" but rest on "material relationships." Even consciousness and ideas derive from economic causes. Marx argues, "The production of ideas, of conceptions, of consciousness is directly interwoven with the material activity and of the material relations of men; it is the language of actual life. Conceiving, thinking, and the intellectual relationships of men appear here as the direct result of their material behavior. . . . Consciousness does not determine life, but life determines consciousness."[47]

Crime

Since the social and economic environment is the source of ideas and ideas are the basis of actions, it follows that people's actions are the product of the environment in which they live. It also follows that people do not have free will; they do not choose their way of life, but their surroundings choose it for them. Thus, although Marx does not make this explicit, people are not responsible for their actions. Individual guilt (and innocence?) is rejected by Marx as an antiquated bourgeois concept. Crime is the consequence of class causation. Whether Marx meant for his ideas to be carried out to their logical conclusion is unclear, but his followers had no doubt about his meaning. For example, Krylenko reasoned that, "every crime is the result of a given social system," thus, for a long time the party considered common criminals as socially friendly elements.[48]

By relieving human beings of responsibility for their behavior, Marxism excuses any act of savagery or terrorism as long as it is aimed against the bourgeoisie. Such acts are rationalized as a liberating revolt against the "fetters" of historically reactionary societies. Even when violence is not consciously political, it is thought to be caused by, and is justified as resistance against, the oppressive strictures of capitalism.[49]

Furthermore, Solzhenitsyn argues, because Marxism does not recognize that evil resides in human beings, and not exclusively in their environment (how else can Stalin be explained; he had the right social origins), it has the tendency to create criminals. For example, the Soviet Union was slow to admit that it had a crime problem. The party hid the whole issue from public view because it was embarrassed. In particular, it did not want the West to gloat over this apparent contradiction in Marxist principles. Only capitalist countries, racked by poverty and degradation, were supposed to have lawlessness. Because the Soviet Union was a socialist society, it should have been free from miscreants. The conspiracy of silence made it easier for criminals to ply their trade. Honest Soviet citizens were never warned of the dangers facing them; thus, they rarely took adequate precautions to protect themselves. A life of crime became very attractive. Outlaws found easy prey amongst the unwitting populace. They were rarely caught, and even when they were, their jail terms were relatively light. By not placing suitable barriers against the lower passions, Solzhenitsyn argues, the Soviet government encouraged those passions to be unleashed; the criminals in spirit became criminals in fact.[50]

Essence and Existence

Solzhenitsyn strenuously rebukes the idea that human beings are determined. He objects again and again to the Marxist claim that essence is determined by existence. He does not doubt that some people allow themselves to be pushed here and there by circumstances. They lived, he says, by the "swinish principle" that existence determines consciousness. This fact does not prove the correctness of Marx's theory, but shows only the lack of spiritual strength in some individuals. "For people of strong minds and spirits," he maintains, "a similarity of paths in life and a similarity of situations" does not give rise to "a similarity of characters." Even under the harshest and most extreme conditions, some inhabitants of the Gulag refused to sell their souls for a piece of bread, choosing instead to cherish their inner freedom of will. There were many such people in the camps, more perhaps than will ever be known, since often they perished. Solzhenitsyn recounts many stories of their tenacious spirit and noble resistance.[51]

It is true, no doubt, that most people make concessions to necessity—this is only human and natural. But Solzhenitsyn criticizes Marx's contention that people cannot help but be reduced by hunger to the level of animals. His character Ivan Denisovich Shukhov best embodies that resilience of character that allows people to survive without being degraded. Despite racking starvation, Ivan Denisovich eats his meager ration slowly, so it can be properly digested. He retains a certain formality in table manners and even refuses particularly unappetizing parts of his soup. In all things it is Shukhov, and not his hunger, in control, showing that people need not be overwhelmed by their needs.[52]

Solzhenitsyn undermines Marx's suppositions concerning human nature in another way. He argues that if existence dictates consciousness, everyone in the camps would have, and should have, become a revolutionary. Conditions in the Gulag were much worse than in the sweatshops and factories of the West. The oppression, suffering, and degradation were immensely greater. In fact, he wonders whether socialism could have sown the seed of its own destruction. Despite this revolutionary kernel within it, the Soviet state was not overthrown, partly because not everyone became resentful of their years as slave laborers. Loyal Communist camp dwellers, who should have been attuned to social inequities, repudiated any hint that their beloved party might have been unjust and should be overthrown, and no experience could change their minds.[53]

Transformation of Human Nature

Marx once commented that "the whole of history is nothing but a continual transformation of human nature." On this postulate rests his hope for the future of mankind. Without it the promise of a better world would be impossible. "For the success of the cause," he writes, "the alteration of man on a mass scale is necessary."[54] Marx had to champion the transformation of human nature, for to look backward into the human race's past was to see a species incapable of forming a perfect society. Marx recognized the truth of Hegel's statement that history was a slaughter bench, but he hoped to change all that. Beginning with the premise that people are determined by the environment, he calculated that when the environment changed, so would human nature. A better future was possible because all the faults and limitations of the past could be overcome. Marx thought less of people in the present—they were neither free nor responsible for their errant ways—because he expected more of them in the future; they could be reformed by perfecting the economic arrangement.

If the sordid history of the attempt to institute socialism in the Soviet Union proves anything, Solzhenitsyn maintains, it proves that human nature cannot readily be transformed. The same urges of greed, lust, and ambition that have motivated people since time immemorial are still with us no matter what the social configuration. A theory that does not take this truth into account is destined to make tragic errors. An attempt to "alter man on a mass scale" solely by restructuring economic relations is foolishness.[55]

What is Human Nature?

For Solzhenitsyn, Marx's conception of man is too narrow. He holds that there is always something in human beings that cannot be fathomed on the basis of class analysis or through causal reasoning; something that is forever surprising. "The bounds of a human being!" he writes. "No matter how you are astounded by them, you can never comprehend." People, "never fit into . . . previously set grooves." Human nature cannot be understood through "simple linear formulations, flat solutions, [and] oversimplified explanations," for it "is full of riddles and contradictions; its very complexity engenders art."[56]

Labor

Marx's view of labor is actually twofold. Labor is productive in the sense that human beings go about changing and shaping nature to their own desires. Labor is necessary in the sense that human beings must satisfy the needs of their bodies. Marx is actually more interested in the first aspect of labor, i.e., man as a creative producer, although he is normally associated with the second, i.e., people driven to revolt by oppression and scarcity. Human labor began, he asserts, as a means of overcoming natural necessity. Once begun, labor quickly became an expression of individual freedom and creativity, a way of conquering nature and putting it to one's advantage. The task of subduing nature obviously was beyond the capacity of single individuals, and therefore the community of human beings was formed—as Marx calls it, man as a "species being." As a matter of convenience and efficiency, the chores of a community were divided according to those who could best accomplish them. No sooner was this division of labor put in place, however, than it began to create problems. People relinquished part of their labor and lost a corresponding amount of control over their lives. Social stratification arose since people with particularly useful skills demanded greater compensation. These distinctions hardened into classes as wealth and privilege passed from one generation to the next.[57]

As history unfolded, the antagonisms established at the origin of social life became more acute. The individual, as worker, had an ever-decreasing influence over what he produced, until, in the final stages of capitalism, he is reduced to an appendage of the machine. The assembly-line worker has a fragmented consciousness because his productive activity consists of no more than repeating the same mechanical operation again and again. And since he has little control over the finished product, he gains no gratification from its creation.

As the society becomes more developed, the worker enjoys less and less of the fruits of his labor. His labor power, as Marx calls it, is wrenched from him by the owners. The meager wages the worker receives are dictated by the market. The owners, in a mad dash to beat their competition and to make a profit for themselves, must reduce costs by lowering wages and are forced to invest their profits (surplus value) into ever more complex machines. The new machines simplify the tasks of labor even more, thus further condemning the workers to mindless repetition and cheapening the value of their labor by eliminating any need for mechanical skill. At the same time the innovations in technology glut the market with goods. In spite of the enormous wealth all around them, the workers are reduced to abject poverty since, as Marx claims to have discovered in his theory of surplus value, capitalism cannot exist without appropriating all the value of their labor except that minimum necessary to sustain their lives.[58]

Labor Theory of Value

Solzhenitsyn argues that the theory of surplus value is a "superficial" account of economics that has gained wide popular acceptance only because few people bother to carefully read the works of Marx. The theory is flawed, he maintains, since "it declares that only workers create value and failed to take into account the contribution of either organizers, engineers, transportation, or marketing systems." In other words, Marx overlooks the role of technical expertise and managerial skill. Moreover, he neglects to pay tribute to forces within the market that tend to ameliorate working conditions. Little wonder Solzhenitsyn calls Marx's economics "primitive."[59]

The Alienation of Labor

Solzhenitsyn partly agrees and partly disagrees with Marx's views on the alienation of labor. He recognizes that people can be degraded by the labor they perform, yet he objects to Marx's assertion that this is an iron law, necessarily true in every case. Even in the camps, he explains, where people received no benefit at all from their work and had no control over the means of production, occasionally they still found labor rewarding. He makes this point through his character Ivan Denisovich. Ivan Denisovich is consoled by his work despite the harsh reality that all the value of his labor is being extracted from him—he is on starvation wages—and in spite of the fact that he has utterly no creative control over the things he is forced to produce.[60]

Interestingly, Solzhenitsyn's novel, which circulated widely during the brief Khrushchev thaw, was attacked by loyal Communists. In line with the Progressive Doctrine, they argued that Shukhov could not have enjoyed his work under such adverse conditions and that he should have refused to work and joined the "true" party members in the camps who were leading the struggle against the cult of personality. Solzhenitsyn scoffs at the latter suggestion and recalls that for loyal Communists, even in the camps, Stalin "remained an uneclipsed sun." To the former assertion he responds that something in human nature finds the process of labor rewarding. He explains:

> such is man's nature that even bitter, detested work is sometimes performed with an incomprehensible wild excitement. Having worked for two years with my hands, I encountered this strange phenomenon myself: suddenly you become absorbed in the work itself, irrespective of whether it is slave labor and offers you nothing. I experienced those strange moments at bricklaying. . . . And so surely we can allow Ivan Denisovich not to feel his inescapable labor as a terrible burden forever, not to hate it perpetually?[61]

As further proof of his contention, Solzhenitsyn considers the difference in the quality of work done in former times with that turned out today. In such a contest, he claims that the past is far superior even though present-day workers are often better compensated. The workers of old may have "ground their teeth and cursed" at the difficulty of their tasks, but their toil gained meaning by the excellence and beauty that it attained and by the purpose to which it was put. Contemporary work, in line with the spirit of equality, aspires to be little more than functional; it serves the greatest number. By failing to reach for the sublime, it loses its capacity to elicit great effort and becomes shoddy and common.[62]

Nor does Solzhenitsyn consider the division of labor to be alienating. Ivan Denisovich, for instance, feels a certain pleasure in the unison of a group effort (although he considers his own work superior to the rest).

In general the division of labor may actually help satisfy the human desire to create, since more can be accomplished in a group than by individual effort. Furthermore, the division of labor can be viewed as a natural outgrowth of the complexity of the human species. Solzhenitsyn reasons that some people are endowed by disposition and conditioning to excel at manual labor, such as Ivan Denisovich, who knew two trades and "could pick up a dozen more just like that," while others become exhausted by the same effort. In part the division of labor reflects the differences in ability and talent that nature establishes within the human race. For all his talk of the variety of social activities that will become available to people after the revolution, Marx's critique of labor does not adequately express the range and depth of human motivation.[63]

Solzhenitsyn also questions Marx's insistence that work is satisfying only when the individual is able to perform many different tasks. He agrees that there may be some truth in this assertion, as the example of Ivan Denisovich shows, but there is also a great deal of satisfaction in doing one thing very well. If people spread their talents over many occupations instead of concentrating on just one, might this not lead in the direction of dilettantism and away from the development of human excellence?[64]

Labor as the Creator of Man

According to Marx the human race is distinguished from the animals by its capacity for conscious production. This activity does not merely serve to satisfy human needs; it constitutes the very essence of the species. Through labor the human race creates itself. Marx writes, "Since for socialist man . . . the entire so-called world history is only the creation of man through human labor and the development of nature for man, he has evident and incontrovertible proof of his self-creation, his own formation process."[65] Solzhenitsyn takes exception to both of Marx's points. He argues that the distinguishing characteristic of the human race is, not that people are conscious producers, but that they are conscious. To be a conscious producer, one must first have consciousness. "Man," he asserts, restating an argument of great antiquity, "has separated himself from the animal world by thought and speech."[66]

He bitterly attacks Marx's claim that labor created man, for it was this premise that became the justification for the Gulag. Since labor constituted man, it was deduced that only labor could reconstitute, or reforge, social deviants. Thus, the Soviet state found a rationale for forced-labor camps. He writes of Engels's discovery, "the human being had arisen not through the perception of a moral idea and not through the process of thought, but out of happenstance and meaningless work (an ape picked up a stone—and with this everything began)." Marx further compounded the error by declaring that labor could reform people. Solzhenitsyn explains that for Marx, "the one and only means of correcting offenders . . . was not solitary contemplation, not moral soul-searching, not repentance, and not languishing (for all that was super-structure)—but productive labor. He himself had never in his life taken a pick in hand. To the end of his days he never pushed a wheelbarrow, mined coal, felled timber, and we don't even know how his firewood was split—but he wrote that down, and the paper did not resist."[67]

To prove his point Solzhenitsyn gives many examples of people who repented their past lives and reformed their ways. None of them were reclaimed by labor. Indeed, the heavy physical labor of the camps in which people replaced machines and from which "the human being" was "once created . . . from the ape," often had the opposite effect, "inexplicably transform[ing] him back into the ape again." Solzhenitsyn mocks the Progressive Doctrine for having ushered into the world the cruelty of the corrective (destructive) labor camps. He compares the exploitation found in the camps to that which existed during the old regime and in the capitalist West, and shows that under Communism far worse conditions prevailed. He ironically suggests that only under the aegis of the Progressive Doctrine did exploitation reach its full potential. To build socialism people were forced to work at or below subsistence level.[68]

Nothing in the bourgeois world could compare to it. Western governments could not marshal sufficient force to keep people in such intolerable conditions for long. They would simply stop obeying, using the "false" bourgeois right of liberty to fend for themselves. Or they would rise up and demand a more equitable share of the nation's resources, which is exactly what occurred during the labor unrest of the twentieth century.

Under Communism, however, power was centralized, making a higher stage of oppression possible. Particularly in the camps, where prisoners could be shot without warning, full extraction of labor was possible at little or no material costs. Prisoners were driven to work by starving them and then dangling higher rations in front of them as a reward for greater effort. Of course, this method had its drawbacks; after about three months prisoners could no longer perform any useful labor and most died. Not even in the darkest days of serfdom was there exploitation on such a scale.[69]

There is an even closer relationship between Marxism and the Gulag, Solzhenitsyn maintains. The camps, he says, are the foundation of Marxist economics. He reasons as follows: Socialism could never have been established in the Soviet Union (or elsewhere) without the assistance of forced labor. How else could people be made to toil and receive nothing in return? The nation was too poor to afford the capital necessary for the vast industrialization planned by the party. It is doubtful whether the state could ever have raised sufficient capital to modernize, since its economic policies crushed individual initiative. To fulfill its promise of material advancement it had no other option but to conscript labor. Was there another way it could elicit the talents "of highly skilled specialists who were willing in addition to live for years in conditions unfit for dogs?"[70]

An objection can be raised that Russia was not an industrial nation, as Marx's theory had expected, when it was overtaken by a premature revolution. Hence, Marx cannot be held accountable for the horrors of modernization that took place in Russia. He had argued no such development would be necessary. This proposition is true enough, although it must be recognized that successful Communist revolts have always taken place in underdeveloped countries. In addition to this discrepancy, Solzhenitsyn unearths an even subtler connection between Marxism and forced labor.

Marx insists that alienation will end only when the necessity for labor no longer exists. He envisages a mode of production that "does away with labor" and asserts that "the question is not the liberation but the abolition of labor." He sees a time when science will fully conquer natural necessity; when man and nature will be one. Labor, instead of a hated torment, will be transformed into a "free manifestation of life." Solzhenitsyn responds that nature is not so easily brought to heel. Its complexities and mysteries are beyond the human capacity to unravel fully. A concerted effort to bring nature totally under human command is likely to backfire, resulting in an ecological disaster of some sort. Nature can never be fully transcended because human beings did not originate existence and have no means of abolishing death; the beginning and the end of being are beyond their control. Yet Marx insisted that alienation would cease and true happiness would reign only through the conquest of nature. Those under Marx's influence, those who accept his goals, are destined to attempt this feat.[71]

Insofar as nature cannot be overcome, Communism, no matter where it exists, is always in the process of being built. Since Communism's economic system is so poor at generating wealth, especially investment capital, it cannot hope to build the machines required to transform the world without forcibly extracting the profits from somebody's labor. It is by this chain of reasoning that Solzhenitsyn forwards his claim: the essence of Marxism is the camps.

In a final verbal thrust at Marx, Solzhenitsyn compares the system of labor that was spawned under Marx's name to Asiatic despotism. He adopts the same expression used by Marx—Asiatic despotism—to describe the most primitive form of social organization, virtually the first stage of historical development. The choice of terms is more than coincidental, since the attributes of Asiatic despotism were said by Marx to consist of "the private arbitrariness of particular individuals," and a centralized state that constructs and maintains a complex and costly waterworks system—a rather accurate description of one of Stalin's pet projects, the Belomar Canal.[72]

Love of One's Own

In an address before the AFL-CIO, Solzhenitsyn said that the *Communist Manifesto* "contains even more terrible things than what has actually been done." Apart from historical analysis and some proposals for minor reforms of society,[73] the *Manifesto*'s major prescriptions involve the abolition of private property, the transformation of the family, and the communism of women. Marx's suggestions for change strike at those things that most people hold most dear—property, family, spouse.

Property

SOLZHENITSYN'S DEFENSE OF PRIVATE PROPERTY

Marx's name and the endeavor to abolish private property have become almost synonymous. In a sense, Marx views private property as the root of all evil. To abolish it would be to rid society of injustice. To be sure, Solzhenitsyn agrees, private property is a kind of selfishness because it gives personal gratification to its owner. However, the abolition of private property will not free the human race from selfishness and greed. In fact, the confiscation of property is likely to jeopardize some very valuable things, including important attributes (virtues) of man's character. "The fundamental concepts of private property and private economic initiative," he writes, "are part of man's nature, and necessary for his personal freedom and his sense of normal well-being." But why is this so?[74]

First, and given the history of Soviet Communism, perhaps most importantly, the private ownership of property acts as a shield or buffer against the arbitrary and capricious whims of those in power (including well-intentioned bureaucrats). Personal property allows individuals to act as independent agents. Because they are free to secure their own livelihood, they are not exclusively or directly dependent on the government for their well-being or life. Moreover, the separation of political and economic power inhibits the government from tightening its grip. It loses a powerful tool of coercion. Since it is not fully in control of the economy, it cannot use the threat of starvation—by taking away one's job, for example—as a way of gaining obedience. Finally, the separation of political and economic activity acts to create autonomous centers of power that, in the nature of things, tend to keep each other in check.

Second, private property increases the likelihood of competence, even excellence, in the professions. In his novel *Cancer Ward*, Solzhenitsyn's character Dr. Oreshchenkov is made to defend private medical practice against socialized or state medicine. Although the views of Dr. Oreshchenkov are not necessarily those of his creator, the arguments that he presents are so compelling that they cannot readily be dismissed.

Oreshchenkov maintains that a doctor, and by implication a member of other trades and professions, "should depend on the impression he makes on his patients, he should be dependent on his popularity."[75] Since patients are likely to seek out the best care available for themselves, such a scheme weeds out incompetent or untalented people. (Who wants to pay for poor health care?) At the same time, it rewards the adroit with renown and, of course, material gain. The good doctor, it seems, is an advocate of the free market.

Obviously, anyone holding such a view is being inconsistent. He is entrusting the care and well-being of others to the personal selfishness of doctors. He is arguing that in one man's breast can exist both a love of others and a love of self. Despite the logical inconsistencies of this position, it does seem to accurately reflect a tension that occurs, to a greater or lesser degree, within every human being. People can and do act selflessly, but it would violate reason to say that is all they worry about. A proper regard for oneself is not unnatural or even ignoble. It merely reflects the desire of every individual for well-being and may even express an impulse toward the perfection of one's ability and character.

Not to compensate people for their hard work or superior ability is likely to lead to mediocrity. The talented may begin to wonder if they should bother developing their skills. If the reward for work of high caliber is no different than for low, will not the able and diligent throw up their hands in disgust and join the crowd? One does not have to bow down to the perfection of the marketplace to see that a rough justice is achieved when people are compensated for a job well done.[76]

Solzhenitsyn shows a strong sympathy for Dr. Oreshchenkov's views. He argues, for example, that the peasants' desire for land was an expression of the dual nature of human striving. He explains, "the peasant masses longed for land and if this in a certain sense means freedom and wealth, in another (and more important) sense it means obligation, in yet another (and its highest) sense it means a mystical tie with the world and a feeling of personal worth."[77] He further points out that farmers who obtained their own land during the N.E.P. produced more than they did either for their former landlords or for the communal farms. They were even likely to learn the most advanced techniques of agriculture.[78]

Returning to Dr. Oreshchenkov's argument, the free market, to a great extent, protects patients (and, by implication, consumers). First, it allows for free choice. Except in a dire emergency the ill can seek out a doctor they prefer, choosing one they trust. A private doctor is likely to be more solicitous than one working for the state because he is dependent for his livelihood on what his patients think of him. A personal rapport is likely to develop in which the patient comes to be treated as a whole person rather than just a sick part.

Under socialized medicine the doctor is under little compulsion to care about the private concerns of individuals; rather, he is pressed to turn out a certain amount of work. Patients are treated as one case in a long line of cases. In rare instances such a system produces exceptionally qualified physicians. More often it yields no more than technical competence. And at its worst, it engenders apathy, since the doctor's salary is paid, regardless. The free market may turn the members of every profession into wage earners, as Marx suggested, but socialism transforms them into something worse, insensitive bureaucrats.[79]

Solzhenitsyn does not subscribe fully to the vagaries of the free market, however. For instance, he does not condone that excessive thirst for wealth that leads some people to oppress others or to sell secrets to their nation's enemies. He seems to argue that the free market works best when the size of businesses is limited and when economic relations between people do not become entirely impersonal. The question that immediately comes to mind is whether such limitations on commerce and industry are practical. What of economies of scale? To this point Solzhenitsyn gives two responses. First, he advocates a "small technology" and a decentralized economy, which, although less efficient, may be more conducive to the human good. Second, he argues that the ills of the free market can be mitigated if people understand that there is something higher than the quest for material rewards—morality should place a check on avarice.

Let us return once again to Dr. Oreshchenkov. Surprisingly, he argues that private medicine is less expensive than socialized. In the first place, he points out that socialized medicine is not free, but is paid for by the levy that government places on people's earnings. If that money were not taken from them, they could use it to pay for medical care, even if that meant having to forgo some luxury. The cost of medical care could be kept down because private medicine is less wasteful. It is not encumbered by the salaries of a large, bureaucratic support staff. Moreover, people are less likely to seek unnecessary care or consultations when they are made to pay for it. However, Dr. Oreshchenkov does not fully endorse a free-market approach to medical care. He believes that truly costly medical treatment is the responsibility of the community.

Solzhenitsyn seems to concur with his artisic creation. In disagreement with Marx, he asserts that the communism of property is wasteful. When things are held in common there is no accountability, nor is there any care for their use. To illustrate this truth he recounts the tale of a *Potemkin* sailor, one of the mutineers, who had escaped punishment and made a good life for himself in Canada as a farmer. When the revolution came to his beloved homeland, he sold everything except a tractor and returned

SOLZHENITSYN ON MARX   103

to his native region. With his tractor and his money he hoped to help build socialism. He enlisted in one of the first communes and donated the tractor for common use. The tractor was driven any which way by whoever happened along and was quickly ruined. The money was rapidly squandered on foolish expenses. Finding himself working harder and all the while growing thinner, the farmer escaped from the land of shared wealth and returned to Canada to begin life over again.[80]

Private ownership, on the other hand, encourages respect for the worth of things, since the responsibility rests squarely with the owner and because the owner must pay for ruined equipment out of his own pocket. (Ivan Denisovich values the best trowel because he is proud of his superior bricklaying. Even though he would not have to replace it, he fears entrusting it to others. So he meticulously hides it at the end of each workday.)[81]

Finally, Solzhenitsyn maintains that abolishing private wealth does away with the possibility of exercising the virtue of generosity. If the state owns everything, then obviously an individual cannot give it away. From a realistic perspective, no doubt, the loss of virtue may be counterbalanced by the gain to common humanity. Yet to Solzhenitsyn this is just one more example of how Marxism undermines the development of human character and the exercise of virtue in the rush to provide for man's material welfare.[82]

THE CONFISCATION OF PROPERTY

As is the case with many of Marx's other forecasts, the confiscation of property has not worked as he predicted. Marx expected that small businesses would have been swallowed up by huge capitalist enterprises when the revolution occurred. But that is not at all what happened. Small holdings were confiscated along with large industries. This is so, Solzhenitsyn argues, because the desire to hold property is so widespread among mankind. Hence, expropriation of property (and this is true even in an advanced industrial country) is likely to injure not just a few bloated capitalists but a large segment of the population.

Solzhenitsyn presents a particularly poignant illustration of this fact in relating the plight of Russia's peasants. Confiscation of their property began as early as 1918 with an edict issued by Lenin. "Those guilty of selling, or buying up, or keeping for sale in the way of business food products which have been placed under the monopoly of the republic . . . [are to be] imprisoned for a term of not less than ten years, combined with the most severe forced labor."[83]

The N.E.P. gave a seven-year respite to the peasants, which many used to enrich themselves and their villages. In the strange tangle of Marxist logic, however, it was these people who suffered the most. Solzhenitsyn estimates that 15 million kulaks paid an extreme price—death—for their ambition, industry, and skill as farmers. On the other hand, the Progressive Doctrine took poverty as a sign of solidarity with the workers. Those who "drank down everything" in vodka and saved nothing were immune from the peasant plague. Sometimes they were even given important posts on the collective farms. There were others who simply did not want to work. They loved possessions no less dearly than the next fellow, but they had too little control over their passions to keep them.[84]

Confiscation of property also has a tendency to destroy artisans and tradespeople, Solzhenitsyn claims. He tells of a former peasant who, by his hard work, was able to open a small sausage factory. When collectivization came the tax man hounded him unmercifully until finally he had little left of any worth. When a survey of the peasant's holdings revealed that some rubber plants in a tub would have to be taken, he hacked them to pieces in disgust. He was subsequently arrested for destroying state property. (The tale does not end there, however. The peasant ended up in the camps working in a sausage factory. This sausage factory was not confiscated, since its only customers were party higher-ups.)

Finally, Solzhenitsyn maintains that expropriation of property excuses and makes more acute the low passion of envy. Those who are jealous of the success of others and "incapable of making anything of themselves except activists" are the ones most likely to carry out expropriation. The urge to expropriate is nourished by a contempt for human excellence.[85]

For example, the property of the monks at Solovestsky Island was confiscated by people acting on the Progressive Doctrine's assumption that priests do no more than prey on others. The monks' cloister had been remarkably successful at agriculture, and had discovered and fished a particularly flavorful variety of herring. The monks were completely self-sufficient, growing all their own food and exporting fish to pay for religious relics. Whom were they hurting? How did their private holdings oppress anyone? Only a desire to show the monks up, to exhibit the superiority of socialism, could have compelled the Bolsheviks to throw these people off their land. However, the socialist commune that took over the monks' property could not grow crops in such an intemperate climate and no one could find where to catch the herring.[86]

THE REEMERGENCE OF SELF-INTEREST

The stated goal of the Marxist revolution was to abolish bribery, corruption, oppression, and the whole tawdry mess associated with the cash nexus. Yet no sooner had the revolution been completed, explains Solzhenitsyn, than sure enough these age-old vices reappeared. As early as 1918 the Commissioners of Supply for the Eastern Front were discovered to have siphoned off millions of rubles into their pockets. They used the money to buy big houses. They rode around on expensive horses and engaged in orgies with women their money had impressed. Even the Cheka was not immune from greed. One very successful agent worked on piece rate.[87]

These incidents all took place early on in the revolution. It could be that they reflect the psychology of a bourgeois background, the initial errors of what Marx calls crude Communism. The problem with this analysis, as Solzhenitsyn vividly shows, is that the quest for material gain and economic privilege became more pronounced as time went on. By 1937 the entire party had become infected with an oligarchic disdain for the life of the ordinary Soviet citizen. Party members sentenced to the camps refused to share any of their extra rations or packages from home with the other zeks. They mouthed the slogans of equality and community, but they would actually have none of it. Their private automobiles, special closed stores, and fine dachas had corrupted them.[88]

Part of the problem was created by Stalin. Trained by vicious bureaucratic struggles and cynical to the core, he understood that money is a temptation few can resist. He preyed on this weakness, paying party officials high wages and then, when his trust in them soured, using their wealth as the basis for a case against them. On the theory that soldiers would fight harder if it were in their self-interest to do so, he allowed the Red Army to plunder the defeated Germans in World War II. Top NKVD officers were rumored to have amassed vast personal fortunes in this way. In spite of the fact that it did no productive labor, Stalin's favorite institution, the secret police, never lacked for material comforts. Its vigilance in uncovering fresh cases was enhanced by the high pay and benefits its members received. Prison chiefs in remote areas virtually lived the lives of ancient potentates, harems and all.[89]

For most of the time the party has held power, Solzhenitsyn argues and the reports from the Communist world now confirm, special privileges were accorded to high party officials. The top echelon enjoyed elaborate apartments, stately summer homes, chauffeured limousines, and the finest clothes and food. Brezhnev even owned an entire lake that he used as a private game reserve.[90]

It is possible that Solzhenitsyn's image of high party officials has been tainted by his years of forced poverty in the camps.[91] The other possibility, the more likely one, is that he understands the system only too well. Certainly the disclosures of party corruption in the Soviet Union and especially in Eastern Europe have borne him out. Few people—especially party members, it seems—can live up to Marx's principles. Such principles defy human nature by asking that people work with no thought of material advantage. They demand that self-interest disappear. But self-interest has not disappeared. Indeed, wherever a Marxist revolution has taken place, self-interest has reappeared with a particular vengeance; the stage of what Marx called crude Communism has never been transcended.

As further evidence of this point, Solzhenitsyn offers the example of the incentive system that had to be reintroduced into the Soviet economy (in fact, into the economy of every Marxist country) as a way of getting people to work. The Soviets merely appropriated the piecework method, once common to capitalism, and renamed it socialist competition. Insofar as the government did succeed in squelching private initiative, it resurfaced as the "second story" economy, black market labor in which craftsmen are paid directly and thereby avoid the impenetrable bureaucratic tangle that accompanies all state-owned enterprises.[92] Evidently, laziness is more a part of human nature than Marx had predicted; it is best overcome by material incentives.

THE PROPER LIMITS OF PROPERTY

Solzhenitsyn labels as a fantasy Marx's hope that the love of private property can be expelled from the human soul. The consequences of that fantasy are visible in the Soviet terror. First an attempt was made to banish forcefully the desire for property by exterminating those classes who were thought to be the standard-bearers of private interest. Later the fantasy reemerged in the rule of people who espoused the ideals of Marx, while presiding over one of the least equitable economic systems on earth. Somehow, under the influence of Marx, people have twisted and warped reality so much that they no longer seem aware of what their actions mean. How else, Solzhenitsyn makes us ponder, can one explain the fact that party officials, entrusted with teaching the masses about the ideology of Marxism-Leninism, would not "lift a finger . . . without payment?"[93]

No doubt Marx would be outraged to learn that his teaching has been put to such use. He had hoped that once property was held in common, people would pursue more humane, nonmaterialistic endeavors. But Solzhenitsyn wonders if things really could have turned out otherwise. In spite of all Marx's talk about the transcendence of property, he does not differ from the bourgeoisie except in one respect. The philosophy that inspired both capitalism and Marxism encouraged the idea that material well-being can somehow make people happy. Indeed, Marx goes a step further in stressing the link between material pursuits and human activity. The real difference Marx has with capitalism is not so much about the ends of life—prosperity is *the* goal pursued by both—but rather about the means of attaining that end. For capitalism, individuals are responsible for their own well-being, for Marx, the welfare of individuals is a communal activity. In truth, the essence of Marx's teaching concerns not so much the abolition but the communal ownership of property.

Little wonder, Solzhenitsyn remarks, that Marxism encourages materialism. "We only have one life" is the motto that has sprung up under its banner, "and we must live it to the fullest." Marx's mistake was that he gave no teaching that would restrain greed, but left that to the good graces of history. He (and other socialists, as well) assumed that people would become selfless once property was held in common. As Solzhenitsyn explains, "In no socialist doctrine . . . are moral demands seen as the essence of socialism—there is merely a promise that morality will fall like manna from heaven after the socialization of property."[94]

The root of Marx's dilemma lies in the assumption that human beings will evolve into something better once universal prosperity is achieved. But what is that something better? Will they become generous, moral people with highly developed characters? If that is the end, as many of the purified Marxists hold, then why is material prosperity necessary at all? After all, Solzhenitsyn and his friends developed their characters while in the camps. It is apparent from everyday life, moreover, that people can strengthen their characters in spite of suffering the most severe poverty. Indeed, it seems that a certain amount of hardship is a positive component in the growth of spiritual well-being. Without it, people are lulled into a false sense of security. They resist confronting their mortality and squander their time on earth in petty pursuits.

What Marx thought to be essential—prosperity—Solzhenitsyn holds, in the most important sense, to be superfluous. Only after everything is lost, he believes, can one fathom the depths of the spirit and enjoy the blessings of complete freedom. He writes of his dawning awareness in the camps, "Own nothing! Possess nothing! Buddha and Christ taught us this, and the Stoics and the Cynics. Greedy though we are, why can't we seem to grasp that simple teaching? Can't we understand that with property we destroy our soul?" By losing possessions one gains the ability to think, to perceive things clearly and impartially. He explains, "A free head—now is that not an advantage in the Archipelago? And there is more freedom: No one can deprive you of your family and property—you have already been deprived of them. What does not exist—not even God can take away. And this is a basic freedom." [95]

Only a person who has suffered a great deal, who has survived the ordeal of imprisonment, can truly value, "the right to move about without waiting for an order; the right to be alone; the right to gaze at the stars that were not blinded by the searchlights. . . . Yes there were many, many more rights like these." Perhaps those who have suffered can better appreciate the sublime pleasures of the mind, those "mysterious flights of the soul which physiologists have never explained." [96]

Solzhenitsyn here seems to contradict what was said above about the virtues of private property. There is a contradiction, but one that reflects human nature and not Solzhenitsyn's oversight. The supposition that one can only be happy after one has lost everything is an extreme position. It would be more acceptable to most people if they had no concern for their daily bread, no care for the welfare of their bodies. If everyone adopted this attitude the human race would soon die out from want of food. There is little probability of that, however. Most people, most of the time, are deeply interested in their personal welfare. A teaching that expects them to be otherwise is a fantasy. But this is not to say that people's physical cares ought to be their only, or even their most important, concern. They need to be reminded occasionally, by the example of individuals who have no tangible goods but who possess a great spiritual strength, that the most necessary things in life are not necessarily the highest things for which human beings exist. If for no other reason, a moral teaching is needed to show people the proper limits of acquisition. At its highest, a moral perspective can even lead them to a full development of their potential.

Marx's teaching places no limits on mankind. It reasons that once people have everything, they will be happy. However, experience does not bear this out. Stalin had everything and he wasn't happy. (Nor does private wealth necessarily lead to happiness, as the lives of some celebrities indicate.) Solzhenitsyn's character Shulubin explains, "Happiness is a mirage. . . . When we have enough loaves of white bread to crush them under our heels, when we have enough milk to choke us, we still won't be in the least happy. . . . If we care only about 'happiness' and about reproducing our species, we shall merely crowd the earth senselessly and create a terrifying society." [97]

Solzhenitsyn's endorsement of private property and material acquisition is a qualified one. Human beings should be restrained by moral considerations and, as the passage cited above suggests, by natural limits. On this point he even acknowledges a difference with bourgeois philosophy, since it has "no incentive to self-limitation." Indeed, its ideas about private property, "would be beneficial to society if only . . . the carriers of these ideas had limited themselves, and not allowed the size of their property and thrust of their avarice to become a social evil, which provoked so much justifiable anger. It was as a reply to this shamelessness of unlimited money-grabbing that socialism in all its forms developed." In a backhanded way he accepts that Marx may have done some good. Solzhenitsyn explains that if nothing else, the October Revolution and the "inhuman experience" that followed taught the ruling classes elsewhere to make compromises. [98]

Solzhenitsyn's position on property can be summarized as follows. He insists that people be allowed to acquire property, since this is a natural desire growing out of their physical existence. Yet he is even more adamant that this not be their only pursuit, since the most important part of a human's being is not physical. The dual nature of human existence is perhaps best expressed by the erstwhile free-marketeer Dr. Oreshchen-kov, of whom Solzhenitsyn writes:

> He had to take frequent rests nowadays. His body demanded this chance to recoup its strength with the same urgency his inner self demanded silent contemplation free of external sounds, conversations, thoughts of work, free of everything that made him a doctor. Particularly after the death of his wife, his inner consciousness had seemed to crave a pure transparency. It was just this sort of silent immobility, without planned or even floating thoughts, which gave him a sense of purity and fulfillment. . . . The image he saw did not seem to be embodied in . . . work or activity. . . . The meaning of existence was to preserve unspoiled, undisturbed, and undistorted the image of eternity with which each person is born.
> Like a silver moon in a calm, still pond.[99]

Family

Marx never actually calls for the abolition of the family. He simply observes in the *Communist Manifesto* that "the bourgeois family will vanish."[100] Marx's opposition to the family is not accidental, however. Communism, by its nature, demands a loosening of family ties. Attachment to family has a tendency to make concern for the well-being of universal mankind less strong. It turns people's loyalty inward toward blood ties rather than outward toward the common good. It promotes a sort of injustice, since family members would rather see their loved ones advance, even at the expense of others and sometimes to the detriment of the general welfare of society. Taken to an extreme, love of family supports nepotism.

A strong connection also exists between family and property. Parents want to give their children all the advantages that their wealth may obtain. They may wish to perpetuate their family line by providing for their posterity after they have died. Needless to say, the desire to secure immortality through family lineage leads to inequality, since the advantages of wealth are passed from generation to generation. That Marx understood this to be a hindrance to equality can be seen in his prescription for the "abolition of the right of inheritance."[101]

All governments must confront people's natural attachment to family.

To a greater or lesser degree every society demands that family members broaden their perspective and look to the general good of the community. If they did not, society would devolve into factional strife based on blood ties. Communism takes an extreme position, however, since it requires that people be at least as interested in the welfare of humanity as they are in that of their own kin.[102]

Solzhenitsyn makes a number of observations about Communism's treatment of families. Although he acknowledges a certain nobility in the fervent attachment to humanity, he wonders whether there may not be something indecent about a commitment that entails neglecting one's own relatives. He tells of a local party secretary, who, as the Organs searched her house prior to her arrest, was more troubled about the incomplete state of the minutes of party sessions than she was about never seeing her children again. The interrogator conducting the search had to remind her to bid them farewell.[103]

Another Communist, a prisoner in the camps, received a letter from her daughter asking whether she was guilty. "Mama," the fifteen year old wrote, "are you guilty or not? I hope you weren't guilty, because then I won't join the Komsomol, and I won't forgive them because of you." Unable to bear her daughter hating the Doctrine of Universal Brotherhood, the mother, who was as guiltless as were millions of her prisonmates, responded, "I am guilty. . . . Enter the Komsomol!"[104]

Solzhenitsyn also protests against the idea that children should be raised in common (which in practice translates into being raised by the state). Marx did not specifically recommend that children be reared in common, yet this proposition can be implied from his assertion that all human relations, including of course those of the family, should become communal. In an ironic way, Solzhenitsyn contends that the camps were a sort of testing ground for Communist proposals. Many infants were born there without the benefit of marriage. Camp authorities discouraged lasting relationships, so fathers rarely were able to see their offspring. Mothers were allowed to stay with sucking babies until they were weaned. After that, parent and child were separated and the state assumed responsibility for rearing the youngsters. Solzhenitsyn reports that these children were often ill-adjusted and soon returned to the camps on their own as juvenile offenders.

There was another example of the communal raising of children. This occurred amongst those young people who found themselves thrown into the camps on one pretext or another. It was no small-scale social experiment. In 1927 nearly half of the population of the Gulag was between sixteen and twenty-four years old. By 1935 Stalin had decreed that anyone over twelve years old could be sentenced as an adult.[105]

These young people were not reforged either by the communal life they were made to lead or by the human-creating labor they were forced to perform. Instead, they were quickly infected by the poisonous attitude of the camps. Without parents to guide them, they became uncontrollable. They lost all capacity to subdue their immediate desires. In their thoughts existed "no demarcation line between what was permissible and what was not permissible, and no concept whatever of good and evil." Perhaps most revealing of all, their capacity for speech was diminished, so that they used only those expressions that conveyed their immediate bodily desires.[106]

Obviously, rearing children in the camps is not completely analogous to a more sympathetic and humane program of communal upbringing. Still, Solzhenitsyn's presentation makes the point that children need the love and direct supervision of parents if they are to mature into decent and normal human beings. The family is the medium by which civility is transmitted through generations. Any scheme that undermines the integrity of the family is also a threat to civility. Since the family is a necessary component of social life, every government (and the ideas on which it is based) must accept certain limitations on what it can achieve. For instance, equality of conditions is impossible because people are naturally attached to their own and seek to pass their privileges on to their children.

The Soviet Union is a perfect example of the tension between equality and family. Solzhenitsyn describes how the upper class (party members or highly paid experts) has used its position to advance the careers and fortunes of their progeny. The Soviet elite is concerned with the same problems that confront parents everywhere—providing their offspring with a good education, finding them a suitable mate and securing them a comfortable job. Ironically in a regime governed by the ideas of Marx, the children of the Soviet well-to-do are more likely to be well situated by their parents than are children in other societies, since almost everything in the Soviet Union is done on the basis of patronage. Once again it seems Communism underestimated the intransigence of human nature.[107]

There is an even greater irony concerning the relationship between the Marxist state and the institution of the family. Solzhenitsyn claims that it was the threat posed against people's families that kept the regime in power. For example, a favorite trick of interrogators was to elicit confessions by threatening to haul people's families in for questioning. Prisoners were kept in line for fear their loved ones would be persecuted. For many years Soviet society was immobilized by the fear of reprisals against the family.[108]

Interestingly, he argues that the people most able to resist despotic edicts of the state were those with no families, hence nothing left to lose, or those with such strong family ties that everything outside the clan was met with hostile resistance. Enough has been said about the former, but he presents an amusing and revealing anecdote about the latter.

After he was released from the Gulag, Solzhenitsyn was exiled to Kok-Terek, where he became a schoolteacher. One of his students, Abdul, belonged to the Chechens, a group of people who "never sought to please, to ingratiate themselves with the bosses, their attitude was always haughty and indeed openly hostile." [109] They viewed all laws, except their own, with contempt and simply refused to corrupt their daughters by obeying the rules concerning mandatory education.

The story begins when Abdul's brother killed an old Chechen woman while robbing her. When his act was discovered he coldly turned himself in to the MVD to escape the reprisals of her family. Under the harsh Chechen law, the dead woman's clan had to take vengeance on some member of the murderer's family. As the next oldest male, Abdul was singled out to take the place of his criminal older brother; he was to be executed. Surprisingly, no one seemed able to stop the vendetta—not the teachers, not the headmaster, not the district party committee, not even the mighty MVD. At last, only the Chechen elders were able to avert bloodshed by sentencing the elder brother to death whenever he came near a Chechen knife. And Abdul "learned all over again that the greatest force on earth is the law of vendetta." [110]

While "Europeans" might scoff at "this savage law, this cruel and senseless butchery," Solzhenitsyn claims that the Chechens can teach us an important lesson. A few of them fell victim to the vendetta, but not so many, and those left behind were strengthened by the harsh example. The law of vendettas created "a force field of fear" around the Chechens, frightening strangers and enemies alike. "Strike your neighbors, that strangers may fear you! The ancestors of the highlanders in remote antiquity could have found no stronger hoop to gird their people," he writes and then wonders, "Has the socialist state offered them better?" [111]

For Solzhenitsyn there is something noble in the fierce attachment to family that ancient cultures foster. If such cultures do not breed sociable, law-abiding citizens, at least they do not produce passive ones. Their people rarely drink from the well of justice, but are refreshed, instead, at the springs of spiritedness. In such societies one's own good, or that of one's clan, is always favored over that of the community; the particular over the general. Hence, these societies rarely enjoy an easy peace. On the other hand, the horrors of mass murder, in which millions meekly march to their graves, are equally unknown.

Needless to say, Solzhenitsyn does not give his unqualified support to the ancient law of blood feuds. In its own way, such a tradition negates anything higher in humanity than an individual's, or a family's, point of view. It leads to anarchy, if not in politics, then surely in morals. Although he is sympathetic to the bonds of kinship, he also recognizes principles of a higher kind. Again his position is inconsistent, but again it reflects an inconsistency found in human existence. People love their own and they love the common good, or some concept of the good, simply. Sometimes the tension between the two loves cannot be easily reconciled.

The object of literature, of a work of art, is to make ideas come to life. The dual nature of human attachments is brought to life in Solzhenitsyn's characterization of the peasant Spiridon. Spiridon is an inmate in the Marvino Sharaska (a research institute inhabited by zeks and the setting for the *First Circle*). He has been incarcerated for happening to fall behind German lines during World War II. Over the years his fortunes have risen and fallen with the various turns in party ideology and the revolutionary events that have overtaken his native land. Both in good times and in bad, Spiridon seems unaffected by the ideas and principles of those in power, be they tsarist, Leninist, or Stalinist. His one overriding concern in life, which he pursues with toughness and cunning, is the security and well-being of his family. Solzhenitsyn writes, "What Spiridon loved was land. What Spiridon had was family. The concepts of 'country' and 'religion' and 'socialism,' which seldom turn up in everyday conversation, were evidently unknown to Spiridon. His ears were closed to them; his tongue would not speak them. His country was—family. His religion was—family. Socialism was—family." Despite his first love, Spiridon expresses a due regard for something higher. When questioned by the philosophic Nerzhin, who proposes that no one "can really tell who is right and who is wrong" since "life changes," Spiridon answers simply, "The wolfhound is right and the cannibal is wrong."[112]

Solzhenitsyn's final position on family may be summarized as follows. In his haste to equalize social conditions, Marx had to undermine attachment to family. By doing so, he advanced ideas contrary to the natural affections of most people. Moreover, he overlooked the salutary effect families have on the transmission of morals and manners from one generation to the next. A philosophy that disdains the bonds of family either will not be obeyed or will be obeyed to the detriment of humanity. Recognizing the necessity of families puts a limit on what can be expected in social life, especially as regards the equality of conditions. People may be drawn to the common good, or to some principle above them, but love of family draws them away from ever fully endorsing it. A decent government can be measured by how sympathetically it endeavors to resolve the tension that exists at the root of our social lives.

The Community of Women

It is not clear exactly what form of marriage Marx envisages in the final stage of Communism. In the short run, at least, he argues that the "hypocritically concealed community of women" of the bourgeoisie would be replaced by an "openly legalized one" of the proletariat. Moreover, he suggests that in the future epoch, humans will have far less exclusive relationships than those commonly practiced in previous historical periods.[113]

It should come as no surprise that Solzhenitsyn tests Marx's ideas in the experience of the camps. He finds that rather than liberating people from the fetters of an obsolete morality, the community of women serves only to degrade them by unleashing the admittedly natural, yet low, passion of lust. He presents the example of Krivoshchek Camp, where five hundred women lived together in a barracks. Officially, men were prohibited from the area, but the ban was ignored by everyone. Women, especially the pretty ones, were propositioned, bribed, and threatened into satisfying masculine urges. Since the barracks was a common one, the acts were performed in the open. This served to further arouse passersby, some of whom were no more than juveniles. The only defense a woman had was to pick a man who could defend her "from the next in line, from the whole greedy queue, from the crazy juveniles gone berserk, aroused by everything they could see and breathe in there."[114] The community of women seems to evolve into nothing more than debauchery.

Solzhenitsyn implies that although the exclusivity of relations between the sexes may not be more natural (in the sense of satisfying natural functions), it is certainly more decent. The superiority of exclusive relationships derives, first, from their being the basis of family life, and, second, from their being a source of self-restraint. Prohibitions against open sexual unions build a healthy sense of shame within people. Such rules teach people to govern their desires rather than be governed by them. In a sense strictures against sex are the first lessons by which adults learn to subdue their desires and impulses so that they may command their own destinies. Finally, while remaining faithful to one's spouse is undoubtedly a difficult task, Solzhenitsyn holds that it is a sign of a certain integrity and even nobility of the soul (even when, as in Nerzhin's case—*The First Circle*—that nobility is futile).[115]

Solzhenitsyn infers that Marx's misunderstanding of the relationship between the sexes stems from his assertion that in the capitalist world, "all passions and all activities [are] submerged in avarice." Hence, the sexual union becomes prostitution.[116] For Solzhenitsyn this analysis puts the cart before the horse. Eros is a far stronger and more enduring passion than avarice. If avarice drives women into the cash nexus of prostitution, the opposite is even more true, for eros drives men into becoming profligate with their money. Solzhenitsyn tells of one fellow who claimed to have had "209 plus" women. To attract them he let "wild money [pass] through his hands." Even the strict discipline of the Organs was easily broken by the power of eros. Prostitutes in the camps were "rich as never before" from plying their wares among the guards. Perhaps even more significant is the lengths to which prisoners went, at times risking danger and even death, in order to satisfy their desires.[117]

The obvious conclusion one draws is that eros does not depend on the economic superstructure. Rather, it expresses itself in ways that may be detrimental to economic rationality. This seemingly insignificant and common-sense observation has particularly troubling consequences for Marx's theory. If eros is free from the causal chain of economic reasoning, may it not be said that it could significantly alter the course of history, and in a particularly spicy way? For example, if a capitalist becomes infatuated with a worker, might not the relationship soften the desire of the capitalist for gain by allowing him to understand the workers' plight? Could this mean that in order to gain better working conditions, the proletariat, instead of forming unions or readying themselves for the revolution, would choose the most attractive individuals from their ranks and send them as lures to engage in physical unions with capitalists as a way of blunting their greed? The scenarios are infinite and quite humorous to imagine. Whatever the case, Solzhenitsyn argues that Marx has made a fundamental flaw in his calculation of the driving force behind human action.

If eros slips past Marx's reasoning from below, love escapes it from above. As is often true, Solzhenitsyn makes his case by use of example. After the camps adopted the practice of separating the sexes, he tells us, relationships sprang up based on no more than a few quickly uttered words, whispered through a wall, or on love letters secretly passed between fences. Sometimes these chance meetings germinated, and people fell in love having never seen each other. Among then were some Lithuanian Catholics, who took their religion seriously. They were married through the walls by a priest, their vows irreversible and sacred.

A Marxist analysis might explain such behavior in terms of social (religious) background. These people would then have been motivated by the ideology of the bourgeois (and remnants of the feudal) society. Objectively, from the perspective of material analysis, their vows were really a way of keeping women in the bondage of monogamy so that they would produce offspring who in turn would become the fodder for an industrial age. An explanation more readily available to reason, however, would hold that their actions had nothing whatever to do either with historical necessity or with economic preconditions. They did it for love.[118]

Solzhenitsyn disagrees with Marx because, on the basis of Marx's ideals, people are punished for their natural love of their own. A decent regime must accept as a limitation on itself this pull of people away from the common good. By teaching people to disregard these limits in the hope of attaining perfect social unity, Marx is responsible for inculcating rash and even cruel expectations. Lest we forget that no Marxist regime has yet to exist without repressing its own people, Solzhenitsyn reminds us that imperfect human nature does not fit into a perfect mold. There will always be those who cannot measure up or those who resist. There will always be a need for some place to put them. Again, it seems, the essence of Marxism is the camps. He explains:

> The Archipelago was, the Archipelago remains, the Archipelago will stand forever!
> Without it, who can be made to suffer for the errors of the Vanguard Doctrine? For the fact that people will not grow into the shapes devised for them? [119]

Philosophy

An objection can be raised against Solzhenitsyn that he sets up a straw man when he criticizes Marx. In attacking Marx he presents statements of Krylenko, Lenin, and Latsis. Clearly, these spokesmen for the Progressive Doctrine were never on an intellectual level with Marx. It is doubtful whether Marx would have endorsed the crude materialism of Krylenko; nor would he have condoned the excesses of Lenin, not to mention Stalin. Perhaps, as Shlomo Avineri suggests, his ideas were too subtle and complex even for his collaborator, Engels, to comprehend fully. Can Marx be held responsible for his ideas being put to bad use?

The misunderstanding and vulgarization of Marx's philosophy could be forgiven him if it were not for his insistence that to have validity, philosophic principles must be put into practice. Prior to Marx, all philosophers had seen their task as understanding the truth about existence. Political philosophy, a subspecies of the broader philosophic pursuit, did endeavor to affect human behavior. However, political philosophers maintained that there would always be a gulf between the best regime that could be constructed in theory and that which could actually be achieved in everyday life. The goal of political philosophy was to suggest what was desirable, but not to mislead as to what was possible. Marx denigrates previous philosophers for making a distinction between thought and action. He proposes that whatever differences exist between theory and practice must be settled in favor of practice—praxis. Indeed, he goes so far as to assert that for something to be true, it must occur in the physical world and not just in the mind. [120]

Immediately a dilemma arises. Just who is to bring this philosophy into being? Philosophers are more than a little rare. For the most part, the human race is made up of those second rate, or worse, minds who misunderstand the nuances of philosophy. It is exactly the Krylenkos and Latsises, the Lenins and Trotskys, and—yes—even the Stalins, who populate this world. If Marx's philosophy has been incorrectly applied, is it not his fault for failing to recognize the capacities of the people asked to do the applying? Solzhenitsyn is cognizant of the gulf between Marx's ideals and the practices of the Soviet Union, yet he does not excuse Marx on that account. He maintains that things could not have worked out otherwise, for Marx's historical analysis led him to the imprudent conclusion that he need not be concerned about the limitations of his followers.

For example, let us consider the idea of premature revolution. Those who forward this argument hold that Lenin perverted Marx's teaching by leading an industrially backward nation into revolution. The Bolsheviks, of course, did not see it that way. They reasoned that if a nation were given the opportunity to skip the capitalist stage of history, with all the horrors and oppression that capitalism entails, it should do so. They came to that conclusion because they believed history to be moving inevitably toward the victory of socialism; hence, seizing the reins of power was a legitimate means of lessening human suffering. But was it not Marx who began this faulty chain of reasoning by writing, in his most popularly read work, that the bourgeoisie's "fall and the victory of the proletariat are equally inevitable?"[121]

The union of thought and action is also deadly to thought, claims Solzhenitsyn. By insisting that all things of importance can be settled at the level of praxis, Marxism reduces human beings to laborers without the leisure to think. It cuts down all that is finest in humanity, because it distracts people, in the everyday tasks of life, from developing the singularly human characteristic, reason.[122] Of course, Marx argues that once natural necessity is overcome through the communism of the means of production, people will use their free time to pursue any of a number of nonmaterialistic endeavors. But by his constant stress on labor as the truly human activity, Solzhenitsyn infers, Marx may have limited the possibility of achieving those other ends.

Whether Marx intended for the highest reaches of thought, philosophy, to disappear after the arrival of Communism is difficult to say. However, he does set out to demolish all philosophy prior to his own. When material reality is depicted accurately, he reasons, "philosophy as an independent branch of activity loses its medium of existence." From this premise he downgrades the importance of philosophy by asserting that for man, "the species being," the metaphysical questions that give rise to philosophic inquiry are unimportant. He advises that investigations into the origin, purpose, or end of life are not fruitful because such questions are mere abstractions that assume the nonexistence of man and nature. He continues, "Give up your abstractions and you will give up your questions. . . . Do not think, do not question me, for as soon as you think and question, your abstraction from the existence of nature and man makes no sense. Or are you such an egoist that you assert everything as nothing and yet want yourself to exist." [123]

As Solzhenitsyn points out, people do ask such questions, for even the humblest of us are egoistic enough to wonder about our own deaths. Thus, not only is Marx's refusal to face the deepest issues of existence profoundly unphilosophic, but it also belies the experience of virtually every living human being.

Even beyond that, Solzhenitsyn explains, Marx's closed attitude toward thought led his followers to repudiate the whole notion of discussion and debate. When it is in their interest, Marxists reserve the right to quash all speech on the grounds that "there are some questions on which a definite opinion has been established, and they are no longer open to discussion." Solzhenitsyn writes that Marxism "uses the neat device of declaring all serious criticism 'outside the framework of possible discussion.' " It "is so devoid of arguments that it has none to advance against its opponents. . . . It lacks arguments and hence there is the club, the prison, the concentration camp, and insane asylums with forced confinement." [124]

Communism's approach to freedom of speech is a perfect example of the bastardization and inversion of Marx's philosophy. Given Marx's stand on the need for praxis, no philosopher in history, Solzhenitsyn forces us to believe, deserves his fate more than Marx.

Atheism

At one point Solzhenitsyn calls Bolshevism "unbridled atheism and class hatred." [125] Communist atheism can be traced directly to Marx. He asserts that belief in God diminishes mankind. "The more man attributes to God," he claims, "the less he retains for himself." Since the human race created the idea of God, it must also destroy that idea. The human species is the highest thing in the universe, and in order for it to fully express its creativity and worth, it must owe its existence only to itself.[126] To prove God's existence is not a simple matter. Perhaps this is why Solzhenitsyn concentrates primarily on the consequences of atheism. He argues that atheism serves, not to elevate people, but to coarsen them. While it may be true that under an atheistic regime everything is permissible, this fact neither enhances human freedom nor encourages noble achievements. Religion supports the idea that every individual has personal worth, a divine spark. Without such a concept, human beings can come to be thought of as "material" or "matter" (Lenin used the term *insects*) that can be used and discarded in building the future epoch.[127]

A particularly troubling consequence of atheism is its tendency to slacken people's self-control, Solzhenitsyn insists. They are less likely to restrain their desires and passions because they see little moral reason for doing so. By unleashing these urges, atheism results in a breakdown of civilization's mores, the mechanism by which society is held together peacefully. Moreover, it is unlikely that people will have the capacity to engage in creative pursuits if they cannot bring their lowest passions under control.

The most dangerous aspect of this disintegration occurs when people are entrusted with power. Without inner moral checks and lacking the concept of divine retribution and reward, their heady position overwhelms and corrupts them. They use their authority for personal gain or for the pleasure they receive from lording it over others. Solzhenitsyn explains, "Power is a poison. . . . But to the human being who has faith in some force that holds dominion over all of us, and who is therefore conscious of his own limitations, power is not necessarily fatal. For those, however, who are unaware of a higher sphere, it is deadly poison. For them there is no antidote."[128] Liberating human beings from the fetters of religion does little to foster creativity. Instead, most people use their newly acquired freedom to indulge their weaknesses.

The Aims of Socialism

Solzhenitsyn is critical not only of Marx's analysis of society, but also of the aims or ends of socialism. Refusing to ride the tide of scholarly opinion, Solzhenitsyn claims that Marxism is not humanism, but rather that everything associated with that doctrine is antihumanism.[129] Obviously, these assertions run counter to a great deal of enlightened opinion in the West, which looks favorably on Marx, not so much for his analysis of economics—in that most agree he was in error—but for the goals he espouses: freedom, equality, and community.

What are the Ends of Socialism?

Exactly what the ends of socialism are Marx never makes clear. The lack of clarity may be due to the prudent caution one should exercise when predicting the future. A reason more consistent with his analysis holds that the future society will be so different from any known to people today that its forms will be impossible to foretell. Marx insists that whatever shape the new society takes, it will be good for people. Hence, they should positively embrace it. The future era will solve "the riddle of history," and bring a true resolution to "the antagonism between man and nature, between man and man, . . . between existence and essence, . . . freedom and necessity, individual and species."[130]

Marx's words sound very nice, but are such things possible? Solzhenitsyn wonders why the ideals of socialism should be adopted when, in practice, they have never been seen or known to exist. Why, for instance, is socialism choiceworthy? There is nothing in Marx's doctrine that proves that socialism and the good are the same. Marx merely criticizes all previous epochs, while insisting that history is moving toward socialism. But what grounds does he have for arguing that things will improve after the revolution? Saying that a thing is inevitable does not necessarily make it beneficial. (Given statistical probabilities and the vagaries of auto travel, either the author of these lines or the reader of them will inevitably get into an auto accident. Does that make it a good thing?) For instance, Marx contends that the division of labor has existed since the beginning of human history. If that is the case, how does he know that its end will make people happy? Marx's materialism, which begins by insisting that only empirical reality is valid, ironically concludes by calling for a social arrangement that has no empirical basis whatever.

Solzhenitsyn goes on to challenge all socialist thinkers on the same account.[131] They all ask that we buy an imagined future sight unseen. Given their lack of clarity on that score, he questions the wisdom of sacrificing the good of present generations for the promised good of an unknown future.

Freedom

Marx has been interpreted to be, above all else, a proponent of liberation—liberation from the cruelty and oppression of capitalism and liberation from the burden of labor itself. As Engels wrote, man must move from the realm of necessity to the realm of freedom. Solzhenitsyn does not accept the standard view of Marx, however. He seems to take the surprising statement in *Capital III*, "the true reign of liberty can only flourish insofar as it is founded on the reign of necessity," as Marx's mature position, and reasons that "the Marxist concept of freedom" is the "acceptance of the yoke of necessity."[132] In other words, Marx is arguing not merely that leisure is a precondition of the good life, but that only after the realm of necessity is conquered by the entire human race can the realm of freedom reign. Solzhenitsyn argues that such a claim dooms people to unceasing labor since it is impossible fully to overcome the demands of natural necessity. Indeed, if Marx were to have his way, human species-beings would contentedly labor to produce what they need, with no thought but of the continued existence of the race—cows happily grazing.

Solzhenitsyn balks at this supposed future of humanity. He maintains that a life dedicated to nothing above the quest for physical well-being reduces people to matter. He describes the hope that prosperity can buy happiness and the desire to exchange personal autonomy for the sake of collective well-being as the temptation of the Grand Inquisitor.[133] Even if such a condition of material bliss could come into being, he doubts whether it would be good for people. Perhaps a world of universal contentment would be so devoid of passionate striving that it would become grotesque.

The more traditional commentaries on Marx insist that he was genuinely dedicated to the liberation of mankind. Accepting, for the sake of argument, that Marx does endorse freedom, Solzhenitsyn asks: The freedom to do what? Freedom is analogous to an empty container; it must be filled with something. It is the end or purpose to which freedom is put, he explains, that determines whether freedom will bring happiness. To enjoy the liberty of unhindered action is certainly a good thing, but to hold that such freedom is happiness is to mistake a precondition of happiness for happiness itself. Moreover, he reasons that human beings are not in need of being liberated, since they possess an inner freedom from birth and they can exercise it regardless of external circumstances.[134]

Equality

Perhaps no aspect of Marx's thought stands out more than his commendation of equality. It is his alliance with the idea of equality, one might suggest, and not his analysis of society, that has caught the spirit of the age and has propelled his philosophy into prominence.

Although it is not altogether clear, Marx seems to accept the possibility of equality of results or ends. He rejects bourgeois natural rights on the grounds that they secure only equality of opportunity. Thus, he claims that they actually encourage inequality of results, since the talented—and more importantly for him, the wellborn—will always rise to the top. He goes on to suggest that differences in ability might be lessened as conventional inequality, in the form of property and class privilege, is abolished. His final formulation, "from each according to his ability to each according to his need," leaves open the issue of whether natural talents would interfere with the egalitarian goals of Communism.

Solzhenitsyn understands the power that the idea of equality holds over people. In *The First Circle* he pictures a young, idealistic Communist making the following address in an attempt to convince a friend of the virtues of the Bolsheviks, "The main thing is they are for equality! Imagine it: universal, complete, absolute equality. No one will have any privileges others don't have. No one will have an advantage either in income or in status. Could there possibly be anything better than such a society? Isn't it really worth all the sacrifices?"[135]

Despite expressing a sympathy with the idea of treating people fairly, Solzhenitsyn maintains that Marxist equality is implausible. It looks toward equality of results, as expressed in Lenin's remark that every cook or housewife should be able to run the state, and overlooks what nature has given us, both the talents and the limitations.[136] It stresses what is most common among people, thereby reducing the impulse toward individual excellence and providing little incentive for the elevation of humanity.

Solzhenitsyn also observes that the egalitarian spirit of Marxism nurtures envy within the lower classes. For example, in the early stages of the revolution some members of the lower classes came to see the destruction of privilege and distinction as their duty. They became so caught up in the urge to level mankind that they increasingly vented their wrath against natural, in addition to conventional, inequality. In fact, it became apparent that natural differences of talent are more frustrating to an egalitarian struggle because they are more difficult to overcome. Solzhenitsyn tells again and again of incompetent people who demanded important posts, for which they were demonstrably unsuited, solely on the basis of their proletarian background. Every sort of skill, especially the technical prowess of engineers, was attacked in the impulse to level Russia's classes. The consequence, as noted earlier, was incompetence on a mass scale, which ruined the economy for years.[137]

Regardless of the initial gains of an egalitarian revolution, Solzhenitsyn reflects, the results are never long lasting. The purpose of a mass movement may be to institute equality, but human beings are constructed so as to seek distinction, position, privilege, and money for themselves. He tells of many instances in which Communists sought to be honored for their dedication to the common people. Inequality of rank became as pronounced under Communist rule as it did under the old regime. However, there was one important difference between the two, according to Solzhenitsyn. Under the old order the upper class had some notion of what a true aristocracy was, both in regard to privilege and to duty; hence, it maintained at least a semblance of justice. The new elite had little awareness of the character of human excellence; it quickly abused its power and thereafter protected its position solely by the authority of its superior force.[138]

Community

According to Marx, the human race can fully resolve its conflicts only by uniting in a universal, spontaneous community.[139] Evidently, he had more in mind than human beings merely living and occasionally acting in common. He argues that individuals gain significance when they act upon others and are acted upon by others. If people undertake self-interested actions that lead to conflict, alienation ensues, since the losers in the struggle will be made to adopt behavior they did not freely choose. Only when every single person on earth acts in unison is social harmony achieved, the relationship between master and slave resolved, and the full potential of the species finally reached.

Marx places enormous importance on social unity because he holds that a person's social relations provide the only source of meaning in existence. There is nothing beyond or above the individual that gives him significance; hence, he must look laterally, to his fellow human beings, to realize his purpose. In common humanity one discovers the whole of which he is a part.

Solzhenitsyn is critical of Marx's notion of community for a number of reasons. First, he argues that although Marx's communitarianism may make him a humanist, of sorts, it is a humanism founded on the lowest common denominator of the race. The only possible means by which all humanity could be united is on the basis of their physical—material—needs; those things that every individual body shares in common. How else could all the differences in politics, language, religion, custom, and culture be overcome? For Solzhenitsyn there is nothing noble or even choiceworthy about a devotion to common humanity. He argues that people are in need of principles that elevate them above their mere physical existence. This is true even if the price they must pay for holding those principles—since inevitably they will differ from nation to nation or religion to religion—is social and political discord. What sort of humanism is it, Solzhenitsyn wonders, that reduces people to beings interested primarily in the survival and comfort of their bodies? Is this concern also not the primary interest of the beasts?

Second, Solzhenitsyn criticizes Marx's notion of community because it is based on materialism. Marx claims to be both a materialist and a communist. Solzhenitsyn responds that the two goals are incompatible. He argues that Marx asks us to share the one thing we cannot share—the pleasures and pains of our bodies. It is true, of course, that we can fulfill each other's desires, in the most intimate of circumstances, for example. Yet we cannot share the actual physical sensation of each other's pleasure. Even more problematic is pain, the most solitary of all experiences. Pain drives our thoughts inward to the self, to our personal distress. Solzhenitsyn captures this truth in his remark, "nobody groans when another man's tooth aches." [140]

Marx even goes so far as to diminish the importance of death. He argues that the individual may die, but the species lives on. He insists that questions about life and death, existence and nonexistence, are fraudulent and egotistical, and therefore should not be asked. Solzhenitsyn rejects Marx's communal perspective of life and death. People may be part of a collective while they are alive, he reasons, but they die alone. The continued existence of the species provides little comfort to an individual whose personal life is about to be extinguished. [141]

Third, Solzhenitsyn questions Marx's assertion that communal action can be both spontaneous and centralized. Once again it is impossible to say exactly what form of association Marx foresaw when the final stage of Communism came into being. However, in the intermediary stage of Communism (and perhaps in the final stage, too), he clearly asserts that all political, economic, and social functions will be centralized.[142]

Solzhenitsyn's story *For the Good of the Cause* centers around some students who voluntarily construct a new science building for their school during their summer vacation. When the job is completed, however, the government takes over the facility for another, more pressing, purpose. Needless to say, everyone involved in the construction is disheartened.[143]

Solzhenitsyn's point seems to be that centralization of power inevitably results in a conflict between the whole and the parts. In such a contest the more powerful central government nearly always emerges the victor. Seeing their fate dependent on a distant, somewhat alien, force and not on their own efforts, people are likely to lose their initiative. If the interference in people's lives becomes too great, they may even become corrupted by it, choosing to live their lives as passive tools of the state. Rather than making people spontaneous, centralization has the tendency to make them dependent and subservient.

Fourth, Solzhenitsyn attacks Marx's hope that the unity of mankind can be made a practical reality. Marx asserts that once class antagonisms, the material basis of conflict, are put to rest, political differences will also vanish. Such an expectation, Solzhenitsyn argues, is foolishly naive. True, human beings act on the basis of their material interests, but there is also a natural division of opinion within mankind predicated on nothing more than different ideas. Marxism is a bad representation of reality because it rejects the independence of human thought.[144]

The worst consequence of Marx's erroneous claim that divergent opinions will disappear after the revolution is that Marxist rulers have been led to believe that those opinions should disappear. Guided by this premise, they have squashed free speech and any form of opposition that has arisen within their countries. "Anyone who is the least bit familiar with Marxism," Solzhenitsyn proclaims, "knows that 'classless society' implies that there will not be any parties." "On the very same day," that Communists agree "there will be a multi-party system [they] suppress every [other] party."[145]

Fifth, Solzhenitsyn questions whether total unity is actually good for people. Marx asserts that "only in community do the means exist for every individual to cultivate his talents in all directions. . . . Only in the community is personal freedom possible."[146] Although Solzhenitsyn does not reject the goal of community per se, he does challenge the assumption that it is ultimately satisfying. For instance, life in the camps was totally communal, but it was not good for the individual, since he hardly had time to think. At one point he calls the communal life he once endured in the camps that of "a herd." He further claims that Communism attempts to "abolish the human essence and deny all individuality to man [by] the forced living in communes, and the incessant dinning of slogans and dogmas." Moreover, since Communism is a threat to the individual, it is also a threat to human creativity. The creative process is an individual endeavor, grounded on the deep insights one gains through solitary reflection. To expect the mass, or any large group of people, to suddenly become original, he concludes, reflects ignorance as to the nature of thought.[147]

In his play *Candle in the Wind,* Solzhenitsyn sets forth his objections to communal life. He says that the assertion people should live for the sake of community reduces itself to the ridiculous conclusion that, "I live for you and you live for me." As appealing as this sentiment of reciprocal affection may sound on first hearing, one is forced to wonder whether it answers the deeper question of why we are alive at all. Solzhenitsyn wants us to ponder the formidable issue of the ends or purposes of human life. If people live solely for the sake of the community, have they done any more than insure the continued existence of the species? Does there not have to be something in life that lifts it above mere survival? After all, what is the meaning of all the eating, sleeping, and procreating that people do? If these functions are the purpose of life, then human beings are no different from the beasts.

Solzhenitsyn holds that socialism is particularly lax in answering these fundamental questions about existence because it defines justice as the equal enjoyment of material well-being. Despite its avowed antipathy toward commercialism, socialism is as guilty as capitalism of making people desirous of material goods. Indeed, it holds that people are unhappy because of scarcity and will be made whole because of plenty. It postpones consideration of what is good for human beings (other than equitable distribution) in the hope that people with full bellies will better be able to answer the question. It diverts people from consideration of moral and ethical issues by making equality of circumstance the one and only moral or ethical principle. Of course, every ethical doctrine holds that those of equal merit should be treated equally. Socialism insists that the only standard one can apply when making ethical judgments is the physical needs and desires of the many. For Solzhenitsyn, to pursue the satisfaction of one's physical urges, with no thought of the proper limits of those desires, is not a mark of morality, but rather, of the lack of morality. Thus he concludes that, "there can be no moral form of socialism . . . [because] ethical principles are not only not inherent in socialism, but are opposed to it."[148]

Solzhenitsyn's blanket rejection of socialism, including the softer variety of the West, seems more than a little harsh, especially to those brought up on the idea that socialism is the only path to social justice. Surely concern for one's fellowman must be thought of as a moral principle. Can those who wish to use government programs to provide for the security of all be lacking completely in moral commitment? In response to Solzhenitsyn, a socialist might say that people cannot develop their souls if they are without the rudimentary necessities of life. It might be correct for Solzhenitsyn to argue that socialists are naive in what they expect from such programs or deluded as to the possibility of social reform; but lacking in morals?

Clearly there is a dispute between Solzhenitsyn and the socialists over the definition of morality. For socialists morality is primarily a devotion to the bodily well-being of others; for Solzhenitsyn it is devotion to principles thought to be eternal, which have the effect of making people interested in the development of their individual character. Solzhenitsyn argues that by stressing what is, in fact, a mere precondition of the good life, socialists have misled people into believing that materialism—equally distributed—is the good life.

Finally, Solzhenitsyn holds that Marxism does not really lead to community. This is so, he argues, first, because it is impossible for any community to treat all its members alike. Theorists of socialism prior to Marx confessed to this lack of universality by admitting that some jobs are so burdensome that no one would volunteer to undertake them. They reasoned that for the good of the whole a special class would be needed whose sole function it was to perform distasteful labor. The Gulag, says Solzhenitsyn, is a realization of this prophecy.[149]

In fairness to Marx, it should be said that he envisaged no need for an underclass within the community, because he expected the complete conquest of nature to transcend labor. As yet, however, nature is far from defeated. Difficult menial tasks remain. Thus, although Solzhenitsyn's criticism of Marx on this point may not be warranted on the basis of theory, it is justified on the basis of practical reality.

Moreover, Solzhenitsyn argues that Marx's goal of a global community is implausible, since internationalism cannot become a true foundation for unity. While acknowledging the nobility of the ideals of internationalism, he holds that there is a practical limit to human affections, beyond which even the highest ideals are likely to become empty rhetoric. The most secure bonds of community are fastened through personal relations. If people know and like their fellows, they are less likely to hurt or take advantage of them. In such a community the harsh demands of duty are softened by feelings of friendship. It seems that in his short story "Matryona's House" Solzhenitsyn wishes to remind his readers that small communities, based on kinship and virtue, can have an endearing quality of civility about them, just as they did when the Greeks first sang their praises more than twenty centuries ago.[150]

Solzhenitsyn is not naïve about the chances of restoring the simple life of small communities. He recognizes that the modern world has made such a return impractical. Nevertheless, he refuses to acquiesce in the belief that the nation should be replaced by a larger political unit. He argues that if devotion to a particular political community is not, strictly speaking, natural to man, it is certainly a commendable second nature. Within nations grow unique cultures that become the basis of a shared life. National culture is the medium by which people communicate, resolve their differences, and learn to live together. It is culture that teaches people to restrain their passions and to make sacrifices for the common good. The irrational and unpremeditated love of one's country is a passion in favor of the common good that counterbalances the all-too-human tendency of people to seek nothing but their own interests.

While the goals of internationalism may exhibit a certain "spiritual beauty," Solzhenitsyn wonders whether mankind can ever reach such heights. Too often, he claims, internationalism destroys whatever national ties exist between people. They are thrown back on themselves and pursue only what serves their own interests. They become isolated. Sacrifice, virtue, and duty become lost in a mass of undistinguished humanity.[151]

The Marxist movement has made particularly grievous errors in the name of internationalism, he argues. It has suppressed indigenous cultures in an attempt to supplant them with the enlightened ideals of socialism. We have already seen the barren results of that effort. Party slogans and propaganda do not constitute a culture, and societies lacking secure bonds, Solzhenitsyn proclaims, can be held together only by force.

Indeed, the Communists' hatred for the nation has backfired more than once. During World War II, for example, slogans of the Progressive Doctrine suddenly disappeared in the Soviet Union and were replaced by messages declaring the virtues of Mother Russia. Almost overnight the old ways were brought back, and even the Orthodox church emerged from the relentless suppression to which it had been subject.

Why this sudden change in the course of history? Solzhenitsyn explains that most people cannot be roused to fight or made to sacrifice for the cause of internationalism. It is too tenuous a goal. He reports that during World War II, when a young zek was asked to enlist in the defense of socialism, he responded, "the proletariat has no fatherland!" To which Solzhenitsyn adds, "Marx's exact words, I believe." [152]

Of course, the Russian people did respond to the call of duty, honor, and country, despite it being raised, in part, to bail out Stalin and his colleagues. Caught, as they were, in the tragic situation of having to choose between the two worst dictators in history, the Russians heeded the call of their country, which is exactly what many of them had refused to do for the cause of international socialism.[153]

CHAPTER V

The Consequences
of Marxism in
the Soviet Union
and Elsewhere

The previous chapter discussed many of the theoretical problems raised by Marx's teaching. This chapter completes Solzhenitsyn's criticism of Marx by presenting the practical consequences that have arisen when Marxist governments have held power. Solzhenitsyn's criticisms were made, for the most part, prior to the reforms that took place in the Communist world during the 1980s. Since these changes have contradicted some of Solzhenitsyn's contentions, an assessment of his views is also presented.

Ideology

It is a matter of some debate whether Marx would have approved of his philosophy being used to answer all of life's mysteries. It is true nonetheless that many Communists have accepted it as providing a complete description of how life should be lived. Indeed, Marxism became the premier ideology of the twentieth century. It supplied the horizon under which a large portion of mankind lived.

Solzhenitsyn is extremely critical of ideology in general and of the ideological commitment people have made to Marx's ideas in particular. He argues that Communism encourages people to stop thinking.¹ They come to accept party doctrine on faith and will not listen to rational arguments that point up its weaknesses.² Instead of critical analysis, loyal Communists are apt to adopt an attitude of "What is real is rational." They deny the evidence of their own senses in an attempt to make reality conform to theory. How else can one explain the party's unwavering support of Stalin? How else can one understand a seventy-year commitment to collectivization, despite its having impoverished the Russian countryside?³ Many Communists have been so blinded by the image of the future perfection of society that they have disregarded the reality confronting them. For instance, socialist realism looks at people, not as they are, but as they should be.

A commitment to Marxist ideology has two other portentous consequences, Solzhenitsyn maintains. First, people under its influence "reject all absolute concepts of morality" and "scoff at any consideration of 'good' and 'evil.'" They replace these ideas with more relativistic terms: progressive and regressive. Whether or not an action is progressive depends on the "circumstances and the political situation." Hence, "murder, even the killing of hundreds of thousands, could be good or could be bad." But who decides what is progressive? Obviously, the people as a whole "cannot get together to pass judgment." Rather, "a handful of people decide," and the rest are expected to follow. If people "are deprived of the concept of good and evil, what will be left?" "Nothing but the manipulation of one another." Loyalty to the Marxist cause also entails a loss of humanity, since members of the cadre, instead of making their own individual judgments, entrust the leaders with that responsibility.⁴ It is truly ironic that a doctrine which begins with complete skepticism about the moral authority of any ruling class, in the end should accept the absolute dominance of the party. Relativism quickly becomes absolutism, for reliance on party dictates is the only measure of whether an action is progressive.

An even more dangerous attribute of ideological fervor, according to Solzhenitsyn, is that people come to believe their own views are entirely correct. They become haughtily self-righteous in rejecting the views of others. Indeed, ideology encourages its adherents to find a scapegoat for all of the human ills. "The same old atavistic urges—greed, envy, unrestrained passion, and mutual hostility" are explained by faulting a certain class or group.⁵ If only those few evildoers over there are eliminated, the committed ideologue insists, the world could be made perfect. "If only it were so simple," Solzhenitsyn responds, "If only there were evil people somewhere insidiously committing evil deeds, and it were necessary only to separate them from the rest of us and destroy them. But the line dividing good and evil cuts through the heart of every human being. And who wants to destroy a piece of his own heart?"[6]

In the past the evil that people did was checked by the need to provide a justification for their actions. Unlike the characters of Shakespeare, Schiller, and Dickens, Solzhenitsyn reasons, few people wished to admit their own profligacy.[7] Since it was difficult to justify breaching widely held moral principles, certain limits were placed on how people behaved. True, many violated moral edicts, then as now, but they perceived their actions as a departure from the norm; hypocrisy was vice's nod to virtue. There were, of course, great villains who went beyond all ethical boundaries, but even they did not attempt to revise the moral code so as to fit their deeds. Quite the contrary, they wallowed in their own malevolence.

The adherents of ideology have no inner restrictions because they earnestly believe that their every action is commendable. "To do evil," Solzhenitsyn writes, "a human being must first of all believe that what he is doing is good, or else that it is a well-considered act in conformity with natural law." The blind acceptance of a creed was how "the agents of the Inquisition fortified their will," just as the European colonizers, Nazis, and Jacobins accepted the infallibility of their own ideals. But it has been in the twentieth century, a time when belief in traditional morality has dwindled, that the contagion of ideology has been most virulent. Is there a better explanation of the mass carnage? Evidently attachment to ideology can utterly destroy the human soul and with it the capacity to do good. Solzhenitsyn claims that most people bob back and forth between good and evil. But there is a threshold beyond which people cannot go and still return to humanity. The threshold is passed when, in the name of the cause, evil deeds are committed to an "extreme degree" or when power over the fate of others is held absolutely.[8]

The ideologue is animated by the goals of his cause; he is continually busied in defense of its ideals. Because he has little time to think, the capacity for deep reflection is lost. He misses the wisdom that came to Solzhenitsyn as he lay "on the rotting prison straw. . . . the line separating good and evil passes not through states, nor between classes, not between political parties either—but right through every human heart."[9] This wisdom led him, "to understand the falsehood of all revolutions in history. They destroy only the carriers of evil contemporary with them. . . . And they take to themselves as their heritage the actual evil itself, magnified still more." [10]

Marxism and the Soviet Union

Totalitarian Dictatorship

One of the most contemptible repercussions of Marxism has been its propensity to inaugurate and justify totalitarian governments. From all that has been said thus far, there can be little doubt that the Soviet Union fell prey to this calamity. However, a question arises as to whether the successors of Stalin moved the Soviet system away from totalitarianism.

Much contemporary scholarly opinion in the West from the 1960s through the 1980s held that only under Stalin was the Soviet Union truly totalitarian. For example, the Sovietologist Jerry Hough argued that the totalitarian structure initiated by Stalin was transformed by Khrushchev and subsequent leaders. In his book *Soviet Leadership in Transition*, published in 1980, Hough stated that "few scholars today think the totalitarian model is an accurate summary of the contemporary Soviet Union." Indeed, it seemed that "many will not even use the word totalitarian. . . . The term most often used," he commented in a parenthetical remark, "is . . . authoritarian, which denotes a more conservative and limited repressive regime." [11] The image one got from Hough was that of a bureaucratic state, which was slow to change, slow to act, and extremely reluctant to alter the status quo. [12]

Solzhenitsyn's description of the Soviet Union under Brezhnev placed it squarely in the totalitarian camp, although he recognized that there are better and worse forms of totalitarianism. [13] Repression softened after the grisly reign of Stalin, Solzhenitsyn reasoned, but not enough to transform the character of the state. He suggested that Marxist regimes travel through stages. At first the leaders of the revolutionary struggle foster an urge to equalize social conditions, which results in a great movement within society. A second stage features the strengthening of the state with the ascendancy of a dictator who is worshiped by his followers. Finally, the tasks of government become routine, and less emphasis is placed on upheaval and change.

This position is in agreement with that of Hannah Arendt, who was the first to recognize that the revolutionary fervor of totalitarian states would eventually cool. She remarks that once faced with "the everyday business of government," totalitarian governments would gradually lose their revolutionary momentum and utopian character. Practical reality would "destroy the fictitious world of their organizations."[14]

Despite the fact that Brezhnev's government was not as outwardly brutal as were its predecessors, Solzhenitsyn argued that all the main ingredients of a totalitarian state were still in place. The ideology was made to dominate people's minds and the secret police their bodies. The party exercised complete control over every aspect of a Soviet citizen's life. There were some outward signs of greater freedom, but whenever that freedom was put to use in a way detrimental to the party's total control, or to further enhance the people's sphere of independent action, it was quickly crushed.[15]

Commentators such as Hough argued that the Soviet Union changed because the top leadership lost faith in the ideology. According to this theory, Marxism continued to be the official doctrine primarily because party leaders could justify their high paying jobs and special privileges only if they remained representatives of Marxist ideals. Solzhenitsyn acknowledged that the party had been corrupt and self-seeking. He pointed out that the obvious discrepancy between the actions and the espoused beliefs of Soviet rulers made them cynical. He depicted a party of about three million people, controlling all the means of oppression and propaganda and looming above a crushed populace. The upper caste was granted every privilege: special stores, secret payments of money, the best houses and apartments, private medical facilities, and free access to health resorts. As payment for these benefits, party members were required to give "unquestioning and obsequious service"; any hint of disloyalty and all the perks were taken away. At the center of this group was the ruling elite, "an oligarchy," numbering about a hundred thousand. They enjoyed unlimited access to material comforts, perhaps living better than the ruling class of old Russia. Moreover, their special position allowed them to pass on privileges to their children.[16]

How could such people still have claimed to be Marxist egalitarians? Solzhenitsyn speculated that in order to justify their high position and the brutal measures that were inflicted on ordinary Soviet citizens in order to maintain it, party members clung ever more steadfastly to the ideology. Ironically, deviation from pure Marxist principles actually strengthened the power that the ideology had over society. If Marxism were abandoned, the party could not have claimed special benefits, and more importantly, past crimes committed in the name of the cause might have been uncovered and the perpetrators punished.

The devotion to ideology may have weakened, Solzhenitsyn wrote in the late 1970s, "but its malignant poison floods our souls and all our life. Ideology is dead, but it still makes us slaves." Even if the leadership no longer believed in Marxism, it was forced to behave as if it did. Why else did it continue to pursue policies such as collective farming, reckless industrialization, and a centrally planned economy? Why else did it arm terrorist groups everywhere in the world? "If no one believes and yet everyone submits," he reasoned, "this demonstrates not the weakness of an ideology but its frightful, evil power." He concluded that "Marxist ideology is the fetid root of today's Soviet life. Only by cleansing ourselves from it can we begin to return to humanity." [17]

He complained bitterly that the ideology forced everyone to live in a sort of fabricated world. Lies were the form of existence within the Soviet Union, since the truth of life did not fit into the ideological principles. "A universal spiritual death" touched the Soviet population. People were compelled to dismiss what they knew to be true in order not to bring down the wrath of the state. Fear of retribution clutched the population so tightly that some proclaimed their loyalty to the lie openly, thereby violating the first tenet of personal integrity. Indeed, what some feared most was "to lag behind the herd and to take a step alone." [18]

The obligatory ideological lie disclosed the insidious nature of Soviet society up until the Gorbachev era. Unlike authoritarian governments, past and present, which require of their citizens little more than supine acceptance of official directives, the Soviet state expected that its citizens make a positive commitment to the ideology. Attendance at ideological training sessions, membership in "voluntary" party associations, and continual public displays of loyalty were the only security against losing one's job, or worse. Furthermore, the lie concealed the violence by which the regime governed. "Violence quickly grows old," Solzhenitsyn explained. People lose confidence in governments supported by it and "in order for it to maintain a respectable face it summons falsehood as its ally—since violence can conceal itself with nothing except lies, and lies can be maintained only by violence."[19] Thus the Soviet state asked more than mere compliance, it sought to possess people's souls.[20]

Another proposition put forward to support the idea that the Soviet Union had altered its nature, held that the leaders were more "liberal." Their main concern, it was said, was to build a healthy economy at home and to avoid a tragedy similar to that which their nation suffered during World War II. Solzhenitsyn rejected this view as bad scholarship. The system, he argued, encouraged a brutal and despotic leadership. Soviet rulers wrapped themselves in the cloak of Progressive mankind, but in truth they learned how to treat people under the heavy hand of Stalin. Before Gorbachev, at least, all the top leaders had gained promotion by stepping over the backs of their interned superiors. Their first successes came by crushing the opposition (mostly imagined) or by mercilessly carrying through the harsh edicts of collectivization.

Solzhenitsyn maintained that it was naive to expect a softer variety of Soviet ruler. The bureaucracy from which any leader arose was replete with patronage and corruption. The processes by which one came to dominate such an organization, therefore, were savage. People of good character were inevitably excluded. He explained, "Never has the Politburo numbered a humane or peace-loving man among its members. The Communist bureaucracy is not constituted to allow men of that caliber to rise to the top—they would instantly suffocate there."[21] Moreover, he argued that because Soviet rulers gained advancement and maintain their position through such brutal measures, they were really all the same. There may have been a struggle for power among them, based solely on personal ambition, he wrote, "but on essentials they all agree."[22]

In the Brezhnev era, no less than in Stalin's time, Solzhenitsyn charged, despotic rule filtered downward so that each province, each factory, each labor union, was the petty fiefdom of some party official.[23] Even beyond that, the style of leadership left its mark on the mores of the Soviet populace. The ruthlessness with which the party retained its privilege and position taught many an important lesson: might makes right. Little wonder crime has been so rampant in Soviet society. The example the leaders have set has been interpreted to mean: if you can get away with it, do it. Only the massive force of the state kept this impulse at bay. Particularly troubling to Solzhenitsyn were the youth, who seemed at times to have learned little from their Soviet education except to take pleasure in cruelty towards the meek and downtrodden.[24]

Solzhenitsyn allowed that some changes were made by Stalin's heirs—the excesses diminished. However, he indicated that the Soviet state could not have survived without massive repression. The camps remained open and functioning, helping to bring natural gas to the West, the insane asylums were treating people crazy enough to doubt that the Progressive Doctrine was the basis of an ideal life, believing instead what their own eyes and ears told them, and the secret police was the most powerful branch of government. As Solzhenitsyn puts it:

> Rulers change, the Archipelago remains.
> It remains because that particular political regime could not survive without it. If it disbanded the Archipelago, it would cease to exist itself.[25]

Yet Solzhenitsyn's analysis appears to overlook the era of reform during the early 1960s under Khrushchev. Khrushchev did not agree with his predecessor. He even denounced Stalin. Solzhenitsyn was a beneficiary of Khrushchev's thaw, and he grants that the volatile leader was out of the ordinary. This, he adds, is the reason why Khrushchev was so quickly removed from office and why he is still a forgotten man in the nation he once governed. Moreover, Khrushchev used the secret police, the camps, and the other forms of repression to restrain opposition to his form of rule.[26] But if the leadership of Khrushchev did make a difference, even for a time, then Solzhenitsyn cannot be correct in saying that all those in power are alike.

What of the present leader, Gorbachev? Solzhenitsyn has made few direct comments on this topic. Tomas Venclova, a visitor to Solzhenitsyn's Cavendish, Vermont, home, reports that Solzhenitsyn is "following developments with interest and not without hope."[27] Gorbachev's ascendancy has presented reason for hope. His calls for *glasnost* and *perestroika* (two terms actually used by Solzhenitsyn in a 1969 letter objecting to his ouster from the writers' union) have fostered anticipation both inside and outside the Soviet Union that true reform may be in the offing. Gorbachev has permitted the publication of Solzhenitsyn's *The Gulag Archipelago, Kolyma Tales* by Varlam Shalamov (whom Solzhenitsyn asked to coauthor *The Gulag Archipelago*), as well as other reports of the cruelties committed by previous Soviet leaders. He has given the Soviet media a much freer hand to print what it wishes, including battlefront coverage of the once taboo topic of the war in Afghanistan. Public demonstrations in independent republics of the Soviet Union, calls for independence in the Baltic states, and protest marches in Moscow itself have been presented on Soviet television. The extraordinary events that led to the collapse of Communist rule in Eastern Europe and the role Gorbachev's foreign policy played in aiding that revolution, reflect that there is true ferment within the party. Communist party meetings in the Soviet Union now regularly air disputes among members. All of this reform indicates that, contrary to Solzhenitsyn's assertions, there are true differences among Communists. Especially worthy of note was the election of the late Andrei Sakharov to the Soviet legislature. Solzhenitsyn even has been asked to join a council that plans to build a monument to commemorate the victims of Stalin.[28]

Solzhenitsyn's silence on these dramatic changes suggests that his judgment concerning the possibility of reform within the Soviet leadership was inaccurate. Of course, no one can predict whether *glasnost* will lead to true openness. It may turn out that Gorbachev will not last, or that he will have to crack down on his opponents. Even if he is sincere in his desire for improvement, Gorbachev is faced with formidable obstacles. He must overcome an entrenched and powerful bureaucracy, a recalcitrant party, a stagnant economy, and, perhaps most difficult of all, long-simmering disputes among the nationalities that make up the Soviet Union.[29]

Why did Solzhenitsyn's evaluation of the Soviet Union misjudge the potential for improvement within the leadership? First, Solzhenitsyn may have been intentionally overstating the evils of the Soviet regime in order to build opposition to it in the West. And it seems that this goal has been partially successful. Second, Solzhenitsyn's analysis made a prediction about the impossibility of reform based on past performance. It is plausible to make such forecasts by postulating the effects that governmental structures have in choosing a nation's leaders. As James Ceaser's fine book on the American selection process demonstrates, the actions that those seeking high position are made to adopt while pursuing office influence the way in which they will exercise power once in charge and even affect the kinds of people that are chosen.[30] Although evaluations based on long-term patterns are possible, there is always a realm of political life that is beyond prediction. Even the best political analysis can deal only with that part of reality not subject to accident. Solzhenitsyn's claim that no humane ruler could arise from within the bureaucracy overlooks the element of chance that is always a factor in controlling human affairs.

Third, the Soviets might have been compelled to pick a more dynamic leader who would attempt to refashion the society because their economic system was near to ruin. As we shall see in what follows, the policies of the post-Stalin leadership nearly bankrupted the nation. Perhaps, the choice of Gorbachev was made, not for the humanitarian reason of providing a better life for the Soviet people, but merely to protect the nation from an economic collapse and the party from international humiliation.

The period of openness under Gorbachev has shown that Solzhenitsyn's views are, at least in part, faulty, yet in a deeper sense they have shown that Solzhenitsyn was all too accurate. *Glasnost* has provided an arena for the airing of grievances against the party. Ironically, the complaints made against the regime, the crimes against the Soviet people, have disclosed that the Soviet Union was more like the picture painted by Solzhenitsyn than by Western scholars. The example of the overthrow of Communism in Eastern Europe has shown that Communism is such a discredited doctrine that it has virtually no public support. It has become apparent that Communists held power in Eastern European countries only by the most cynical use of force and intimidation.

Further Consequences

According to Solzhenitsyn life under the Marxist-inspired post-Stalin leadership was bleak and dismal. First, government policies impoverished the nation. Solzhenitsyn claimed that 40 percent of the population lived in a state of poverty. Food was normally rationed in some way. There were persistent shortages. Many people lived on inferior diets: high in starches, low in nutrients.[31]

Lack of private initiative was perhaps the most important explanation for the Soviet economy's abysmal record. The farming population, bound to the land by the internal passport system, was held in a condition of virtual serfdom. Without proper incentives, collective-farm labor was done in a slipshod manner. Perceiving little hope for advancement, the young sought to leave the kolkhoz by whatever means possible. In sum, the collective-farm system was so inefficient that it could not produce enough food for the nation.[32]

The economy as a whole was organized in such a way that it stifled excellence and innovation, except in government-sponsored projects, such as the military, where scientists were given a free hand to copy Western technology. Large industries had such ponderous plants, the consequence of government investments, that they could not readily adapt to new technology. Even small businesses, such as trades and services, were nationalized, making minor household repairs a bureaucratic nightmare. As a result, an illegal, but officially overlooked, "second story," or underground, economy flourished. Since shortages in one commodity or poor coordination of goods in another often resulted in economic dislocation throughout the entire nation, the underground economy thrived. The Soviet people were compelled to undertake lawless activities as the modus operandi of their economic life.[33]

Adding to the problems of an already beleaguered economy was the cost of training and supporting the Organs, the largest police force in the world. Despite having lost some numbers since its zenith under Stalin, the KGB managed to secure a healthy portion of the Soviet budget. Moreover, The KGB's wards, the zeks, added to the inefficiency of the system. As Solzhenitsyn made poignantly clear, slavery is not a cost-effective means of production.[34]

The state's lack of success at producing abundance should not be taken as a lack of intent to have done so. Quite the contrary, the overwhelming compulsion behind the Marxist ideal was to insure physical well-being through increased industrialization and productivity. The result of this intense urge to modernize was to dramatically increase pollution of all kinds, to strip the nation of its natural resources with no thought for the future, to press women into the labor force in order to perform the most backbreaking and tedious jobs, and to disfigure cities in a foolish attempt to "plan" urban life.[35] Little wonder that *restructuring* has become the watchword for the current Soviet leadership.

Solzhenitsyn also noted that Russia's once formidable cultural heritage was continually under attack. The arts were scrutinized to a degree unheard of in former times. Not only were artists prohibited from expressing certain ideas, they were expected to take an active role in propagating the doctrines of the party. Worst of all, sterile party pronouncements replaced the once rich Russian language.[36] The language of Pushkin, Gogol,

Tolstoy, and Dostoevsky was brutalized because, unlike the old regime, the Soviet state left no breathing space for creativity to flourish. Moreover, the traditions and folkways of the village, which for centuries had taught the ordinary people how to live, were ridiculed by local party officials. People were distracted from developing their spiritual potential by the constant blare of the radio and the loud speaker. Propaganda stunted their minds; "voluntary" ideological sessions took up their precious leisure time. They were taught to believe in the virtues of materialism. They were kept from pondering the meaning of life—and of death.[37]

Despite its troubles at home, Solzhenitsyn argued, the leadership spared no expense to stir up trouble abroad. Although he recognized the need for national defense, he maintained that the vast Soviet military capability served no rational purpose except that of an offensive tool. The West, he insisted, did not wish to threaten Russia and would have quickly reduced its arms if the Soviets showed some initiative.

The source of the Soviet's expansionist policies, he stipulated, was none other than the ideology that proclaims that "socialism" is truly possible only on a worldwide scale. Hence, the leadership sought, wherever feasible, to expand its power, influence, and territory. It supported any terrorist group that might be used to undermine the stability of the West. It exacerbated local and regional conflicts to gain a foothold for its ideology everywhere in the world.[38] Tragically, it did all this by depriving its own citizens of the necessities of life. Solzhenitsyn concluded that "the forces of the entire Soviet economy are concentrated on war," a statement made prior to the invasion of Afghanistan.[39]

Only the naïveté of the West kept the idea of détente alive. In the Soviet Union there was no détente. Away from the main cities, in the places where the Western press was excluded, the media were continually presenting war propaganda.[40] The obvious intent was to frighten the population into making sacrifices for the future socialist victory over the forces of imperialism. The less obvious intent was to secure loyalty; fear of war is a powerful means of attaching people to the regime. How, Solzhenitsyn asked, was such a government to be trusted? Could a government be trusted to keep its pledges to disarm or to observe its treaty agreements when it did not obey its own constitution?[41]

For Solzhenitsyn the Soviet Union was the worst regime in human history. Hitler, whose reign is most often held to be the pinnacle of evil, was a mere disciple of Stalin. (Stalin actually helped the Nazis to establish their power by circumventing the Treaty of Versailles and training German officers.) The Nazis and the whole Fascist movement quickly burst onto the world stage, its barbarity was recognized, and it vanished. Communism was better disguised. It has murdered far more people, but Marxist doctrine still holds sway, especially in Western intellectual circles.[42]

Solzhenitsyn argued that only the other Communist dictatorships have rivaled the Soviet Union in evil. By comparison the authoritarian societies of the right were mere juvenile delinquents of terror. He pointed out that since they could not control the flow of information fully, their atrocities eventually met with resistance at home and condemnation abroad. For instance, he compared the sentences given for suspicion of terrorism in South Africa, the pariah of the international community, to those administered in the Soviet Union. In South Africa, which he acknowledged as an unjust society, any person suspected by the government of fermenting social unrest was likely to be detained without trial for three months; in the Soviet Union a similar offense might have netted one an incarceration of from three to ten years.[43] Robert Conquest wrote in support of Solzhenitsyn's analogy, "To compare the suffering of Greek [prior to the restoration of democracy in the 1970s] and other right-wing governments with those of the Soviet Union is something in the nature of saying a gross and unprovoked assault, such as punching someone on the nose, is the same as boiling him in oil."[44] Moreover, governments on the right have been overthrown, Solzhenitsyn explained, but no Marxist government, which sunk deep roots into a nation, had ever been put out of office. The revolutions in Eastern Europe mark a new era in the history of Communism, one that seems to refute some of Solzhenitsyn's analysis. Still, the details of how Communist leaders maintained their positions in those countries show that Solzhenitsyn was correct: the regimes were very brutal and dangerous.

Solzhenitsyn even contends that authoritarian societies of the right may nurture important spiritual principles within them. He infuriated liberal opinion in the West by praising Franco's Spain for preserving its Christian heritage. In 1975 he warned that reforms should proceed gradually in that nation and that at all costs revolution should be avoided.[45] There is little doubt now that Solzhenitsyn was correct in his appraisal, especially if one considers the slow but steady gains Spain has made to reach democracy.

The Worldwide Marxist Movement

In a statement many in the West would likely consider either naive or an antiquated holdover of Cold War mentality, Solzhenitsyn claims that Communism is radically hostile "to mankind as a whole" and that it is "irredeemable. . . . there exists no 'better' variants." He continues, "it is incapable of growing 'kinder,' . . . it cannot survive as an ideology without using terror. . . . consequently to coexist with Communism on the same planet is impossible. Either it will spread, cancer-like, to destroy mankind, or else mankind will have to rid itself of Communism."[46]

In the West such statements have long ago been discarded as anti-Communist hysteria. Sophisticated critics argued that Communism was far from monolithic; it showed a divergence of views as varied as in the West. Solzhenitsyn was aware of the differences among the followers of Marx, yet he argued that in the most important ways they were "frightening" in their "unity and cohesion."[47] A fundamental goal of Communist parties, wherever they existed, was to destroy the social order of the West, he maintained. Even where they acted as minority parties in constitutional democracies, their real purpose was to attain power and abolish all opposition. Their seeming loyalty to the nation was a ploy, made expedient by their lack of strength.[48]

Once in command, "all Communist parties . . . have become completely merciless."[49] Their aim, Solzhenitsyn wrote, "(whether in the U.S.S.R., in China, or in Cuba) is to force the people to serve them unfailingly as a work force, or, if need be, as a fighting force."[50] It is as if Communist leaders were compelled by the inexorable logic of their ideology to proceed through the various stages of upheaval, dictatorship, and terror until finally achieving the status of bureaucratic repression— the phase of Soviet development even under Gorbachev.[51]

No doubt an objection can be raised against Solzhenitsyn's position. For example, it is inaccurate to say that the government in China was the same as that in North Korea, or that Hungary did not grant its citizens more freedom than did Albania. An objective appraisal of Communist nations uncovers a great many differences among them. Moreover, reforms within the two leading Communist powers, China and the Soviet Union, show that Solzhenitsyn's claims are wrong. And yet, for the first seventy years in which Communist regimes held power, none were willing to relinquish the party's power, even in the face of massive popular opposition. Whether the era of reform can be sustained in the Soviet Union and China in the face of all the dangers that liberalization poses to the ruling elites is a question that only time will resolve.

What seemed to worry Solzhenitsyn most about Communist nations was that they were united on the basis of their governing principles. From that perspective they were all joined in the common hope of implementing the ideas of Marx. But, as we have seen, Marx's ideas cannot be brought into being without tragic consequences; hence, all Marxist governments had to oppress their own people. Communists were constrained in their ability to pursue Marxist goals, not by any limitation that the doctrine placed on them, but either by the resistance of indigenous national cultures or by the limits nature itself places on the activities of human beings. In the former case, for example, Communist leaders in Poland found themselves faced with an enormously popular Catholic church, while in Yugoslavia the various nationalities were resistant to complete subjugation by the party. Thus the party's appetite for complete domination was everywhere the same, but in some places it was checked by the vestiges of the former culture. In the latter case, the Chinese are perhaps the best example. During the Cultural Revolution, the party attempted the creation of the new socialist man, a deed accomplished by equalizing all of Chinese society. The resultant confusion, lack of order, and loss of incentive caused a famine of vast proportions. When the party cadre itself began to feel the shortages, enough momentum was gained to reform the system.

Communism in the West

What of Communists in the West, have they not shown themselves to be militantly opposed to oppression, especially against the poor, and in favor of liberation, especially for the downtrodden? Solzhenitsyn acknowledges that Communism "disguises itself as humanitarianism," but he contends that the ideology somehow narrows and hardens people's souls so that they fail to recognize the suffering that they themselves inflict. As is his way, he tells a story to make his point.

While he was still living in his native land, the Soviet media buzzed for almost a year with stories of the arrest and incarceration of the radical American college professor Angela Davis. The Soviet Union was inundated with news of the injustice done to her and of the suffering she experienced in prison. Soviet schoolchildren were asked to sign petitions for her release.

As we know, Angela Davis was released. Although American prisons are far from perfect, her discomfort was minimal as compared to that of the inhabitants of the Gulag. Still, she was invited to recuperate at a Soviet resort. While she was there, some Soviet and Czech dissidents addressed an appeal to her in the hope that she might intercede on behalf of a number of people thrown into prison as the result of their protests against the Soviet invasion of Czechoslovakia. "Comrade Davis," they wrote, "You were in prison. You know how unpleasant it is to sit in prison, especially when you consider yourself innocent. You have such great authority now. Could you stand up for those people in Czechoslovakia who are being persecuted by the state?" Comrade Davis responded, "They deserve what they get. Let them remain in prison." To which Solzhenitsyn comments: "That is the face of Communism. That is the heart of Communism for you." [52]

Obviously, this one story does not prove that all Communists become hardened to the misery of others. Yet Solzhenitsyn maintains that it is indicative of a tendency among dedicated Marxists to become cruel in pursuit of their goals. Not every follower of Marx has become ruthless, yet, Solzhenitsyn points out, far too many than can be safely ignored have become so. All doctrines produce narrow-minded, self-righteous fanatics, but Marxism engenders more of them.

If Communism is such a vile and degrading doctrine, how has it continued to exist? Why have people put up with it? Solzhenitsyn offers a number of suggestions. First, as we have seen, it has "inhuman strength." Second, it is philosophically and rhetorically allied with the three most popular currents in the twentieth century—material well-being, equality, and liberation. Finally, as we shall see in what follows, it has been aided by the West.

Solzhenitsyn on the West

Solzhenitsyn's discussion of Marxism's influence on the politics of the East is certainly controversial, yet by comparison, his analysis of the contemporary West has stirred an even greater debate. He has been called "confused" and "uninformed." His views are said to be those of a "religious fanatic." He complains that after his commencement address at Harvard, he was told to "get out of the country."[1]

Despite the storm of protest that his remarks have raised, Solzhenitsyn claims to be a friend of the West. However, he is not, as he says he once was, a worshiper of the West. A friend, it can be inferred, is likely to be more objective in his appraisal than one who worships. He would not, as a worshiper might, turn a blind eye to his friend's faults. In this regard, a friend of the West might acknowledge its strengths, but also point out its weaknesses in hope of correcting them. A true friend might even be compared to a doctor. The medicine he prescribes may be "bitter" to take, but it is given in the spirit of doing the patient some good. Solzhenitsyn understands his criticism of the West in precisely this way. He explains, "I am not a critic of the West. I am a critic of the weaknesses of the West. I am a critic of a fact we can't comprehend: how one can lose one's spiritual strength, one's will power, and possessing freedom, not value it, not be willing to make sacrifices for it."[2]

This chapter will begin with a practical discussion of Solzhenitsyn's arguments against certain policies that the West has adopted toward the Soviet Union for most of that nation's history. It will then investigate his views on the sources of "misunderstanding" that have led Western scholars and statesmen to make incorrect choices concerning the East. In particular, it will focus on the theoretical problem that Solzhenitsyn sees as the root cause of the West's shortcomings. Finally, it will examine some of the major criticisms that have been leveled against Solzhenitsyn's ideas and will speculate how he might respond to these attacks.

Why Aid Totalitarianism?

Almost from the outset of Communist rule, Solzhenitsyn claims, the West aided the totalitarian government of the Soviet Union. As exemplified by the first exploratory trips of Armand Hammer during the Bolshevik revolution of the 1920s, Western capitalists provided material assistance to a government incapable of furnishing even the bare necessities of life to its citizens. Without the foodstuffs and technological expertise of Western business, Solzhenitsyn said, "the clumsy and awkward Soviet economy could never cope with its difficulties."[3]

Western capital restored Soviet factories, helped with construction projects, built automotive and tractor factories, and provided foreign aid in the form of low-interest loans. This assistance was "economically indispensable," he maintained, because the "Soviet economy has an extremely low level of efficiency. . . . What is done" in the West "by a few people and a few machines . . . takes tremendous crowds of workers and enormous amounts of material" in the Soviet Union. The system has been so inept that it could not deal with all its problems at once. "War, space (which is a part of the war effort), heavy industry, light industry, and the need to feed and clothe its people," all pull the economy in different directions. The gaps, those things that have been lacking, have been supplied by the West. What sort of country is it, he asked, that has nothing to sell? Heavy equipment, complex technology, and even agricultural products are purchased abroad. Except for military equipment, the Soviet economy has nothing to sell except "that which God put in the Russian ground at the very beginning."[4]

Solzhenitsyn argued that the aid given by Western business often was used to support agents of the secret police in its never-ending crusade to crush its own citizens.⁵ Western aid was also turned into weapons of war, which, given the regime's long-term goals, were the means by which capitalism was to be destroyed. Solzhenitsyn claimed that the shortsightedness of Western business people derived from "a burning greed for profit that goes beyond all reason." They seemed destined to fulfill Lenin's prophecy that capitalists would be hung on the rope they once sold to socialists.⁶

Business has not been the only culprit, according to Solzhenitsyn. The governments of the West also have given substantial support to the Soviet Union. In World War II, for example, the democracies sent Stalin vast supplies. They raised up one dictator to defeat another. If the West had been truly steadfast, he argued, it could have conquered Hitler without building up the Soviet economy and bringing Stalin to world prominence. After all, what did the West gain by an alliance with Stalin? Germany was defeated, but as a consequence Europe was divided, its eastern half subjugated, and Poland, for whose freedom the war was begun and so many lives were sacrificed, was reduced to virtual slavery. In their own countries, he explained, Churchill and Roosevelt may be honored as statesmen, but in Eastern Europe they are considered "shortsighted" and "stupid" for having given away the freedom of so many people whose destiny was in their hands.⁷

It is "incomprehensible to the ordinary human mind," he continued, that the Western powers should have ceded so much to the forces of totalitarianism at the conclusion of World War II. He reasoned, "Victorious states always dictate peace: they create the sort of situation which conforms to their philosophy. Instead ... President Roosevelt ... gave unlimited aid, and then unlimited concessions. Without any necessity whatever the occupation of Mongolia, Moldavia, Estonia, Latvia, Lithuania were silently recognized at Yalta. After that, almost nothing was done to protect Eastern Europe, [thus] seven or eight more countries were surrendered."⁸

The West's situation after World War II deteriorated even further, he argued during the 1970s and early 1980s. "Country after country" was yielded by the Western powers so as not to disrupt "their agreeable state of general tranquillity." In particular, Western lack of resolve was exhibited in Vietnam, where "two of the great powers of the West—France and America—tried their strength" against the forces of Communism "and both in turn have quit the field." Such wars of "national liberation" were particularly dangerous to the West, he predicted, for Western public opinion turned against resisting Communism in the Third World, thereby giving Communist leaders an open road to global domination. A "calm and impartial comparison" between the West's strength in the 1970s and in 1945 showed that the West's power slipped while the East's increased. The West's "spirit of resistance," its "position throughout the world," and "the confidence" that "the neutral 'Third World' " had in it "have been weakened." On the other hand, "the communist system has spread over huge areas."[9] And "its powerful enemies . . . have been destroyed." While some argued that Communism "is ready to collapse," he argued prior to the fall of Eastern European Communist governments, it "has always managed to keep its balance."[10]

Solzhenitsyn contended that détente, the policy of compromise between East and West made fashionable by Henry Kissinger, was an example of the West's lack of prudence. He agreed that détente was necessary "as air," since nuclear war is a horrible prospect, but he found that East-West relations, particularly during the 1970s, fell far short of détente.[11]

The West's shortsightedness was best epitomized by SALT (Strategic Arms Limitation Treaty), accords that put a ceiling on the amount of certain kinds of nuclear weapons that each side could deploy. These treaties also had the effect of recognizing the status quo in relation to the division of Europe. In an effort to gain peace for themselves, the Western powers entered into agreements that accepted Soviet domination of Eastern Europe, effectively legitimizing the enslavement of half a continent. Solzhenitsyn asked: What sort of signal was this to send totalitarian rulers? If Europeans were unwilling to resist, even symbolically, the encroachments of a tyrannical force of occupation against their fellow Europeans, one was led to wonder if they truly were ready to defend their own freedom.

There were even more serious problems with the concept of détente, Solzhenitsyn insisted. First, he argued that détente did little to moderate the war that Communism waged against its own people. What sort of détente was it, he asked, that allowed the Gulag to exist, doctors to destroy dissidents' brains with injections of drugs, and the entire Helsinki human-rights watch-group to disappear?[12]

Second, détente, as it came to be practiced in the West, depended on the Soviet leaders keeping their word. But, according to Solzhenitsyn,

Soviet leaders never kept their word, or they did so only when it suited them or when they had to. Real détente was impossible unless the power of the Soviet rulers could be checked. But who can guarantee that "détente will not be violated overnight?" Soviet leaders were not controlled by public opinion. There was no adversary press and only under Gorbachev has there been any hint of a freely elected parliament to insure that agreements were not broken on a whim. Thus, there was no "way to insure compliance." Solzhenitsyn's own experiences with the authorities during the forced-labor-camp revolts at Ekibastuz and later when he became world famous have convinced him that the word of Soviet officials can never be taken at face value. There was always an intrigue. Every action, every position, was taken for the sake of some political advantage, or for propaganda purposes. Nothing was ever done for pure and selfless reasons. The goal was always to gain favorable publicity at home and abroad.[13] He explained, "Khrushchev came and said, 'We will bury you!' . . . Now, of course, they have become more clever. . . . Today they don't say 'We are going to bury you,' now they say 'Détente.' Nothing has changed in Communist ideology. The goals are the same as they were, but instead of the artless Khrushchev, who couldn't hold his tongue, now they say 'Détente.' "[14]

Third, he argued, real détente would be possible only if some provision were made to reduce the ideological struggle against the West conducted in the Soviet Union. Peace would be unachievable, Solzhenitsyn claimed, if each day the state-run media decried the Western nations as aggressors and imperialists. Such propaganda created an asymmetry of forces. In the West, the hope for a peaceful reduction of tensions tended to soften public opinion toward the Soviets. The need to stand firm was undermined, and the need to support military preparedness was questioned; hence, the West was often "outplayed" at the bargaining table. The "ideological warfare" of the Soviet Union was intended to whip up hatred and fear of the West and thereby justify further sacrifices for military expenditures. An end to the ideological war was, therefore, the first step toward a lasting peace.[15]

There are policymakers and commentators on international relations, epitomized by such writers as Hans Morganthau and George Kennan, who take a more "realistic" approach to the conduct of East-West relations. They argue that in foreign affairs it is not important to consider a nation's ideology, for all nations have the same goal: to pursue their own interests. Proponents of this view would agree with Solzhenitsyn that it is foolhardy to depend on the good graces of Soviet leaders. Instead, they contend, Western policy should be based on the common interests of East and West. Accordingly, this group has sought to reduce tensions, to slow the arms race, and to divert resources into much-needed domestic programs. Both sides would see the advantage in pursuing such goals, it was reasoned; hence, both would have an equal interest in détente.

Solzhenitsyn's analysis casts some doubt on the "realist school's" approach. In challenging the realist school, he argued that the interests and actions of Communist rulers depended on the principles they espoused and on the character of the individuals involved. In both cases, as has been pointed out, the interests of Marxist leaders seemed to be at odds with those ideals cherished in the West. For example, he explained that both the Soviets and the West accept economic prosperity as an important goal. This seeming agreement of interests disguised the fact that Soviet rulers pursued their goals ideologically. For instance, they followed a policy of central planning for seventy years, despite its having impoverished the nation. Surely, he argued prior to the era of "restructuring," it was in the interest of party officials to abandon an economic program that had an unbroken history of failure and to adopt a system, private ownership, that has had a phenomenal record of success. Solzhenitsyn concluded that they did not change to the more efficient model, choosing instead to deprive their own people, because their actions were dictated by the ideology.[16]

Moreover, the Marxist ideology spread its influence far beyond the borders of the Soviet Union. It was not the Soviets, but indigenous Communists, who were responsible for the Cultural revolution in China, the genocide in Cambodia, the repression in Vietnam, and the suppression of Solidarity in Poland. The same type of events occurred with frightening regularity in lands separated both geographically and culturally. Thus, there can be nothing else to blame but the ideology.[17]

Solzhenitsyn argued that leaders who orchestrated such incidents could not remain free from their poisonous effects. For the most part, the life's experience of Communist rulers consisted either of bloody revolutionary struggles or vicious and occasionally deadly bureaucratic intrigues for power. Upon obtaining rule, Communists routinely sought to oppress their own people. Solzhenitsyn made us wonder whether the word of such people should be respected. Would not the same mentality that fostered oppression at home necessarily spread to their attitude toward international affairs? Was the interest of people who proclaimed themselves to be the salvation of mankind, yet who cynically presided over a totalitarian system intent on stripping every vestige of freedom from humanity, truly to be measured by the same standards as applied to the West?

For Solzhenitsyn the answer to these questions was clear. He declared that it was incorrect to attribute a rational, Western calculation of interest to Communist rulers, since they were dedicated to a program of internal oppression and external expansion. "The main goal of Communism," he wrote, "is an irrational and fanatical urge to swallow the maximum amount of external territory and population, with the ideal limit being the entire planet. . . . And it is symptomatic that Communist imperialism (in contrast to the earlier colonial variety) does not benefit or enrich the nation that it [conquers]." [18]

Unlike tyrants of old, who were restrained in their designs by practical limitations, Communist leaders were spurred on by an ideology that justified global conquest as a means of fulfilling its historical promise. Solzhenitsyn explains, "No personal tyranny can compare with ideological Communism, since every personal tyrant attains a limit of power that satisfies him. But no single country is enough to satisfy a totalitarian Communist regime. Communism is a type of virtually incomprehensible regime that is not interested in the flourishing of a country, or in the welfare of its people. On the contrary, Communism sacrifices both people and country to achieve its external goals." [19]

The true interests of the West-could be served, he insisted, only when Western policymakers acted on the supposition that "Marxism is hostile to the physical existence and the spiritual essence of every nation. It is futile to hope that a compromise with Communism will be found, or that relations will be improved by concessions and trade." [20]

Solzhenitsyn offered a number of policies that the West could pursue to forward its long-term interests. First, he forewarned that diplomacy, no matter how clever, and concessions, no matter how broad, could never serve fully to civilize the Soviet leadership. [21] He attacked the carrot-and-stick approach formulated most clearly by Henry Kissinger during his tenure in office. Of course, Kissinger did not suppose that the United States could influence the internal practices of the Soviet Union. But he did argue that the Soviet leaders' conduct of foreign affairs could be altered, their aggressive impulses blunted, and their actions towards other nations made to conform to the standards of the world diplomatic community. When they acted civilly and kept their word, Kissinger proposed, they would be rewarded with trade, loans, and technology. When they acted badly, they would be punished by having the flow of these things cut off. Kissinger realized that, for the short run, Western assistance might be used to build up the Soviet military, but he calculated that in the long run the leadership would be taught to keep their trust and to become a partner in the diplomatic community—playing by the rules. In sum, the leverage gained by aiding the Soviets could be used to humanize their international conduct.[22]

Solzhenitsyn stated that diplomacy alone could not tame the grand designs of Soviet rulers, but necessity could. If only the West stopped helping the Soviet government and refused to sell it the things it needed, it would have been forced to loosen its grip. It would have made real concessions or face total collapse. It would have become part of the world diplomatic community, not on account of the skills of a single statesman, but because objective conditions would have compelled it to moderate its behavior. In that regard Solzhenitsyn presented one of his ironic challenges to the East by asking the West to:

> at least permit this socialist economy to prove its superiority. . . . allow it to show that it is advanced, that it is omnipotent, that it has defeated you. . . . stop selling to it . . . for ten or fifteen years. . . . then see what it looks like. When the Soviet economy is no longer able to deal with everything, it will have to reduce its military preparations. . . . the system will be forced to relax. . . . stop helping it. When has a cripple ever helped along an athlete?[23]

It could be argued that Solzhenitsyn did not disagree with Kissinger's goals, but he reasoned that they were impossible to achieve unless a crisis of the severest form unsettled the security of the Soviet leaders. It is possible that the military buildup, tough rhetoric, and renewed economic strength of the United States during the Reagan years forced such a crisis.

Along with an economic boycott, Solzhenitsyn suggested that the West use its "mightiest weapon," radio broadcasts to the East, and engage in a war of ideas. He hoped that the West would put a wedge between Communist governments and their people by encouraging feelings of nation-

alism. He deduced from past experience that strong feelings of nationalism would undermine the stability of every Communist state, forcing the
leaders to moderate their actions both at home and abroad.[24] One need
only look to the unrest in the Baltic states and Armenia during the late
1980s to understand how prophetic Solzhenitsyn's statements were.

Critics of such a policy did not doubt that the West could stir up turmoil in the Soviet Union and even more in Eastern Europe, but they worried that social unrest would drive Soviet rulers to take desperate measures. Rather than lose their power and privilege, these critics predicted,
party leaders would be willing to take a reckless action against the West.

Solzhenitsyn understood that to engage the East in a conflict of ideas
entailed some risks, but he claimed that the dynamics of Communism
made the quest for expansion and global domination inevitable.[25] He
thought that some sort of confrontation between East and West was inevitable. The West could be victorious in that struggle only if it enlisted
the support of the enslaved peoples of the Communist world, who—
prior to the uncoupling of Eastern Europe from the Soviet empire—
outnumbered those of the Western alliance.[26] The West could not avoid
a confrontation with the East, Solzhenitsyn believed, it could only choose
when and with what weapons—ideas now, military force later—the battle should be conducted. With a certain rhetorical flourish, Solzhenitsyn
summed up the point as follows, "Communism is a denial of life; it is a
fatal disease of a nation and death of all humanity. And there is no nation
on earth that has immunity against Communism. To improve or correct
Communism is not feasible. Communism can only be done away with by
the joint efforts of the many peoples oppressed by it."[27]

As a final practical suggestion, Solzhenitsyn argued that the West
should deal with Communist nations from a position of strength and
with a policy of firmness. Firmness, he claimed, was the one tactic that
Communist rulers understood. The rough-and-tumble of bureaucratic
politics and the harsh necessities of keeping a totalitarian government in
power taught them to take advantage of any weakness and to respect
only strength. When confronted with resoluteness and determination,
Solzhenitsyn extrapolated from his own tumultuous experience, they
retreat.[28]

On the other hand, practical calculations of interest were not sufficient
to forestall an advance by the East or to avoid a catastrophe for the West.
Behind any successful policy, he maintained, there had to be a purpose

that made that policy worth defending. Hence, the West had to realize that by opposing Communism it was not merely promoting its own way but was protecting morality. If the West refused to take a moral stance, it would undermine its capacity to defend itself. (We employ arms, they employ arms; thus both sides are equally evil, or more rightly, foolish.)

We might infer, then, that for Solzhenitsyn the "realist" school of international relations was not realistic. By focusing exclusively on power relationships between states, realists failed to recognize the true nature of Communism, and therefore were incapable of maintaining a steadfast resistance to that movement. After all, if one teaches that all states pursue pretty much the same goals and that the character of states must be discounted when considering foreign affairs (our side is not much different from their side), it is natural that people should become bewildered as to the need for sacrifice. Without a moral perspective from which to judge, the global conflict waged for the soul and mind of the human race resembled a self-centered game, played to gratify the egos of the super powers. Therefore, Solzhenitsyn recommended that in the conduct of external affairs, "One cannot think only on the low level of political calculation. It is also necessary to think of what is noble, and what is honorable." [29]

In the end, decisions that take their bearing from moral principles actually would serve the interests of the West better than those based solely on practical considerations. Only if the West would cast its struggle against Communism in terms of good and evil, he argued, would it be able to muster sufficient will to withstand the "inhuman strength" which threatened to extinguish its way of life. "And how surprising it is," he said, "that a practical policy computed on the basis of moral considerations [turns] out to be the most far-sighted, the most salutary." [30]

Sources of Western Misunderstanding

If Solzhenitsyn's analysis is correct, many in the West seriously misjudged their adversary. How could this have happened? He argues that a major triumph of Communism was to gain a foothold in the West through misunderstanding and deceit.

An important component in that victory was the ability of Communist nations in general, and the Soviet Union in particular, to control the flow of information to the West. [31] Until—during the reign of Gorbachev—the party began to disclose some of the disagreeable aspects of Soviet society, little reliable information was actually available about what went on in that country. Westerners were not allowed to travel freely or given access to areas outside the major cities. When impromptu meetings did occur between Western journalists and the average Soviet citizen, either they were staged by the KGB or an agent was close at hand to insure that nothing derogatory was said. Indeed, reporters were consistently fooled into believing conditions were better than they actually were. The real poverty and oppression existed in the countryside, from which outsiders were prohibited. Even clandestine meetings with dissidents were an insufficient means of collecting unbiased information, since most were urban dwellers who were in the dark themselves about what went on elsewhere.[32]

As examples of his point, Solzhenitsyn explains, first, that the full extent of Stalin's fanaticism was not recognized in the West for many years, that the 1962 Tambov peasant revolt was never reported, and that even today the vast majority of Soviet dissidents, not to mention non-Soviet resisters, are not sought out by the Western media and their views are rarely heard.[33]

Second, there is a tradition in the West of speaking ill of national Russia. The faults of the Soviet system are said to be a manifestation of Russian character and of the Russian people's willingness to endure tyrants. Soviet expansionism was blamed on the traditional geopolitical interests of the nation—the desire for warm water ports, for example—or on the legacy of oppression and imperial adventure held over from the tsars.

Perhaps these factors did play a role in forming Soviet behavior, but Solzhenitsyn asks why the analogy to the past is made only in the case of Russia. Did not all the nations of Europe—indeed, virtually every nation on earth—have a tyrant in their past? Why in the case of Russia do despotic tsars explain and exculpate Soviet dictators? France had Napoleon, Rome the Caesars, but no one suggests that such examples would give a satisfactory explanation of present-day tyrants in those countries. Moreover, blaming Soviet expansion on the past misrepresents European history. When the Russian Empire was at its height, every other European power also was engaged in empire building. If the logic by which Soviet expansionism is explained were applied universally, then the sun would still be refusing to set on the British Empire. In fact, Soviet designs have been far greater than were those of any tsar, Solzhenitsyn argues. The

Soviet Union has endeavored to extend its influence and domain throughout every continent on earth.[34]

Blaming Russia for the faults of Communism "comforts the entire
West." Solzhenitsyn reasons, "If the horrors of the U.S.S.R. stem, not
from Communism, but from the unfortunate Russian tradition, . . . then
the West has nothing to fear. It follows that nothing bad will happen. If
socialism does overtake them, then [it will be] a virtuous socialism."[35] It
cannot be forgotten that the atrocities of the Soviet Union are not unique
in the Communist world, and it is impossible that Russian national flaws
could be held responsible for events in Albania, China, North Korea,
Cuba, or Cambodia, to name just a few nations.

Third, Solzhenitsyn argues that it is hard for any people to understand
the suffering of another across national and cultural barriers. This is particularly true if one's own situation is safe and prosperous. He explains
that it is difficult for the affluent to comprehend the suffering of others
because they are too intent on prolonging their "well-being for as long as
possible at any price." In this regard, the West is not alone. It is simply
an "appalling human characteristic" that people are often indifferent to
the plight of others. This trait—to be caught up entirely in one's own
concerns—is an aspect of human nature "against which religious books
and many works of literature warn us."[36]

How many witnesses from Communist countries would it take, Solzhenitsyn wondered during the Brezhnev era, before the West was shaken
from its easygoing attitude? How many stories of camps, of murder, and
of repression were necessary for the West to comprehend the nature of
Marxism and to understand the character of its adversary? He asked
whether it was necessary that another Berlin Wall be built before the
West saw the true nature of Communism. (And one wonders if everyone
in the West will understand Solzhenitsyn's point now that the Wall has
been torn down.) At some point, he argues, it should have been admitted
that Western indifference and naïveté towards Marxism's vices were
merely self-deceit.[37]

Finally, and most importantly, he argues that a true awareness of the
nature of Marxism has been clouded by the intellectual agreement that
many in the West have with the ends or ideals of Marx's philosophy. The
ideas that once were the foundation of Western culture, he maintains,
have come under attack. As a result they have moved in a particular
direction—a direction that has made Marx's principles of liberation,

equality, and material well-being more and more acceptable as the sole criterion for judging the worth of human life. In order to comprehend fully the reasons for this acceptance, it is necessary that we investigate Solzhenitsyn's analysis of Western philosophy and ideals.

Crisis of the West

The Movement of Western Thought

According to Solzhenitsyn, "today's world" is facing a crisis of momentous proportions. The clearest manifestation of that crisis has been the rift between East and West. Yet there is a fissure, he says, which "is both more profound and more alienating" than any "political conception." It is doubtful that this danger can "be eliminated through successful diplomatic negotiations or by achieving a military balance." Moreover, the rift threatens to swallow both East and West into its ever-widening chasm. For Solzhenitsyn problems that the East and West share are more dangerous than the political differences that divide them. He writes, "This deep and multiform split threatens us all with an equally manifold disaster, in accordance with the ancient truth that a kingdom—in this case, our earth—divided against itself cannot stand." [38]

But what crisis could be worse than the present antagonism between the superpowers? What is the source of this crisis? How did it originate? What are its possible effects?

The source of our plight, holds Solzhenitsyn, is the result of modern culture having "lost the concept of a Supreme Complete Entity." [39] At one time this concept: had served "to restrain our passions and our irresponsibilities"; had given us the courage to resist evil; had supplied a criterion by which to judge actions right or wrong; had made us aware that there were more important things in life than the satisfaction of physical desires; and, not least importantly, had endowed our lives with meaning and purpose. One is led to wonder why a concept so beneficial to human life ever came into disrepute.

Solzhenitsyn maintains that the "spiritual" aspect of human existence was not overwhelmed all in one stroke—in fact, there are remnants of the spirit existing within Western culture today. However, belief in the spirit was challenged and finally undermined by ideas that came to be the fundamental premises of modern culture.

There are, he explains, certain nodal points in human history at which time people reassess their way of thinking and acting, and set a new course for the future. One such shift was reached at the end of the Middle Ages. It occurred as a reaction against an "intolerable despotic repression of man's physical nature in favor of the spiritual one."[40] The philosophies of the Renaissance and Enlightenment recoiled from the "excesses of Catholicism"[41] and proposed that, instead of God or nature, man himself should stand as the center of the universe.[42] The medieval ideals, he writes, "pulled us, drove us toward Spirit, by force, and we naturally rejected this, jerked free, plunged into Matter. Thus began a long epoch of humanistic individualism. Thus did civilization begin to be constructed on the principle: man is the measure of all things. The whole inevitable path enriched the experience of mankind immensely."[43]

The ascendancy of the human species would be possible, it was reasoned by the philosophers of the Enlightenment, if that which is said to be higher than human, hence, beyond human control, were rejected in favor of that which humans could sense, i.e., the material world that could be brought under human command. This feat was to be accomplished in a number of ways.

First, mankind had to be released from the bonds of ecclesiastical servitude. During the centuries of Christian rule, church leaders had done little to combat superstition, prejudice, and ignorance among the people. Quite the contrary, the clergy retained its influence by keeping the flock backward and innocent. In a deeper sense, the position of the clergy rested on a belief that existence was governed by immutable edicts issuing from God. For the religious person, human beings were only one part of His creation, and their duty was to accept life as it was given to them.

The Enlightenment philosophers revolted against this supine acceptance of human fate. They calculated that the squalid conditions in which most of the race lived could be conquered once the power of the clergy was broken and all people learned to think for themselves. Furthermore, the belief that human beings should not tamper with divine laws had to be destroyed. Rather than understanding themselves as part of nature, people would see themselves as its lord. In this way, the laws of nature could be studied and then put to use satisfying people's physical needs. They could be relieved of the constant struggle to provide for the necessities of life. Degradation, poverty, and ignorance would be at an end.

Second, the human race as a whole was to be enlightened as to the benefits of intellectual endeavors. No longer would the continual questions and inevitable skepticism of the philosophic enterprise undermine belief in and commitment to the established political order. The struggle between philosophy and the practical life, best exemplified by Athens' trial and execution of Socrates, was to be settled by stripping the intellectual pursuits of their normative content and by using their discoveries as a means of increasing material bounty. These twin goals could be achieved if philosophers did not take part in the controversy over the best form of political association. By abandoning the question that had so intrigued philosophers of antiquity, "modern" philosophers would seem less threatening to the political community because they would no longer present themselves as one of the many groups contending for power. Indeed, their primary concern would be to assist the human race by making the scientific discoveries that would bring material benefits to all.

However, this seeming lack of political ambition on the part of philosophy was more apparent than real. The Enlightenment philosophers reasoned that they could conceal their true influence over what people thought and how they acted, if the political and ethical horizon they established was popular with the vast majority of mankind. Although in practice this turned out to be no mean feat, in theory it was quite simple. Give people what they want: peace and material comforts. Science was to be turned into technological inventions that would relieve man's estate. At the same time, a stable political foundation was to be constructed by turning people's attention away from matters that were likely to make them combative (for instance, theological disputes) and towards those things that would make them peaceful (for example, commerce). Dedication to religion and morality was to be replaced by a rational calculation of self-interest, and concern over spiritual matters was to be kept a strictly private matter.[44]

Commenting on the optimism that many felt would be achieved if people were liberated from spiritual restraints, Solzhenitsyn writes, "Once it was proclaimed and accepted that above man there was no supreme being, but instead that man was the crowning glory of the universe and the measure of all things, man's needs, desires, and indeed weaknesses were taken to be the supreme imperatives of the universe. . . . in the course of several centuries this philosophy inexorably flooded the entire Western world, and gave it confidence for its colonial conquests."[45]

The early twentieth century marked the high point of the Western ideal. Since that time, however, one catastrophe has followed another, until it seems that living at the brink is the norm of our age. Two world wars, the revolution of 1917 that initiated the struggle between East and West, the threat of nuclear annihilation, widespread crime in the midst of plenty, pollution, materialism, and alienation have all served to undermine the optimism once so common when, at the beginning of this century, the promises of the Enlightenment seemed to be at hand.

What was the cause of this rapid, one might say breathtaking, decline? For Solzhenitsyn the reverses are a consequence of the Enlightenment's principles having reached their natural limits. He writes, "The West kept advancing steadily in accordance with its proclaimed social intentions, hand in hand with dazzling progress in technology. And suddenly found itself in its present state of weakness. This means that the mistake must be at the root, at the very foundation of thought in modern times."[46]

Solzhenitsyn's account of the process of Western decay can be explained as follows: A fundamental tenet of liberalism, the original political philosophy to emerge from the Enlightenment, held that human beings cannot, thus should not, be trained in virtue. It is not that liberalism failed to comprehend the need for self-restraint of a certain kind, but it doubted that the traditional understanding of virtue was practical. Virtue demanded that people not be guided by their passions and desires, but conform instead to higher moral principles. But, because passions and interests have their origin in people's physiological makeup, they are very strong motivations. Moral principles, having no such physical support, are felt less urgently. According to liberalism, the call to virtue, so customary in the Middle Ages, was little more than high-toned hypocrisy. For while everyone paid lip service to the commandments of morality and religion, most obeyed the stronger urges of their bodies.

Moreover, the kind of virtue that liberalism criticized was not the somewhat narrow concept, consisting of a number of "do nots" (e.g., do not steal, do not murder), that we have today. Virtue had a broader meaning, which, while it included those universal "do nots," also placed positive demands on action. The virtue of a thing was its particular faculty and its highest form or excellence. We sometimes use the concept in its traditional way when we say, for example: "The virtue of a race horse is to run fast." This statement connotes an ability on the part of race horses to run fast and a notion that when they are acting as they should (excellently), they can run faster than any other horse.

To apply such a concept to human beings raises important difficulties. What is the virtue of man? What is his particular faculty? What is his excellence? The answers to these questions are inevitably controversial. Indeed, liberalism maintained that in the previous two thousand years no moral philosopher had come up with a fully adequate explanation of virtue. The result was that there were different conceptions of the virtue of man, all claiming to understand his nature, and all wishing to train him to a certain kind of excellence. These theoretical differences spilled over into political life, most visibly during the religious wars of Europe. In other words, the very concept of virtue opened up theological struggles and political upheavals, which, as mentioned previously, the Enlightenment wished to put to rest.

As a replacement for virtue, liberalism proposed that people be taught law-abidingness. This was to be achieved in two ways. First, institutions would be constructed that, while not hindering people's desires, would channel them in ways conducive to public peace. Second, an environment favorable to acquisition would be created. Citizens would learn that their interest lay in the continued existence of the state. It was reasoned that people who enjoyed prosperity would be unlikely to engage in subversion or revolt.

The Enlightenment's principles found their political expression in the doctrines of liberalism. The satisfaction of human desires could best be accomplished, according to liberalism, if people were left alone to pursue their own interests in their own way. All unnecessary hindrances standing as a barrier to people's ambition were to be removed. The government's major functions were to enforce contracts and to insure that the contest for economic gain did not go so far as to upset the peace. The fundamental goal of such a state was to secure a realm of liberty so that in their private lives, people could live as they chose—hence, the name liberalism.

Despite the dazzling success that this philosophy has achieved in unleashing human ingenuity, Solzhenitsyn maintains that it has also set free some unsavory human traits. The freedom that liberalism so cherishes has given free reign to "pride, self-interest, envy, vanity, and a dozen other defects," which, along with our positive attributes, are so much a part of human nature. This tilt toward evil seems to be at odds with what the original proponents of liberalism had expected. They reasoned that once people overcame prejudice, superstition, and above all the constant demands of natural necessity, they would use their newly won freedom to aid in the progressive betterment of the human condition. The advocates of liberalism held this belief, infers Solzhenitsyn, because their "anthropocentric" and "humanistic way of thinking . . . did not admit the intrinsic evil in man." Thus societies founded on liberal principles left, "Everthing beyond physical well-being and the accumulation of material goods, all other human requirements and characteristics of a subtler and higher nature . . . outside the areas of attention of state and social systems, as if human life did not have any higher meaning. Thus gaps were left open for evil, and its drafts blow freely today."[47]

As support for his proposition, Solzhenitsyn points out that despite their unprecedented wealth, every Western nation seems to face an intractable problem with crime. This unexpected phenomenon has occurred, he explains, because freedom is more easily abused by our lower passions than it is exercised wisely for the cultivation of our higher attributes. Without the requisite principles to limit and guide our ideas and actions, decadence easily overtakes virtue because good must be nurtured, while evil flourishes all on its own.

A second consequence of Enlightenment philosophy has been the rise of materialism, what Solzhenitsyn calls "the cult of well-being." It is fair to say that the original premise of liberalism did not necessarily lead to an overly acquisitive society. Liberalism left open the question about the proper ends of human life. Whether individuals sought to become wealthy, or whether they sought some other goal—say, artistic creation or a life dedicated to the mind—was entirely a matter of personal choice. Yet, given the reality of what interests most people most of the time, it was a foregone conclusion that liberty would be used for personal gain. Solzhenitsyn reminds us of a verity proclaimed by virtually every moral teaching: material goods, alone, cannot make people happy. Rather than satisfying people's needs, an overabundance of goods tends to sharpen the appetites. People lose sight of the proper limits of consumption. They dash madly about competing with one another to acquire more, always more. "This active and tense competition," he explains, "comes to dominate all human thought and does not in the least give rise to spiritual development." Indeed, the quest to achieve happiness through material gain is futile, for human desires are limitless. There is always a better stereo, a faster car.[48]

The "humanism" of the modern world has done little to humanize mankind, Solzhenitsyn concludes. The unlimited freedom it bestows on people has come to undermine their ability to make moral judgments. Those who still insist that limitations be placed on human desires and passions are branded fanatics, intent on foisting their narrow-minded beliefs on an unwilling populace. With few moral grounds for restraint, natural human desires (especially avarice) and passions (especially envy) have been unleashed to an excessive degree. Just since World War II, Solzhenitsyn argues, the extent of industrialization has exceeded that of all previous ages. Humanity is awash in a sea of commercial goods, while corporations rush to introduce new products that satisfy virtually every desire. The world's natural resources are being used up in a futile attempt to satisfy fickle and limitless appetites. Placing himself squarely among the ecologists Solzhenitsyn complains, "Having placed man as the highest measure—imperfect man, never free from self-interest, self-love, envy, and vanity, man has given himself up without measure or restraint to Matter—we have arrived at a littering, a surfeit of garbage. We are drowning in terrestrial garbage. This refuse fills and obstructs all spheres of our existence."[49]

Although mankind gained much from the Enlightenment, Solzhenitsyn argues, it also lost something. At the core of that philosophy is nothing that elevates human beings above a concern for their physical needs. Human beings could be conceived of as very smart animals who create an environment conducive to their well-being. Similar to other animals, however, there is little beyond staying alive, commodiously if possible, that gives life purpose. Solzhenitsyn laments, "We have become hopelessly enmeshed in our slavish worship of all that is pleasant, all that is comfortable, all that is material—we worship things, we worship products. Will we ever succeed in shaking off this burden, in giving free reign to the spirit that was breathed into us at birth, that spirit which distinguishes us from the animal world?"[50]

Solzhenitsyn acknowledges that the Enlightenment did not transform people into materialists all at once. He seems to agree with Tocqueville's assessment that the morals of an earlier age continued to hold great sway over the human conscience. In fact, the freedom secured as the result of the Enlightenment's political philosophy allowed religion to flourish as a private pursuit, acting as it always had to form people's characters and to restrain their desires. The vast edifice of the Judeo-Christian heritage continued to inform people about the proper limits of their freedom and about the responsibilities they owed to each other and to the community. Slowly but inexorably, however, the West's spiritual reserves were eroded. Concern over material gain, so much a part of the Enlightenment principles, began to overwhelm people's regard for the spirit. The public ideals of easygoing morality, the quick profit, and unlimited freedom invaded people's private, religious beliefs. More and more the premises of the Enlightenment encouraged the hope that "politics and social reform" could bring about human happiness. Indeed, since the Enlightenment's ideals "did not admit the existence of intrinsic evil in man," many came to believe that religious restrictions were an unnecessary hindrance. They reasoned that religion could be discarded altogether and that human beings could create morality for themselves.

The emancipation of the human race from moral constraints has proceeded apace with an ever higher standard of living and ever newer and better technological marvels. Despite the increase in wealth and the widespread enjoyment of "the rights of man," the last few generations have discovered that the price to be paid for freedom from religious restraint is very dear. Every age has its cruelty and injustice—such is the nature of the race—but in the twentieth century people have inflicted vaster crimes on their fellow human beings. No other era has reached the momentous scale of suffering. No other period has succumbed to totalitarian movements. All this, Solzhenitsyn maintains, is the result of the diminution of religious belief.[51]

The decline of Western culture's dependence on a "Supreme Complete Entity," Solzhenitsyn's term for the Divine, has also driven the more progressive elements within society to adopt more and more extreme positions on the public issues of the day. Ideas such as liberation, equality, and the possession of material well-being (often labeled development when applied to the Third World) have gained popularity, and in turn, have become the basis for social movements. Not only have these ideas served as rallying points for the overthrow of the hierarchical traditions of the aristocratic age, but they have undergone a transformation and radicalization themselves. Some social critics have come to believe that absolute freedom, full equality, and uninterrupted abundance are not only the birthright of humanity but possible to achieve in practice. Without higher moral standards to serve as the ordering principles of human life, all restrictions on personal freedom seem illegitimate, every distinction between higher and lower desires is thrown into doubt, and a dedication to anything other than physical well-being is thought to be unnecessary.

Once moral criteria gave a clear demarcation between liberty and license. Those who persisted in abusing their freedom were thought to have it rightly taken away. But today those strictures have been loosened. All is permitted except what is proscribed by law. But law, even when supported by sufficient force, has been shown to be an inadequate means of controlling human behavior. Without some notion of morality to give them guidance, those who make the laws have difficulty deciding right from wrong. Furthermore, as Solzhenitsyn points out, the law provides no basis for the internal check on citizen behavior that is the hallmark of a civilized society.[52] He states:

> in early democracies, as in the American democracy at the time of its birth, all individual human rights were granted on the grounds that man is God's creature. . . . freedom was given to the individual conditionally, in the assumption of his constant religious responsibility. Such was the heritage of the preceding one thousand years. . . . even fifty years ago, it would have seemed quite impossible . . . that an individual be granted boundless freedom with no purpose, simply for the satisfaction of his whims.[53]

Once standards existed by which to assess and to emulate great character and noble deeds. Today, Solzhenitsyn alleges, those measures have been eroded by the incessant demands for equality. This tendency toward leveling has occurred to the point that, "an outstanding, truly great person who has unusual and unexpected initiatives in mind does not get any chance to assert himself; dozens of traps will be set for him from the beginning. Thus mediocrity triumphs under the guise of democratic restraints."[54]

Once people had faith that there were higher pursuits than the gratification of physical desires. Presently, Solzhenitsyn argues, belief in those goals has been weakened. Replacing the "higher view of life" is a hedonistic perspective based on the idea that "you only live once." But the quest for bodily pleasures can become a never-ending trap from which the human spirit finds it difficult to escape.[55]

As demands for greater freedom, equality, and abundance have increased, Solzhenitsyn argues, the political expression of those demands has become more radical. Thus, there has been "a general transition from liberalism to socialism."[56] Although Solzhenitsyn never spells out in detail how this transition occurred, nor whether the term *socialism* refers to all of the varieties of socialism practiced in the East or in the West, it is possible to deduce his arguments on these two issues.

Obviously, liberalism's vision of the world was realistic, since people did use their freedom to produce prosperity on a scale that transformed how the race lives. Yet liberalism set off a reaction against itself. The continual pursuit of money and the constant jarring of interests caused some people to draw back in horror.[57] They saw that while liberalism tended to make everyone materialistic, it succeeded in making only a few people rich. Even more disturbing was the disparity of wealth endemic to a liberal society. Indeed, in its original and pure form, liberalism seemed incapable of fulfilling its promise to better the lot of mankind. The few rich used all their resources to oppress the many poor and to keep them in a state of economic dependency, making them a cheap source of labor.

The appeal to socialism was a direct result of the failures of liberalism. The latter sought to make people happy by increasing the stock of goods available to mankind, a feat made possible by giving material incentives to inventive genius. The former intended to make people content by equitably distributing the fruits of human creativity. The essence of the dispute lay in this: liberalism depended on material rewards as the spur that would drive people to produce greater abundance. Socialism surmised that differences in wealth would result in differences in opportunity, making it impossible for all people to share equally in the material bounty.

Liberalism set forth no moral criterion or standard above the human will by which to justify the social hierarchy that the freedom to acquire property was likely to create. Of course, it did put forward the notion that the ingenious and diligent are entitled to the greater benefits their abilities could earn them. In other words, given equal opportunity—in the form of equal rights—natural talent and determination would provide a proper basis for distinction. There is some truth to the assertion, but socialism attacked liberalism by arguing that equal rights cannot insure equal opportunity, since some people have a greater advantage at birth; they are born into rich families. Hence, socialism concluded that all differences in rank were unjust.

The process of self-criticism within Western thought did not cease with socialism's assault on liberalism. Solzhenitsyn explains that the interrelationship among social philosophies is such that:

> the current of materialism which is farthest to the left, and hence more consistent, always proves to be stronger, more attractive, and victorious. Humanism which has lost its Christian heritage cannot prevail in this competition. Thus during the past centuries and especially in recent decades, as the process became more acute, the alignment of forces was as follows: Liberalism was inevitably pushed aside by radicalism, radicalism had to surrender to socialism, and socialism could not stand up to communism.[58]

The absence of unifying moral principles has led to the progression from liberalism to socialism in another way. In former times the inequalities that were a part of social life were thought to be ordained by God or nature. Putting aside the historical defense of social hierarchy for our purpose, one can see that moral principles of whatever kind justify inequality, since some people live up to the moral standards, while others do not. Without commonly held ideals, however, there is no basis for distinguishing between good and bad, better or best. All differences between people are illegitimate—all are conventional. Socialism solves this dilemma by reducing questions of moral worth to issues of bodily need. That is, we all have bodies. Those bodies have needs that must be satisfied if life is to continue. Thus, there is a moral imperative in satisfying those needs equitably.

Finally, the very liberty from which liberalism derives its name has served to undermine that philosophy. If the belief that all are entitled to their opinion is taken seriously, then, anyone's ideas are as good as anyone else's. There are no opinions of greater worth than others. The opinion that liberalism is the proper political order for mankind is thrown into doubt. And if there is no ground from which to make authoritative judgments, all ideas of morality merit the same respect—equality reigns. With no principles to support authority, even the authority underlying liberalism, all forms of inequality are suspect. Here again socialism solves this problem by recourse to what is most common and visible in our lives—our physical being. While moral and ethical precepts have always been subject to much controversy, it is difficult to deny the fact that all human beings are equally in need of providing for the necessities of life. Socialism is more consistent in recognizing this fact.

For Solzhenitsyn, the increased dependence on political and social movements as the way of finding purpose in life, the transition of political ideals to more and more radical forms, and the barren hope of finding happiness in material possessions are all natural outgrowths of the "autonomous, irreligious humanistic consciousness" first established in the Enlightenment philosophy. Thus there is an intimate connection between East and West. Both denigrate, "our most precious possession: our spiritual life. It is trampled by Party hucksters in the East, by commercial ones in the West. This is the essence of the crisis: the split in the world is less terrifying than the similarity of the disease afflicting its main sections."[59]

The Consequences of the Crisis to the West

What problems face the West as a result of the spiritual crisis of modern culture? According to Solzhenitsyn there are a number of troublesome ones.

First, he claims that the intelligentsia of the West has shown a marked sympathy for the aims of socialism. The newest, boldest, and most progressive abstract notions of social justice appealed to the intelligentsia's way of thinking. He writes that the "tendency of ideas to continue on their natural course made people admire them."[60] The intelligentsia's infatuation with leftist causes, he alleges, made many of them turn a blind eye to the faults of the Soviet Union and other Communist nations.

> The Communist regimes in the East could endure and grow due to the enthusiastic support from a number of Western intellectuals who (feeling the kinship!) refused to see communism's crimes, and when they no longer could do so, they tried to justify these crimes. The problem persists: In our Eastern countries, communism has suffered a complete ideological defeat; it is zero and less than zero. And yet Western intellectuals still look at it with considerable interest and empathy, and this is precisely what makes it so immensely difficult for the West to withstand the East.[61]

It is an overstatement to say that Western intellectuals advocate the Soviet system—although during the 1920s and 1930s many certainly did. The vast majority abhor the repression and injustice so characteristic of Soviet life. On the other hand, as Solzhenitsyn points out, many Western intellectuals have been more reticent about blaming the Soviet Union's ills on its Marxist ideology. He explains:

> Since the unmasking of the Soviet system, Western concepts have retreated from trench to trench. First they abandoned Stalin and shifted all the blame into a mythical Stalinism which never existed. Then, with a heavy heart, they abandoned even Lenin: if everything bad stemmed from Lenin, it was not, they argue, because he was a Communist, but because he was Russian. Since these are all Russian perversions, what has the West to fear? . . . The West's intellectual sympathy [for Marxism] is also conditioned by the common source of their ideological origins: materialism and atheism.[62]

Ideological affinity for progressive ideas has led many Western intellectuals to support Marxist movements, such as wars of national liberation. The process is almost always the same. A Marxist revolution arouses great sympathy within the intellectual class. Its goals are defended, its fervor supported. As the revolutionary fire cools and the centralized bureaucratic state comes to dominate all life in the nation, intellectuals lose faith and return to their theorizing—until the next revolution breaks out. Since intellectuals are the opinion leaders of society, the population in general has become confused in its capacity to recognize the founding of totalitarian regimes.

Intellectuals have backed Marxist uprisings not so much because they are Marxist themselves but because these movements have taken the correct stance on the issues of our time.[63] They have attacked existing societies from the left and have spoken out in favor of greater freedom,[64] more equality,[65] and increased material well-being.[66]

Of course, few intellectuals would attempt to force social reform as far as it has gone in the Soviet Union or in China under Mao. Yet many agree that socialism, purged of the excesses, is the true path to social justice. To which Solzhenitsyn replies:

> The decline of contemporary thought has been hastened by the misty phantom of socialism. Socialism has created the illu-

sion of quenching people's thirst for justice: Socialism has lulled their consciences into thinking that the steamroller which is about to flatten them is a blessing in disguise, a salvation. And socialism, more than anything else, has caused public hypocrisy to thrive; it has enabled Europe to ignore the annihilation of 66 million people on its very borders.[67]

Obviously, there is a difference between socialism of the Soviet variety and that practiced in the West. Solzhenitsyn recognizes the difference, but maintains that Western socialists are guilty of not resisting Communism as vigorously as they might, and certainly not as strongly as the more conservative groups have. Moreover, since the ideas behind socialism rest on Enlightenment principles—indeed, represent their culmination—they incline people to adopt a materialistic attitude toward life. In doing so, they diminish people's spiritual strength and, as we shall see in what follows, make them less inclined to lay down their lives in defense of freedom or any other principles. And people lacking faith in a higher spiritual purpose may be tempted to reform the world to conform to some vision of earthly perfection—as did the most idealistic followers of Marx.[68]

A second serious problem facing the West, Solzhenitsyn warns, is a loss of courage. During the 1970s, he argued that "A loss of courage is the most striking feature that an outsider notices in the West today. . . . Political and intellectual functionaries . . . [offer] self-serving rationales as to how realistic, reasonable, and intellectually and even morally justified it is to base state policies on weakness and cowardice."[69]

Solzhenitsyn recognizes the problem of liberal societies first brought to light by the English philosopher Thomas Hobbes: a way of life that rests on the protection of physical well-being has difficulty prompting people to exhibit the virtue of military valor. If life entails little more than the gratification of one's desires, why should people endanger those pleasures by placing their lives in jeopardy? After all, it is most difficult to partake of any of life's pleasures if one is dead. Yet, "to defend oneself," Solzhenitsyn writes, reminding us of the harsher side of life, "one must also be ready to die; there is little such readiness in a society raised in the cult of well-being."[70]

All too often, he complains, the West has backed down from the challenges of totalitarianism. The "spirit of Munich" has infected our age. The West's once high principles are mocked and labeled reactionary. Its once high purpose no longer serves to rally its citizens from their private concerns. In the face of an implacable foe, the West has become increasingly confused and paralyzed. It has sought to gain a respite of peace and security by making concessions. According to Solzhenitsyn it has deluded itself into believing that compromises with evil are noble and moral attempts to avoid conflict.[71] "Behind all this," he warns, "lies that sleek god of affluence, now proclaimed as the goal of life, replacing the high-minded view of the world which the West has lost."[72]

One of the most devastating effects of the West's loss of spiritual balance, Solzhenitsyn insists, is the ascendancy of moral relativism. He says that inhabitants of the present generation are left with the small change from the gold coins of their parents and grandparents. For ages people lived together with the understanding that some things were good and others bad. True, different countries and cultures held different things dear, yet all shared the belief that moral judgments not only were plausible but were the ground from which all other opinions sprang. In the modern age, particularly the twentieth century, the idea that there are moral standards has come into disrepute. Choices between good and bad, noble and base, even true and false are said to be culturally bound, historically determined, or a matter of personal preference. One could almost go so far as to say that the relativism that pervades contemporary thought has become nihilism, the doctrine that there is no truth and that existence has no meaning. Except for the fact that modern culture retains an unshakable faith in the capacity of science to cure all our social ills, nihilism would be an apt description of our intellectual horizon. However, since the debate is over which of the many competing "values" should determine how to use the discoveries of science, the terms *relativism* or *moral relativism* are more accurate descriptions of the contemporary ethos.

But how did we reach such a state? How were the once so optimistic tenets of Enlightenment turned into the disheartening notions of relativism? Solzhenitsyn once again seems to find the answer in the "transition of ideas." More specifically, his argument in *August 1914* against the Kantianism of Tolstoy suggests that he understands the philosophy of Kant to be a critical factor in the introduction and general acceptance of relativism into the mainstream of Western thought.

Stated briefly, Kant had been roused from his easy acceptance of liberal ideals by the attack made on those principles by the French philosopher

Jean-Jacques Rousseau. In particular, Kant objected to the position, put forward most strongly by Hobbes, that unless otherwise restrained by the state, people would always seek their own interest. Such a view of human motivation held as one of its corollaries that moral behavior, indeed the concept of morality itself, rested on the power of the state to compel citizens to act in ways not destructive of the public good; peace was founded on force, virtue on fear. Through his investigations, Kant hoped to find a foundation for morality that did not rest on some force external to the individual making a moral choice. He claimed to have discovered that foundation in the categorical imperative.

The categorical imperative grows out of the constructs of human reason. It exists in human beings a priori and, therefore, makes the individual agent responsible for his moral choices, not some external power. It is also universal; any reasonable person can understand its nature. Indeed, to rid itself of the charge that the individual agent may be acting for his self-interest or as the result of some external threat of retribution, the agent acting under the provisions of the categorical imperative can have no thought of himself or of the consequences of his action. Therefore, the categorical imperative must be contentless and completely exclude, so as not to introduce a self-interest based on personal or cultural bias, moral values that grow out of the experience of an individual or a particular culture. Facts can in no way affect one's values. Put simply, it is each thinking and acting in terms of all.

In order to maintain the validity of moral judgments based on the categorical imperative, Kant had to show that human beings could not make evaluative judgments based on empirical evidence (one could not infer the "ought" from the "is"), for this would mean that one people's moral code could be superior to another's, opening once again the wound that gave rise to the religious wars of Europe. Most of the philosophy and theology prior to Kant had made ethical judgments on the facts, of course. But Kant attempted to show that this was nothing more than idle speculation. Taking the place of an ethics grounded in practical experience and prudence was a universal moral code founded on the capacity of the human reasoning power to make entirely impartial judgments.

Despite the high hopes and good intentions of Kant's philosophy, it was quickly overwhelmed by the transition of ideas. Marx attacked Kant's ideas on at least two fronts. First, Marx turned Kant back on himself by showing that even the a priori judgments, which Kant thought would be immune from bias, were actually determined by the economic structure of a particular historical epoch. Hence, there were no grounds from which human beings could justify making moral decisions—all such choices were culturally and historically determined. Second, insofar as the universalism of Kant did reflect the future of the race, it was naive, because it provided no mechanism or historical agent, such as the proletariat, for its coming into being.

Marx does not reject all of Kant's thought, however. Instead, he accepts the notion that each should think in terms of all, but radicalizes the doctrine by maintaining that the categorical imperative could be made to have a material manifestation. Put simply, each should work for the good of all. Indeed, Marx goes so far as to say that human beings could be truly human only when they abandoned the pursuit of personal gain and labored to produce for the good of the community. In making this argument, Marx reasoned that animals strive to produce for their physical well-being, but humans have the capacity to work for the sake of the universal. Thus, people could make themselves free if they cast off the chains of self-interest and personal desire so prevalent in the rest of nature and thought more of others than themselves.

From Marx's perspective, capitalists would become more humane after they gave up private enterprise. While capitalism could make individuals rich, it necessarily compelled them to pursue their own interests. Thus the richest capitalist was engaged in an undertaking no different from that of the lowliest insect. To be human, one needed to transcend the merely animal in human nature. One could be sure that the merely animal was transcended when one thought, not at all of oneself, but only of others. In capitalism a person was forced to treat himself and others merely as a means. He treated himself as a means to survival and others as commodities of exchange or consumers of products from whom wealth would be derived. Such a person would be alienated from his truly human capacity in much the same way that a person who acts selfishly, and not according to the categorical imperative, is not wholly rational and thus not wholly human.

Solzhenitsyn's characterization of Tolstoy shows that his ideas were transcended in practice in exactly the same way Kant's were in theory. Tolstoy's universal "love commandment" helped undermine the traditional views of morality that grew out of Russia's cultural past. But the more progressive of the Russian revolutionaries quickly came to see Tolstoy's views as antiquated and even dangerous to the cause of the revolution, for they inhibited social upheaval. Moreover, they were seen as naive, for the teaching of goodwill towards others was ineffective when measured against the armed might of the government. Finally, as we have seen, the Communist party of the Soviet Union attempted to implement the ideas of Marx by creating a universal state based on the material community of mankind.[73]

The consequence of the "transition of ideas" has been the rise of: Marxism, which holds that all morality, except that which brings the revolution, is illegitimate; social science positivism, which holds that values can never be inferred from facts; and rationalistic humanism, which holds that only universal values are legitimate. The practical result of these three teachings is to make moral valuations impossible, or, in the case of humanism, to make valuations so difficult—since they abstract completely from self-interest—that they are all but impossible. Thus, all limits that traditional morality had placed on people have been undone. Despite the avowed humanism of the age, it has experienced inhumanity and brutality on a scale unknown in former times. Not even value-free science has been a total success. The discoveries that were intended to alleviate human misery have burst through those limits and now threaten to extinguish the race that created them. Evidently, the gold coins of our forebears have not been spent wisely.[74]

Relativism has also undermined the West's much-cherished principles of tolerance. Without some notion of morality, tolerance knows no limits and, therefore, is turned into indifference. If people deem themselves incompetent to make ethical judgments, or think that it would be wrong to impose their values on others, in fact, they are legitimizing the activities of those who, in Michael Novak's words, "prefer torture, rapine, systematic murder, authoritarianism, and slavery." Despite these dire consequences, Novak maintains, in his defense of Solzhenitsyn's position, that "there are millions of people. . . . In the vast middle range of our society," who refuse to acknowledge any moral codes that are "universal and binding upon us all."[75]

Solzhenitsyn concludes that relativism is an ignominious end to the optimism of the Enlightenment. Not only does relativism undermine all yardsticks by which human beings judge their actions, it raises doubts that human life has any meaning and purpose whatever. The triumphant march of technological progress seems to have been a hollow victory, and the human race is left with little but emptiness.

The Turn Upward

Solzhenitsyn maintains that the ideas that began in the Enlightenment have run their course. While they have "enriched" us along the way, they have now reached an impasse. "Today it would be retrogressive," he writes, "to hold to the ossified formulas of the Enlightenment. Such social dogmatism leaves us helpless before the trials of our time." [76]

To Solzhenitsyn it seems that the world is facing a juncture similar in scope and intensity to the one that initiated the modern age. If an ecological disaster does not overtake us, surely a spiritual one will. The evil that lies close to the human heart cannot be resisted adequately on the grounds that the Enlightenment set down. Human beings must know that there is something worth struggling for before they are willing to struggle in its defense.

A spiritual revival is necessary if the West is to avoid repeating the mistakes of the East or to escape gradually declining into decadence and despair. The rejuvenation of mankind can begin only when the central flaw of modernity's philosophy is exposed. Human beings cannot find meaning in existence or be made happy merely by acquiring material objects and by nurturing their physical beings. Solzhenitsyn postulates, "If, as claimed by humanism, man were born only to be happy, he would not be born to die. Since his body is doomed to death, his task on earth evidently must be more spiritual." [77]

Once it is recognized that nature can never be so fully conquered as to overcome the impermanence of life, the age-old longing for an attachment to something imperishable will cause people to embrace anew the concept of a "Supreme Complete Entity." As to exactly how this process of spiritual recovery will occur, Solzhenitsyn is unclear. But, as we shall see in the next chapter, he claims that there are a number of sources of spiritual strength; included among them might be the reaction of the human race to the specter of universal tyranny. Whatever course is taken, a change in the direction of human history will not be a simple matter, for it will take great effort and much vision to plot a course that neither curses "our physical nature, as in the Middle Ages," nor tramples "our spiritual being . . . as in the Modern Era. This ascension is similar to climbing onto the next anthropological stage. No one on earth has any way left but—upward."[78]

Criticisms of Solzhenitsyn

Solzhenitsyn's assessment of the West has drawn a great deal of negative commentary. These criticisms are presented here for three reasons. First, for purposes of evenhandedness, it is appropriate to offer some of the problems that Solzhenitsyn's ideas raise. Second, the arguments against Solzhenitsyn help us better understand his position and aid us in perceiving some of the misunderstandings that have surrounded his pronouncements. Finally, these sections give the author an opportunity to detail some of his own questions and misgivings about Solzhenitsyn's judgments.

It was said that Solzhenitsyn's views: (1) would lead to a renewed Cold War; (2) called for the West to liberate Russia; (3) may have initiated a nuclear holocaust; (4) did not accurately reflect the world situation because they overlooked the Third World; (5) left no room for diplomacy, compromise, and conciliation; (6) misrepresented America's so-called moral retreat from Vietnam; (7) were not sufficiently informed about the West; (8) were influenced by a particular strain of Russian nationalism that refuses to see any virtues in the West's way of life; (9) painted America in too admirable a light and thereby discounted the role America played in beginning and sustaining the tensions between East and West; (10) would cause a resurgence of anti-Communist hysteria because they were a simplistic characterization of the world situation; and (11) were too expansive and thereby overstate his case.[79]

1, 2.   Solzhenitsyn rebutted the first and second criticisms directly. He argued until the late 1980s, at least, that the Cold War had not ended in the Soviet Union and to revive it in the West was only to reflect an existing condition of political reality.[80] A comparison between the Brezhnev years and the era of *glasnost* certainly supports Solzhenitsyn's contention that tensions between East and West were originated in Moscow. Those who maintained that he advocated the West liberate Russia are inaccurate. Quite the contrary, he insisted that the East had to free itself. He merely asked the West to cease aiding Communist governments in oppressing their citizens.[81]

3. The threat of nuclear war, everyone can agree, is a terrifying danger. All are united in opposing such a war. The real debate is over how much we are willing to pay in order to avoid it. Solzhenitsyn argued that one course, capitulation, was actually not safe at all. Given the history of the Gulag and the likelihood of what would happen if the West were conquered, he led his readers to wonder whether a quick death was not preferable to a slow and agonizing one. Moreover, he warned that too many in the antinuclear movement were willing to sacrifice moral principles for the sake of peace. For instance, he was particularly critical of the founder of the antinuclear movement, Bertrand Russell. His slogan, "Better red than dead," Solzhenitsyn asserted, lacks all ethical content. Russell's principle reduces life to mere survival and counsels people to submit even if it means losing their human dignity.[82]

While Solzhenitsyn accepts the yearning for peace as a noble purpose, he would not pursue it at any price. For him, there are things in life—integrity of the soul, for example—that make life worth living. Without these things, life would become intolerable. The things in life that make it worthwhile are, in a sense, more important than life itself and may very well be worth dying for.[83]

In addition, it is important to note that Solzhenitsyn doubted that a nuclear war would take place. He reasoned that the Soviet rulers had gained too much power and prestige in the international arena to risk it all in a nuclear exchange. Moreover, he reminded Westerners that the Soviet leaders were materialists, and to them life was all that mattered.[84]

Then too, he insisted, mankind as a whole has a marked instinct for survival. As proof he cited the case of the Nazis, who despite their wickedness, never used their stockpiles of nerve gas, for fear of Allied retaliation. Rather than direct confrontation, Solzhenitsyn postulated that East and West would struggle in proxy wars, fashioned after Vietnam and fought in the Third World. He reasoned that these clashes would be a means for the East to gain ground on the West without provoking a costly reaction. The wars in El Salvador and Nicaragua seem to have borne out his prediction.

4.   As to the politics of the Third World, Solzhenitsyn was acutely aware of the contest being waged there between the ideals of East and West. He recognized too that the nations of the Third World would prefer to be left alone to settle their own problems. However, he claimed that the dynamics of Communism made expansion inevitable, and that many Communist states, particularly the Soviet Union, sought to exacerbate local and regional problems and to use the resulting confusion for their own benefit. He also recognized that Marxism has been an attractive doctrine to many in places where poverty has been great and class distinctions have been prevalent. Yet he questioned whether a system of government—Communism—should be adopted that would make conditions worse for most people.

5.   The argument that Solzhenitsyn's proposals left many diplomatic and practical matters unresolved has much truth to it. For example, how was a tough policy toward the Soviet Union and other Communist countries to be carried out? Was the West to have no dealings at all with Communist rulers? Were we to show our utter contempt by ignoring them? If a policy of neglect were adopted, how was the West to express its firmness? Unless we were willing to start a war each time the Soviets acted precipitously, was not some form of diplomatic leverage, in which both sides had an interest in accommodation, necessary to show our displeasure? Finally, was single-minded firmness always the best course? For example, it was not simply Solzhenitsyn's strength of will that allowed him to "butt the oak" (the actual title of his autobiography, *The Oak and the Calf*, might be translated "the calf that butted the oak") and remain alive, but also Kissinger's formidable negotiating skills and, one can surmise, a deal not to use Solzhenitsyn's works on the broadcasts to the East, that secured his release.[85]

To balance these practical considerations, it must be added that Solzhenitsyn was less interested in laying down actual policy than in stiffening the resolve of policymakers. He may have succeeded. Certainly the 1980s showed a change in attitude among Western leaders toward the Soviet Union. In particular, American diplomacy toward the Soviet Union was backed up by a much-strengthened military capacity.

6.   Solzhenitsyn was very critical of those who believed that America's defeat in Vietnam was a moral victory. He warned early in the Paris negotiations that if the United States capitulated, a tyrannical government from the North would come to dominate all aspects of life in the entire nation and would extend its power over neighboring states. He predicted that the scale of human suffering inflicted by the newly installed Communist government would far outweigh the misery caused by the old regime or even by the war. Sadly, events in Southeast Asia since that time seem to have borne out his prognosis.[86]

7.   Solzhenitsyn responded directly to the charge that he did not know the West. He claimed that the West is easy to know, even for an outsider, because it is so open. One need only read a newspaper, listen to the radio, or watch television to gather all the information one needs. But for Westerners to understand the East, Solzhenitsyn said, turning the argument around, was virtually impossible. The East was cloaked in secrecy and very little news escaped.[87]

8.   As if to prove the point that the West has lost its intellectual bearings, some commentators rejected Solzhenitsyn's arguments, not on the basis of their substance, but rather because they are culturally determined. Tracing Solzhenitsyn's position to a particular strain of Russian thought, these scholars claimed to understand Solzhenitsyn better than he knows himself.

Putting aside the issue of whether cultural determinism does not reduce itself to nonsense (Is everything culturally determined except the idea that things are culturally determined?), there are serious flaws in the "Solzhenitsyn is part of the Russian tradition" argument. To assert that Solzhenitsyn cannot understand the West because he comes from an alien culture, would also mean that Westerners cannot fathom Russia, since its ideas are foreign to us. To be consistent, cultural determinists would have to admit that even recognizing the tradition of another culture (never mind placing some one within it) is next to impossible.

Of course, this is not at all what these critics wished to say. They really wanted to argue that Solzhenitsyn does not understand the West because he is culturally biased and because he has had few contacts with the Western way of life. But, perhaps these commentators proved more than they wished by their assertion. Despite the isolated way in which he chooses to live at his home in Vermont, he has experienced far more of the West than any Westerner has of the Gulag, or of Soviet life in general (he once took an unaccompanied auto tour of the United States and, of course, he can read).[88] Given that fact, should we not listen to what he says about the dangers of Communism? But the cultural determinists really wished to have it both ways. Not only did they claim to have a greater knowledge and appreciation of the West than does Solzhenitsyn, but also a fuller understanding of the Russian tradition and of who belongs to it.

It could be that the determinists did not wish to extend their determinism generally, but meant it to apply only to Solzhenitsyn. In that case, as Delba Winthrop points out, it does not matter where his ideas come from. The real test is how well his arguments reflect the truth.[89]

Moreover, Solzhenitsyn claimed not to have been influenced by either the tradition of Russian nationalism that developed in the eighteenth and nineteenth centuries or the Russian messianism that became intertwined with devotion to the Russian Orthodox church. He explains, "As for, 'historical Russian messianism,' this is contrived nonsense: it has been several centuries since any section of the government or intelligentsia influential in the spiritual life of the country has suffered from the disease of messianism. Indeed, it seems inconceivable to me that in our sordid age any people on earth would have the gall to deem itself 'chosen.' "[90]

Solzhenitsyn's connection with the whole tradition of Russian nationalism seems even more remote if one considers his proposals for the future of Russia. He favors freeing Eastern Europe and breaking up the Soviet empire into its separate nationalities. He would have Russia turn inward and concentrate on building a viable economy. He argues that Russia should seek isolation from international affairs in order to recoup its spiritual strength and recover from the ravages of Communism, a task that would require "150 to 200 years of external peace."[91]

Solzhenitsyn's detractors do have a point when they argue that he lays all the blame for his nation's ills on Marx and Marxism and hardly any at all on old Russia's traditions or history. Surely, Solzhenitsyn cannot believe his nation was free from the flaws that affect every human creation. Perhaps it would be better, from Solzhenitsyn's perspective, to argue that there are weaknesses in the Russian national character, just as in the character of every other nation, and that Communism has been able to use and exploit those defects to its own advantage.

9. It should not escape notice that those who attacked Solzhenitsyn because he does not appreciate the West enough are contradicting those who criticized him for supporting America too much. This division of opinion would be more comprehensible if it were not for the fact that on occasion the same people made both criticisms. Perhaps, this problem of interpretation arises because Americans are accustomed to criticisms from the left, but become confused when confronted by a powerful voice on the right.

In response to the critics of the United States' role in world affairs, Solzhenitsyn asserted that America is "most magnanimous, the most generous nation in the world." Of all the countries in the West, he claimed, the United States has done the most to preserve world order. Twice it helped European democracies win wars and twice it "raised Europe from post war destruction." For "thirty years it has stood as a shield protecting Europe while European countries counted their nickels to avoid paying for their armies."[92] Yet despite America's obvious strength, he wondered whether it is suited for the role it has been forced to play in world affairs.

For centuries, Solzhenitsyn argued, the European continent ruled the world through the power generated by its ideas. That power has dissipated, partly as the result of two world wars, but more importantly because the ideas that thrust Europe to the forefront of world events have now run their course. Leadership has passed to the United States, itself a child of European thought. It has had to shoulder responsibilities for which it never asked, for which its principles make it unsuited, and for which its history has made it ill-prepared.

Solzhenitsyn seemed to have some doubts about whether this nation will bear up under the strain. He has, of course, settled here. He offered his views of America most clearly in a 1975 speech (poorly attended) before the United States Congress. The address skillfully endeavored to elevate the lawmakers above the parochial concerns of party and region by explaining to them that although they were elected to represent their constituents, their decisions affected the whole world. Specifically, he reminded them that millions in the East had no voice in government, and all their hopes rested on the policies that the United States adopted.[93]

Solzhenitsyn's general position may be summarized as follows: A truly farsighted policy must recognize that freedom is indivisible. The world cannot exist half slave and half free. Such a state of affairs is too contradictory. Either the East will shake off its yoke of bondage, or the West will be harnessed with chattels of its own. If ever the West loses sight of the difference between itself and the East, or if it comes to doubt that value judgments of the kind that attribute superiority to one way of life, as opposed to another, are impossible to make, then the West will not be able to defend its own highest principles.[94]

10. Because Solzhenitsyn is so adamantly opposed to Communism, many of his critics were fearful that if his sentiments spread to the United States populace at large they would rekindle the anti-Communist hysteria of the 1950s. What startled these critics about Solzhenitsyn's presentation of Communism was that even its strongest opponents during that era, for example, John Foster Dulles, actually may have underestimated its evil and the threat it posed to the West. Such an opinion is startling for two reasons. First, it throws a wholly different light on United States foreign policy in the post World War II era, especially the tragic events of Vietnam. Second, it conjures up memories of the red-baiting tactics of Senator Joseph McCarthy.

Many Americans feel a revulsion toward the McCarthy era because they realize that anti-Communist hysteria posed a threat to civil liberties and injured the careers of a number of innocent people. One is tempted to say that the demagoguery of Senator McCarthy established a prejudice against anti-Communism in an important segment of the intellectual class of America. Indeed, nearly everyone critical of Solzhenitsyn's views raises the specter of McCarthy against him. Until this prejudice is overcome, the ghost of McCarthy will haunt fair-minded discussions of Solzhenitsyn's work.

It could be that Solzhenitsyn has never confronted this issue directly because he knows little of that period. It is more likely that he is disdainful of the whole topic. During the time a few Hollywood writers and actors were losing their jobs in America, Solzhenitsyn and most of his fellow Russian artists were helping to build socialism, against their wills, in the Gulag. The comparison speaks for itself. It is also conceivable that he has ignored these criticisms because they are unfair to him. Solzhenitsyn does not adopt the tactics of McCarthy. He does not unscrupulously implicate innocent people in an attempt to resist Communism. As Norman Podhoretz has pointed out, the real crime of McCarthy was that he wrongly accused people of being Communists. McCarthy's demagoguery should in no way color the attitude one has toward people who are actually Communists. Thus, it may not be hysteria to oppose a doctrine that has a record of producing such inhuman evil.[95] Solzhenitsyn explains, "That which is against Communism is for humanity. Not to accept, but to reject this inhuman Communist ideology is simply to be a human being. Such a rejection is more than a political act. It is a protest of our souls against those who would have us forget the concepts of good and evil."[96]

Yet, Solzhenitsyn's opponents may have had a point when they accused him of simplifying the world situations into "evil" Communist governments and "good" non-Communist ones. First, the Communist world is not unified, but has deep political divisions among its members. If Communist governments are all alike, as Solzhenitsyn claimed, then what can explain these political disputes? If pure power politics is the source of these divisions, then the ideology cannot be the only motivation behind the action of Communist states. Second, Communist governments are not all alike in their internal policies. True, all are oppressive, but some more than others. If commitment to Marxism is the one common characteristic of these states, again, how can one account for the differences among Communist nations?

For example, does Solzhenitsyn's analysis help us understand Deng Xiaoping's reforms in China? There, the Communist party led the way in introducing free market-mechanisms into the economy. It loosened its political grip on the society and has even allowed some criticisms of Marxism to surface. Whether these initial liberalizations will bring a true transformation of China is still not clear—the interest of the party cadre may yet put an end to the reforms, as occurred during the crackdown on student demonstrations in 1989. What is clear, however, is that China has undergone changes that run directly counter to the ideology of Marx.

The same kind of modifications have begun to occur in Gorbachev's Soviet Union. Calls for freer expression and a more decentralized economy have been heard from within the party hierarchy. Some of the crimes of the past have been described in the Soviet national media. Political corruption has been exposed and the perpetrators given jail sentences.[97]

According to Solzhenitsyn's analysis such changes within Communism should have been impossible. He has warned that no Communist party will allow its position to be questioned and any reforms that do so will be brought to an immediate halt.[98] Evidently Solzhenitsyn was incorrect in his assessment. A number of factors might account for this mistake. First, as stated in the previous chapter, commentators on political events cannot predict the course of future events with certainty. One can make assessments based on trends visible in past performance, but there is always a realm of existence that escapes prognostication. Thus, given Communism's history of cruelty and oppression, Solzhenitsyn could not anticipate a weakening of its resolve in some places and its actual collapse in others. The unforeseen course of future events caused Solzhenitsyn's analysis to go astray. However, while the West should be pleased with the startling fall of Communism in Eastern Europe, these events should not lead to undue euphoria. The reforms of Communism may quickly and unexpectedly be reversed, as they were in the Chinese People's Republic.

Second, Solzhenitsyn may have underestimated the intransigence of human nature. As we have seen, Solzhenitsyn (perhaps more forcefully than any other contemporary commentator on human affairs) argues that many of Marxism's tenets run counter to the strongest longings of human beings and that a commitment to ideology overwhelms even the most commonsense observations about human motivations. However, ignoring the aspirations of people cannot be continued without cost. As the movement toward *perestroika* makes clear, the Soviet economy virtually bankrupted itself in an attempt to implement the principles of Marx. At some point even committed Marxists had to acknowledge the inadequacy of policies that were impoverishing the nation, as seems to have been the case among many reform-minded Eastern European Communist party leaders. Therefore, change to an economic system that relied on greater decentralization and introduced mechanisms to reward personal initiative was both necessary and probably unavoidable. Although Solzhenitsyn did not expect that the natural desires of people would triumph over impractical ideals so soon, he did point out that human nature cannot be abolished or transformed even with the greatest application of force.

Third, the Soviet economy was so backward that it could not compete with the West. This fact threatened the Soviet Union's military strength. While most Western nations had moved to greater flexibility in their economies, the Soviet Union maintained ponderously large plants equipped to produce primarily the manufactured goods needed for heavy industry. But in the age of computers, when new designs and technologies can be fabricated on terminals, the ability to retool quickly is essential.

Not only could the Soviet economy not cope with these rapid innovations, but its political system, which restrained the free exchange of information, inhibited the introduction of computers into the society. As the Soviet economy fell further and further behind its Western rivals, its military position became more and more tenuous. Perhaps this inability to compete with Western technology explains what can only be termed a Soviet obsession with halting America's Strategic Defense Initiative.

Fourth, Solzhenitsyn's remarks may have actually influenced the course of events in his homeland. The publication of *The Gulag Archipelago* in the West had the effect of discrediting the Soviet system and Communism in general. Although the aftermath of *Gulag* was most strongly felt among French intellectuals, it also seemed to harden attitudes taken by the general public against the Soviet Union. The fear and distrust that its stories of atrocities planted in the popular culture may have played a role in bringing strongly anti-Communist governments to power in Germany, Great Britain, and the United States. A consensus formed in favor of a vigorous military buildup; nearly one trillion dollars was allocated for defense in the United States alone. The British, Germans, and Italians elected governments openly hostile to the Soviet Union. Clearly this heightened military competition overmatched the already burdened Soviet economy. The result was a new willingness on the part of the Soviet leadership to seek diplomatic accords that slowed the arms race and, of course, a dawning realization that innovative economic measures would be required if the stagnant Soviet economy was ever to contend with the West.

Although Solzhenitsyn has said very little in regard to these transitions, his evaluation of Communism would make it seem doubtful that long-lasting change can take place under the aegis of the party. In many Communist nations social and economic conditions have deteriorated to the point of near catastrophe. Thus, as has been suggested, not to alter past policies courts disaster. Yet if the hierarchy loosens its grip and allows the pent-up forces within society even a limited autonomy, it also places its authority at peril. The past failures of Communism, combined with its history of treachery and ruthlessness, have so discredited the party that granting any amount of liberty to those under its power will result eventually in a movement for its overthrow. As has been made absolutely clear in the nations of Eastern Europe, virtually no one trusts the Communists. Moreover, both the Soviet Union and China have maintained their empires by suppressing the nationalist aspirations of their respective ethnic minorities, as the Soviet Union did by subjugating Eastern Europe. A shift toward liberalization of those relationships surely will unleash a grass-roots movement to replace the party with a government less tainted by past mistakes and more sympathetic to nationalist sentiments.

Moreover, if the party abandons its Marxist ideals of social and political equality in the name of the efficiency of free-market exchanges, then it has to abandon any moral authority by which it can claim to rule. Why, after all, should citizens be willing to obey a ruling group whose legitimacy rests on a discarded doctrine? The only possible method by which it can maintain its superior position is by the application of naked force. Faced with a genuine revolution, the party may be compelled to haul in the reins of reform in order to preserve its power.

11. Occasionally, Solzhenitsyn falls into the disturbing habit of overstating his case. For example, at one point he claims that there has been "a total emancipation" from Christianity. Elsewhere he states that there is a "universal sympathy for revolutionary extremists." In neither instance do Solzhenitsyn's dramatic statements seem correct. There are many people who cherish their Christian beliefs, and work hard to live by them. There are as many people who abhor extremism.

Perhaps, Solzhenitsyn intended no more by these statements than to drive home his point with a rhetorical flourish. Whatever the case, these unqualified judgments tend to weaken his arguments and make him vulnerable to the charge that many make—that he is a fanatic.[99] As a careful reading of Solzhenitsyn's *The Oak and the Calf* shows, Solzhenitsyn plans everything he does carefully, and it may be that he consciously intended to overstate the strength and ferocity of the Soviet Union and to underestimate the reserves of the West in order to stir up Western public opinion.

Whatever his true intentions, Solzhenitsyn's assertions about the West's loss of will do not seem altogether accurate. It may be true that within the intellectual community a certain dislike for spirited actions holds sway, but among the citizen body as a whole there are great reserves of patriotic sentiment—duty, honor, and country are still held in high regard. Perhaps Solzhenitsyn recognizes this, for he qualifies his appraisal of the West by specifically naming "the ruling and intellectual elites," as those who have lost their courage to the greatest degree.[100]

There is a sense in which the dichotomy between intellectuals and average citizens shows only too clearly the validity of Solzhenitsyn's analysis of the loss of will and its relationship to the movement of Western thought, detailed above. Intellectuals are exposed to the latest and most progressive ideas and traditionally have been the standard-bearers of Enlightenment aspirations. It should not be surprising, then, that from among this group have arisen those who look upon patriotism and civic courage as naive jingoism. In the contemporary era they have been the leaders of virtually every peace movement. In spite of the massive Soviet arms buildup, such groups invariably counsel the disarmament of the West. Most disturbing, many intellectuals have shown a marked sympathy for political and social movements of the left. Despite all the evidence coming to us from such examples as the Great Cultural Revolution in China, the murderous rule of Pol Pot in Cambodia, the enslavement of half of Europe, and, of course, the nature of the Soviet system, that fondness for principles of the left remains largely undiminished.

On the other hand, during the 1980s many citizens in Western nations showed that they were far from enthusiastic about disarming their own countries while aiding those who publicly decry their way of life as evil. Perhaps this is because such people are less affected by the latest wave of progressive idealism, and base their judgments on common sense instead. Although such anti-Communist leaders as Ronald Reagan and Margaret Thatcher were not popular among the intelligentsia, they were elected by large popular majorities.

Finally, Solzhenitsyn's supposition that Western culture is about to collapse seems to fit in that category of dire prediction initiated by Malthus. Philosophers as diverse in views as Marx, Nietzsche, and Heidegger have proclaimed that the West was about to fall—yet, it still remains. Perhaps there is sufficient resolve within the West for it to last for some time yet. The sources of that strength derive from religion, which remains a powerful influence on people's opinions; from an attachment to the principle of freedom, which is most apparent when freedom is most in peril; and from a natural inertia, which makes human beings unwilling to change their way of life too radically.

Of course, he may be right. Intellectuals have used their formidable powers of persuasion with great success in spreading progressive principles among the people. In the West, religion has become as much an engine for social change as it is a source of spiritual authority. The principle of freedom has been used to defend ideas that are antithetical to the concept of freedom. And attachment to the way of life of the West based on an assertion of its superiority over other ways of life—for example, that of the East—is held to be narrow-minded and bigoted.

Still, it is hard to conceive of the West collapsing. Nonetheless, this difference between the author and Solzhenitsyn may be the result of my lack of imagination. The most difficult of all intellectual tasks is to look beyond the horizon of one's own culture while peering into the future. A belief that the West can survive may be among those yearnings of the heart for one's own way of life that were also experienced by monks at the end of the sixteenth century as they contemplated the meaning of the Renaissance.

On a Revival of the Spirit

I t is often said that Solzhenitsyn criticizes the programs and ideas of others but never proposes anything of his own. This claim misunderstands Solzhenitsyn's project. He holds the commonsense view that people's opinions lead them to act. The ideas that inform those opinions exert a crucial influence over human behavior. Solzhenitsyn does not overlook the other motivations in life, such as the desires and passions and the longing for love, beauty, and honor, but he maintains that ideas shape people's responses to these factors. Given this view, he attempts to change what he considers evil behavior by undermining the ideas that support it. The first step in such an enterprise is to shake people's confidence by jarring the contemporary wisdom. The more difficult next step is to supply a new basis for people's actions and a new goal for them to work toward. Solzhenitsyn admits that he is engaged in an effort to force a change in the way people act. He says at one point that an artist is a second government.

Spiritedness

The task of laying out a new path is particularly difficult in the modern world. Even a mind of the first order is confronted with an Herculean undertaking when called upon to overcome the contemporary ethos of moral relativism. People are skeptical, not just of new ideas, but of any principles that claim to be universally true. Seeing that all the precepts of the past have been overturned and that the various systems of belief today contradict one another, many have concluded that there are no grounds for trust in anything. If people's horizon is not nihilism—a conviction that holds nothing to be true or right—it is merely because they have not fully thought through their position.

Much has been written about Solzhenitsyn's effort to reawaken the spiritual side of life. It is equally true, perhaps more so, that he wants to invigorate the spirited element in human nature. Spiritedness is an aspect of the soul closely allied with anger. It causes people to strike out at anything that threatens what they hold dear, such as family, homeland, or principles. Spiritedness has another element, in that it provokes people to seek honor for themselves in the service of the community, even at the risk of their own lives.

To promote spiritedness, Solzhenitsyn relates stories, often in a bitterly satirical style, that are intended to outrage the reader. Not only are we led to doubt the ideas that he attacks—for example, those of Marx—but we also are made to feel a sense of righteous anger against the evil deeds that those ideas have encouraged. Solzhenitsyn appeals to people's reason, but he does so by summoning their passions. He aims above all at animating that passion which defends and nurtures justice and goodness. There are any number of examples of this in his writings, but one, concerning the fate of the kulaks, best illuminates the point and merits quoting at length.

> This chapter will deal with a small matter. Fifteen million souls. Fifteen million lives.
>
> They weren't educated people, of course. They couldn't play the violin. They didn't know who Meyerhold was, or how interesting it is to be a nuclear physicist.
>
> In the First World War we lost in all three million killed. In the Second we lost twenty million (so Khrushchev said; according to Stalin it was only seven million. Was Nikita being too generous? Or couldn't Josif keep track of his capital?) All those odes! All those obelisks and eternal flames! Those novels and poems! For a quarter century all Soviet literature has been drunk on that blood!
>
> But about the silent, treacherous Plague which starved fifteen

million of our peasants to death, choosing victims carefully and destroying the backbone and mainstay of the Russian people— about that Plague there are no books. No bugles bid our hearts beat faster for them. Not even the traditional three stones mark the crossroads where they went in creaking carts to their doom. Our finest humanists, so sensitive to today's injustices, in those years only nodded approvingly: Quite right, too! Just what they deserved![1]

But why does Solzhenitsyn want to anger people with such a story? Why does he want to evoke a sense of righteous outrage or spiritedness? Is not such a passion upsetting to public peace? Could people under its spell become so enamored of their own way of life and their own moral principles that they would be willing to strike out blindly and zealously at others? Is not spiritedness the root cause of war?

To begin with, Solzhenitsyn inspires a sense of righteous indignation as a means of teaching his readers that there are such things as morality and justice. The pervasive spirit of relativism in contemporary life has led many to doubt that there are common human standards for judging ethical conduct. Yet somehow people can be drawn into condemning certain acts as unjust. People may not be able to decide what justice is, but they can be made to feel the sting of injustice. It is almost as if there was a natural physiological response to experiencing the misery of others—which is why Solzhenitsyn counsels people to listen to their hearts and not just their heads. Indeed, this sensation is exactly what his artistry hopes to elicit. Having conceded that much, his readers are compelled to ask how human beings can understand injustice if they have no idea of its opposite. Do we not know what injustice is because we have an awareness that something is lacking? Must we not then have some idea of what justice is? It is by this reverse method that Solzhenitsyn seeks to accomplish his goal. A reaction against injustice and inhumanity may be only a first step, but it is intended to show people that in practice they are not relativists, and thereby to move them towards a positive acceptance of moral criteria.[2]

Second, spiritedness is a passion that contributes to a sense of community. Sometimes, no doubt, this sentiment can be turned to petty concerns, such as to defense of party or faction. Yet more often, spiritedness breeds a feeling of civic responsibility. It combats the all-too-human desire of people to seek nothing but their own self-interest. It rests, in part, on love of one's country, one's way of life, and one's people. Thus, although it is a passion and not wholly rational, it gives rise to high-minded, even noble, actions taken on behalf of others.[3]

Third, spiritedness is essential as an antidote to the crass materialism of the modern age. It animates people, making them concerned with pursuits of a higher and finer sort than the mere continuation of their physical existence. If not the highest of human virtues, spiritedness can induce that greatness of soul on which heroism rests. Solzhenitsyn's tales of resistance to oppression and escape from imprisonment, particularly in *Gulag Archipelago III*, portray people fervently dedicated to their principles. They are resolved to risk hunger, deprivation, even death rather than allow their wills to be crushed.[4] Their souls have an inextinguishable fire that lights the way towards those aspirations that enrich humanity. For example, to understand what a true love of freedom entails, one need only turn to the deeds of Solzhenitsyn's indefatigable friend Georgi Tenno and his perpetual attempts to escape from the camps. Indeed, it is a testament to all that is finest in the human spirit that Solzhenitsyn and the other survivors from what once was heralded as the Marxist utopia could remain unbroken in the face of such fearsome evil, holding aloft all the while the banner of freedom and justice.[5]

Despite all their difficulties, Solzhenitsyn's heroes are truly alive, while those who sit on the sidelines, afraid to raise a finger for fear of losing their lives, are spiritually dead. Without spiritedness, Solzhenitsyn warns, human beings can become a "herd"; they follow closely behind the pack so as not to be singled out. If they become too cowardly to stand up even for the truth, they will lose their humanity; thus it is that a "spiritual death" can overtake them. In an open letter to his countrymen Solzhenitsyn attempted to fortify them against their rulers. He entreated them to stop reciting the party's lies and then challenged them as follows: "And if we get cold feet even taking this step then we are worthless and the scorn of Pushkin should be directed at us: 'Why should cattle have the gift of freedom?' 'Their heritage from generation to generation is the belled yoke and the lash.' "[6]

In the West, Solzhenitsyn argues, spiritedness is also needed, for the struggle to maintain human freedom and dignity is never an easy task. Yet the West considers itself too civilized and intelligent for this primitive passion. It prides itself on its humanity towards others and its concern for the welfare of every individual. No Western nation wants to inflict suffering, particularly in an age of instantaneous communication when the anguish of the victims is visible to everyone.[7]

The West's principles, despite their original premise that people would protect their own lives, have now been extended to encompass everyone's survival. Thus, these codes of conduct have given rise to a strong sentiment of pacifism, for one way to protect one's own life is to strive for a completely peaceful world. While Solzhenitsyn recognizes the noble instincts of true pacifists, he complains that many who extol these principles do so in order to conceal their own interests.[8] More importantly, the West's reluctance to commit itself to military action against inhuman regimes does not reduce the sum total of human suffering. Those conquered and subjugated under tyrannical governments are forced to endure the worst forms of despotism and terror. How can founding governments worse than the ones they replace be a victory for morality? Solzhenitsyn argues that the morality born of Western pacifism takes no responsibility for what happens as the result of inaction. It is, to use Max Weber's term, the ethics of intention. Solzhenitsyn's morality is grounded on the disquieting fact that some forms of government, especially Communist regimes, tend to oppress their own people. Peaceful intentions will not work, for abandoning the struggle against inhumanity allows, indeed encourages, this oppression to occur. When making a decision about whether military force should be exerted, Solzhenitsyn would have us calculate the nature of the regime to be opposed (for example, taking into account the dismal history of Marxist rule). His is the ethics of responsibility.

No one can doubt that when we are directly answerable for inflicting pain and death on others the consequences will rest heavily on our consciences. But this sense of inner self-restraint of which the West is rightly proud can easily become a source of irresoluteness. To infuse Western public opinion with the strength of will necessary to make the difficult choices of political life, Solzhenitsyn has attempted to breed a spirited hatred of Marxism. Except by adopting some of Marxism's passion, he has claimed, there is no way for the civilized world to resist the barbarism that confronts it.

Solzhenitsyn was particularly worried that the West had lost heart immediately after the United States defeat in Vietnam. In order to reinvigorate spiritedness in the West, he went on the road, so to speak, giving many public addresses intended to undermine the legitimacy of Marxist regimes and to bolster the sagging morale of the Western powers. In those lectures he acknowledged that resistance to Communist uprisings and expansion was fraught with danger. But, Solzhenitsyn asserted again and again after his exile to the West, the high-minded road was safer in the long run than the path of least resistance. Was it not better to stand fast in the present, he asked, than to face an invincible foe in the future? He argued that an impartial reading of history showed that Marxist leaders take any sign of weakness as a cue to advance. Continual vacillation could only lead to further encroachments, to further losses of power, to more concessions, and to final defeat. He reminded his audience of the atrocities that the Progressive Doctrine might commit if there were no one left to oppose it.[9]

The world situation did not have to slide so far, he predicted. If the West remained firm, Communist rulers would have backed down. For example, Solzhenitsyn pointed out that West Germany's Prime Minister Adenauer's tough political negotiations with Khrushchev "initiated a genuine détente."[10] Marxist rulers fear spiritedness, Solzhenitsyn reasoned, for the party can remain in power only so long as people acquiesce to its commands. As with other forms of despotism, the party preys on people's weaknesses. However, once they refuse to pay any price for survival, the party loses its strength and must retreat. Tyrants have the courage of bullies. When on top, they are relentless, but they quickly lose heart when tested by an implacable foe. Solzhenitsyn gave no guarantees, of course, but he reasoned that the West could take some succor in the examples of Lenin, who caved in to German demands, and even of the mighty Stalin, who could not conquer Finland and who panicked during the Nazi advance.[11]

> You misunderstand the nature of communism. The very ideology of communism—all Lenin's teachings—are that anyone is considered a fool who does not take what is lying in front of him. If you can take it, take it. If you can attack, attack. But if there is a wall, then go back. . . . You defended Berlin in 1948 only by your firmness of spirit, and there was no world conflict. In Korea in 1950 you stood up against the communists using only your firmness, and there was no world conflict. In 1962 you compelled the rockets to be removed from Cuba. Again it was only your firmness, and there was no world conflict.[12]

It would be premature to credit Solzhenitsyn with having caused the decline of Soviet power. Yet it is significant to note that after the various

parts of *The Gulag Archipelago* began to be published, public opinion in
the West hardened against the Soviet Union and nearly all of the nations
in the Western alliance chose governments hostile to Soviet aggression.
The United States, in particular, elected the most conservative and fervently anti-Communist president of the postwar era. Not only did Ronald Reagan challenge and ridicule the Soviet system, but his administration spent enormous sums on military preparedness, seemingly to back
up the president's tough talk.

Initially, the Soviet leaders belittled Reagan's rhetoric and his military
buildup. They labeled him a cowboy and a warmonger and did all they
could to separate the United States from its European allies. Yet it is
possible that the Soviet leaders began to believe their own rhetoric. After
years of vacillation in the West, the Soviet leaders were confronted with
a strong anti-Communist alliance and a popular president of the United
States, who proclaimed that Marxism belonged on the trash heap of history. The Soviet economy was clearly overburdened with military expenditures and unable to compete with the revitalized free-market system of
the West. In what must have been a moment of self-doubt, the Soviet
leaders turned to a new leader who could both make a deal with the West
and bring life to the economy. In other words, the Soviets yielded.

This line of argument is difficult to prove, but it is given credence by
one undeniable fact. While the leader who was the least sympathetic to
the Soviet regime was president, the Communists selected the leader who
has been, thus far, the most willing to make domestic reforms and to
transform Soviet foreign policy. To state the proposition plainly, if Solzhenitsyn's writings stiffened Western resolve and that firmness helped
bring about a change in leadership in the Soviet Union, then Solzhenitsyn
had an important hand in bringing Gorbachev, with all his reforms, to
power.

Sources of the Spirit

Life is very dear and few people are willing to risk danger in vain pursuits. People must have strongly held principles and high purposes if they
are to put their existence in jeopardy. But what gives rise to these sentiments? What are the sources of the spirit?

According to Solzhenitsyn there are a number of springs of inner strength. One rests on attachment to family, country, or, more generally, the individual's wider community. Family ties evoke spiritedness by appealing to the natural desire to protect and nurture loved ones. Strong national ties are rooted in the mystic connection that human beings feel toward the place of their birth (or their adopted land) and the generations past, present, and future who inhabit it. The bond of community is nourished by traditions and customs that prepare the citizen for the burden of civic responsibility. The greater that bond, the less people feel isolated and alone. They may even deem it their duty, in order to protect the country's way of life, to sacrifice themselves for the good of the whole.

Another source of spirit seems to be a gift of nature. Some people are blessed with such tenacious character that they will not crack even under the severest pressure. Solzhenitsyn tells of people who, rather than wilting in the confines of the Gulag, actually came to flourish there. The stiffer the test, the greater their resistance, and the more their inner strength grew.[13]

Since nature produces only a certain number of people with immovable wills, the rest of humanity must look elsewhere to attain strength of character. The most common support of the soul is religion. It rests on the belief that human life is given meaning and purpose by a divine plan. The rewards of this life—money, position, even happiness—are considered of less importance than abiding by God's will. Religion turns people away from the daily care of their bodies and towards the protection of their souls. It makes people spirited, as well as spiritual, by teaching that a fate worse than death may befall those who sell their souls to save their bodies. Solzhenitsyn tells again and again of the courage and determination of members of the various religious sects in the camps. Try as it might, the state could not dim the eternal light that dwelled within them.[14]

Finally, there is a category of people who are animated by a dedication to certain ideas. Indeed, it has been the commitment to the various manifestations of Enlightenment ideas that has driven the modern world on its course. The enormous appeal of Marxism derives from its being the most progressive expression of the Enlightenment ideal. However, if this dedication becomes too extreme, one may be led to become an ideologue. This is especially true when the doctrine counsels no self-restraint—as in the case of Marxism. But it need not go that far. The classical philosophers could be distinguished from other human beings by their peculiar love of ideas, and they were hardly ideologues.[15]

Self-Restraint

While spiritedness is usually associated with an assertion of the will, it does have elements of self-sacrifice. Spirited people must keep their desires in check if they wish to accomplish something higher. Rather than being pushed and pulled by impulses, such people must practice self-control in order to set goals of their own choosing. If, as in the camps, they cannot control external events, at least they can govern those things within their power. The heroes of the camps refused to grovel before their captors, even when rations were short and death seemed near. Self-restraint actually affirms the more noble aspects of human life—hence, its connection with spiritedness—for it establishes people's freedom of will over the petty concerns of practical life and the deadening effects of materialism.[16] "The main thing," as Solzhenitsyn "spells out" for us, is to "live with a steady superiority over life."[17] It should be noted that Solzhenitsyn uses the word spirit to express the concepts of both spiritedness and spiritual. In fact, the two are closely connected. For him, an acceptance of spiritual principles is almost an exertion of will. Those who believe in a spiritual realm are very likely to be spirited in its defense.

The road upward from matter to spirit is not without trials, however. Most people need to be forced into restraining their physical appetites. A personal crisis is often the occasion for a thorough examination of conscience. For instance, Solzhenitsyn reports that when people came face to face with the grief of prison life, often they were made to exert the "highest form of moral effort," one that "has always ennobled every human being."[18]

In agreement with Christian moralists, Solzhenitsyn affirms that suffering can be a good thing. People who are riding high, filled with their own success, rarely feel the need to consider the requirements and aspirations of others. They are deceived by their own pride into believing themselves infallible. They easily become self-righteous and arrogant.[19] Solzhenitsyn does not discount the value of a comfortable life. He realizes that modest prosperity can lead many to generosity, while deprivation can inspire great cruelty. Yet his own experience has taught him that only after a fall do people engage in true soul-searching and thus become aware of moral limitations. Their smugness and complacency shaken, they begin to open themselves to compassion and even wisdom.[20]

Since self-limitation is most often learned by the force of circumstances, then the most extreme deprivation provides the most insightful lesson. It is not surprising, therefore, that the Gulag taught a number of its citizens the secrets of self-sufficiency. In order to adapt themselves to the short rations, prisoners had to achieve mastery over their hunger. They did so "as far as possible" by "lifting" themselves "into higher spheres." Putting pleasures of the body behind them, they partook of the more sublime enjoyments of the mind. Solzhenitsyn writes of his experience in Lubyanka prison: "A weightless body, just sufficiently satisfied with soup so that the soul did not feel oppressed by it. What light and free thoughts! It was as if we had been lifted up to the heights of Sinai, and there the truth manifested itself to us from out of the fire. . . . And there we suffered and we thought, and there was nothing else in our lives."[21]

But in the camps, ascent was not easy. Prisoners found themselves at a crossroad. They owned nothing and had little hope of possessing anything in the future. They were utterly dependent; their fate was in the hands of others. Thus their thoughts could not be turned to the normal activities of everyday life. Either they had to ascend toward the beautiful and eternal, or sink toward the all-consuming desire for food.[22]

Of course, most people were simply degraded by their term in the Gulag, but for some it provided a rare opportunity. For perhaps the only time in history, much of the educated class of a nation was made to live the sorrows of the underprivileged class. Rather than imagining the pains and woe of others, they actually experienced them. Unlike the often semiliterate lower classes, who understood suffering but could rarely find a spokesperson to write of their plight, the Russian intelligentsia was educated and could convey its travail to others. Solzhenitsyn maintains that, for this reason, Russia would produce a literary and artistic movement the likes of which have rarely been seen, if only the government would lift its censorship.[23]

There is an ironic justice to Solzhenitsyn's claim that the camps have raised up a class of people who are unmoved either by the materialistic appeals of Marxism or by its threats to their lives. Their self-control and fearsome spirit makes them formidable enemies. He calls them *lichnost,* people with fully developed characters.[24] If the Marxist dictatorship is ever overthrown in the Soviet Union, it will be these people who lead the way. It is only fitting, one supposes, that Marxism should sow the seeds of its own destruction.

Self-Limitation in the Modern World

Sadly, Solzhenitsyn proclaims, it is not only Communist nations that are in need of self-limitation. Much of modern political philosophy is constructed on the idea that happiness can be attained by insuring an ever higher standard of living and thereby fulfilling people's every desire. New ways to produce more goods, it was hoped, could bring about infinite progress for the race.[25]

Solzhenitsyn repeats the truth expressed most clearly in Aristotle's *Ethics:* it is not how much wealth one has but to what end one puts it that is important. Because acquisitiveness too easily becomes avarice that knows no bounds, human beings can never be fully satisfied by material possessions. While the Enlightenment philosophy held out the hope of gaining happiness by conquering the material world, Solzhenitsyn hearkens back to the tradition that guided people to turn inward and conquer themselves.

As Fernand Braudel's history of premodern societies makes evident, in the ancient world people were constrained to limit themselves because there were not enough material things to go around. Either they practiced self-control or they coveted the fixed store of goods available to others. The philosophy of the Enlightenment attempted to end chronic shortages by unlocking the mysteries of nature. Science and technology were to increase nature's bounty.[26]

To a great extent the experiment was a success, but, as with almost all other things in life, there was a price to be paid. Citing the evidence of various groups of ecologists and scientists, Solzhenitsyn argues that the world may soon face an ecological disaster. The misguided optimism of the modern world, he asserts, has caused us to overpopulate, overproduce, and overindustrialize. We are polluting the world in a senseless effort to produce wares we really do not need.[27]

At some point, he suggests, the earth will reach its productive capacities. People will be forced once again to think in terms of limitation and not expansion. Their energies will have to be spent on the development of inner strength rather than on outward signs of success. Solzhenitsyn asks if there is not a realignment of human culture in the offing. If productive limits are reached, the shortage of goods is likely to precipitate a revolution against Enlightenment principles. A moral and spiritual revival would then occur, for people would be driven to despair and they would have no place to turn "except . . . upward."[28]

As with all predictions of impending doom, it is easy to criticize Solzhenitsyn's.[29] After all, Malthus, who might be called the theoretic progenitor of modern-day ecologists, was proved wrong. He underestimated the capacity of technological innovation to solve the problem of overpopulation. For that matter, the suppositions of the deChargin Society and the Club of Rome, on which Solzhenitsyn bases his dire forecasts, to this point have proven inaccurate. The shortages of the 1970s did not lead to a reevaluation of Western thought. Quite the contrary, it has become apparent that the market adjusted in such a way as to actually harvest an abundance of natural resources.

Yet these signs of strength in the West do not entirely refute Solzhenitsyn's position. What will happen, he makes us wonder, if, as forecast, the world's population doubles in the next twenty-five years? Under such conditions, can there be an ever-increasing standard of living? Are there no outer limits to expansion and progress? Can human ingenuity overcome the inevitable depletion of the world's natural resources?

Solzhenitsyn insists that some adjustments to the Western way of life may be coming in the years ahead. The anxiety resulting from a serious economic or ecological crisis could very well initiate a period of soul-searching. Thus, as Delba Winthrop points out, Solzhenitsyn's argument in favor of self-limitation rests on "the nature of nature" as well as "the nature of man."[30]

Those who contend that Solzhenitsyn is conservative on every issue are wrong. In agreement with the ecological movement, Solzhenitsyn would have us adopt a "small technology," which aims at a stable rather than an expanding economy and at cleaning up rather than polluting the environment.[31]

Finally, he argues that the optimism of the Enlightenment philosophy is already beginning to wear thin. The more hopeful advocates of its ideas had promised that people and society would become better once they were emancipated from natural necessity and allowed to develop freely. The inaccuracy of that forecast is all too apparent if one considers the history of this century or looks at the problems facing virtually every Western society today. At the same time that unprecedented standards of living have been achieved, crime of all kinds has actually risen. Rather than making people better, affluence seems to have weakened their moral fiber.[32] Thus, the notion that people can be reformed merely by enhancing the material environment is now seriously in doubt. The recognition that the sources of human motivation run deeper than people's surroundings, Solzhenitsyn suspects, will lead to a reexamination of the very foundations of the modern edifice.

Repentance

Spiritedness directs people to assert their wills, defend their community, and resist injustice. However, it can become a source of arrogance that is used to injure others. While Solzhenitsyn wants to animate people's spirit, he does not want to weaken their moral responsibilities. In his essay "Repentance and Self-Limitation," he reiterates his oft-stated belief that the dividing line between good and evil runs through the heart of every person. No nation, class, or party is totally good or completely evil. Such a truth demands that we "search for our own errors and sins" rather than placing every problem on the shoulders of others. Only when we acknowledge our own faults, can "spiritual growth" begin. History makes apparent that repentance is difficult. "All throughout the ages," Solzhenitsyn writes, people have "preferred to censure, denounce and hate others, instead of censuring, denouncing and hating" themselves. The hope for repentance is even dimmer today. Commercialism blinds people to the need for such an attitude, and Marxism vigorously rejects it altogether. Moreover, for "all countries which previously suffered oppression and now fanatically aspire to physical might," it "is the very last feeling they are about to experience." Yet given "the white-hot tension between nations and races we can say without suspicion of over statement that without repentance it is . . . doubtful we can survive."[33]

Repentance is difficult not only "because we must cross the threshold of self-love, but also because our own sins are not easily visible to us."[34] Overcoming our natural vanity requires courage, especially in a situation where we are the first to repent.[35] The outward sign of repentance is forgiveness, and it may even induce generosity and magnanimity.[36]

An attitude of repentance is likely to produce moderate, self-sacrificing, even pacific behavior. Does this not mean that he counsels people to accept evil? Clearly this seems to conflict with Solzhenitsyn's earlier stated intention, to make people spirited in defense of justice.

Repentance can become "counter productive," he claims, if, as in the case of the prerevolutionary Russian intelligentsia, people acknowledge sins only within their own group or nation. This attitude may cause an intellectual paralysis that results in people abdicating to others their responsibilities for making choices. Thus, it is equally a mistake, although a less common one, to see only good in others and to overlook their evil. He concludes that full repentance is possible only when both sides limit themselves, when it is mutual. Obviously, an ideal of this type is impractical, especially in the anarchy of the international arena.[37] The best one can hope for is a middle ground between the hardness of arrogance and the softness of surrender.[38]

In the West most of the criticism of Solzhenitsyn has come from those who consider his strident opposition to Marxism an indication of his fanaticism. In truth, he is strident, but as his stance on repentance makes clear, it is unfair to label him a fanatic. He asks that we strike a balance between assertiveness and self-sacrifice; in other words, he calls on people to be prudent. Indeed, he calls for a "prudent self-restriction."[39]

He is no less aware than other moral teachers of how complex it is to make ethical decisions. He understands that innocence and guilt are often difficult to sort out (as his views on Russo-Polish relations and his attitude toward West Germany show).[40] He presses his case against Marxism so strenuously, not because he is blind to the faults of Communism's opponents or unaware of the dangers of righteous indignation, but because he has experienced, firsthand, the full fury which that doctrine reserves for human beings of extraordinary character and people who resist its commands. He appreciates that the calculation of a prudent person must change from case to case, implying a knowledge of circumstances and, perhaps, wisdom about ends. Yet even the most moderate people ought to take heed if their adversary is unusually vicious. While most situations call for a response roughly between temerity and timidity, in extreme situations only audacity will do. The evidence presented throughout Solzhenitsyn's work, but most clearly in *The Gulag Archipelago*, is meant to convince prudent people that Marxism tramples all that is finest in the human spirit, and that if they wish to protect human dignity, that doctrine must be defeated.

But how are people to decide when an action is appropriate? On what basis should they make such judgments?

Morality

Moving against the tide of "social sciences, . . . particularly the more modern of them," Solzhenitsyn argues that it is possible for human beings to make correct moral valuations.[41] For instance, he writes that the concept of justice is "inherent in man," and is not relative to one's "own way." The "voice of justice" can be "recognized" by those who "recognize the voice of their own conscience." Furthermore, "convictions based on conscience are as infallible as the internal rhythm of the heart."[42]

Despite his reliance on conscience as the ground for morality, Solzhenitsyn does not seem fully to endorse St. Thomas's view that the capacity to discern good from evil is imprinted on the soul. Rather, he observes that it is a common human trait to evaluate things on the basis of whether they are: "noble, base, courageous, cowardly, hypocritical, false, cruel, magnanimous, just, unjust, and so on."[43] The argument against the ability to make such valuations holds that there is no natural or divine support for these distinctions. But Solzhenitsyn contends that human beings are also part of nature, and it is in their nature to make such judgments—man is an evaluating being. Of course, people's mores will differ from political community to political community, but this does not contradict the fact that moral judgments are possible. Rather, it points once again to the importance of political communities in helping to establish moral sentiments.

The argument that supports our ability to make moral judgments may never rest on apodictic demonstrations, but, Solzhenitsyn asserts, it is certainly no weaker than the argument put forward by those who claim such judgments are impossible. No one, in his or her private life, is a thoroughgoing skeptic. If one is human, one naturally holds some things to be better than others, and in doing so, one shows that it is reasonable to assume that standards of judgment do in fact exist.[44]

Obviously, the natural argument in support of morality is far too subtle to hold great sway. Indeed, Solzhenitsyn is a staunch proponent of the religious way of thinking. For most of mankind, religion is the ultimate source of moral truth. It reminds people to abandon their earthly cares, at least for awhile, and give their thoughts over to "life eternal." It raises them above the level of animals by making them aware that all who live are destined to die, and that the meaning of life must have more to do with the development of the soul than the care of the body.[45]

Solzhenitsyn is most often taken to be a spokesman for Christian ideals. There is no doubt that he understands and even fosters religious sentiments. Whether he is himself a Christian writer is a deeper and perhaps irresolvable question. He joined the Orthodox church in 1970, rather late in life and only after his character had been formed in the camps.[46] We have no reason to doubt his piety, but in his public works he rarely invokes the authority of revelation. He chooses instead to rely on appeals to unaided reason.[47]

It is important to note that Solzhenitsyn is less interested in stressing the differences between the religious and philosophic ways of thinking than he is in showing their similarities in comparison with the modern understanding of life. As Charles Kesler points out:

> He is, in many ways, the greatest living representative of the West, an avatar of the West's most ancient and honorable principles. . . . having witnessed the diminution of man by modern science, and . . . having known that greatness of which the human soul is capable even in the most terrible circumstances, it's not surprising that he could reappraise, indeed resurrect, the almost forgotten alternative to modernity: classical and early Christian political philosophy.[48]

Solzhenitsyn reminds us of what is finest and noblest in the Western tradition. Contrary to the contemporary positivist belief that law is the only grounds for judging actions good or bad, he argues that morality is higher than law. Morality is not inchoate and amorphous, while the law is clear and complete. Law is the "human attempt to embody in rules a part of the moral sphere which is above us all."[49]

He makes us face the once commonly held truth that people are responsible for their own souls and their own actions. No social arrangement, no matter how closely it approximates justice, can ever resolve every human dilemma. There can be little doubt of the importance of justice, yet there is a realm of human activity that transcends political life. Politics is only secondary to the development of human character (and perhaps even to the fostering of friendship). The form of government that allows and encourages the fullest development of human potential is the best regime. Yet, no government can complete a task for which every individual is personally responsible. Politics is incomplete; it points beyond itself to the higher purposes of life. At best it can establish an atmosphere that may help people achieve integrity of character and in some instances may even induce greatness of soul.[50]

He recalls for us that no individual can be "the creator of an autonomous spiritual world." If a person accepts nothing "above himself," and instead "hoists upon his shoulders the act of creating this world and of populating it, together with total responsibility for it," he "collapses under the load." Not even a "mortal genius can bear up under it."[51]

Finally, Solzhenitsyn revives the idea that human beings are capable of using their intellects to discern good from evil. He attempts to show that we can make rational choices and that we can judge the relative worth of different forms of government. For example, we can perceive the difference between totalitarian, autocratic, and democratic regimes. We can then adjust our policy to aid the friends of freedom and dignity, while opposing its enemies.

Obviously, reason cannot fathom all of life's mysteries, but it can help guide people to choose the appropriate actions for any given situation. Perhaps more importantly, it can teach them the proper limits that life places on their expectations. In truth, the exercise of the mind is a purpose all to itself. Since humans are separated from other beasts by their capacity for speech and reason, it follows that those who develop those peculiarly human skills are the most fully human.[52]

The Form of Government Solzhenitsyn Favors

Solzhenitsyn's insistence that he is not a political scientist has great credibility. For example, he does not present an ideal or best form of government by which to judge the relative worth of actually existing states. He has not made an attempt to collect his thoughts on politics into a unified whole. Despite his lack of organization, he does make many suggestions concerning the proper arrangement of political life.

He may have forsworn for practical reasons the opportunity to present the ideal regime. The philosophy of the Enlightenment has led many people to believe that the ideal political order can be brought into being and that, by reforming political institutions, all human problems can be resolved. This is especially true of people who do not believe in God. They are sometimes tempted to create an earthly substitute for heaven. But, as we have seen, this aspiration steers people down the wrong path. It overlooks inner, spiritual improvement, which is a more important source of human motivation and for which the individual is personally responsible. In a sense, Solzhenitsyn wishes to diminish what people expect of politics, while raising their expectations of themselves. With such a goal in mind, presenting an ideal form of government might serve only to lead people astray.

His moderation in this respect derives from an organic conception of the development of communities. In *August 1914* he makes one of his characters ask: "Who is conceited enough to imagine that he can devise ideal institutions? The only people who think that are those who believe that nothing of significance was ever done before their own time."[53] It is arrogant, his character asserts, to imagine that a perfect social order can be instituted, because "history is not governed by reason. History is irrational. . . . history is a river, it has its own laws which govern its flow, its bends. . . . The bonds between generations, bonds of institutions, traditions, customs, are what hold the banks of the river bed together and keep the stream flowing."[54]

The life of each nation, the argument continues, is somehow independent of those who wish to control it.[55] A country's culture consists of millions upon millions of decisions concerning the proper way of life, made by generation after generation of its inhabitants. Traditions put a check on what reformers can do to change the way of life of a people. Although Solzhenitsyn's novel admits that "one kind" of social order is "less evil than others," and "perhaps there may even be a perfect one," it warns that "the best social order is not susceptible to being arbitrarily constructed, or even to being scientifically constructed."[56] Those who wish to alter society radically, according to some abstract ideal, are naive about the possibilities of positive change and ignorant of the wisdom that is stored in the folkways of a nation.[57]

Solzhenitsyn is not, however, in total agreement with those who look to the traditions of their community as the true source of moral standards. He rejects the absolute correctness of one's own way; he does not adhere to the belief that prejudice is of higher value than reason; and he claims that a return to the past would be foolish.[58]

If there is a perfect form of government, bringing it into being is a matter of chance, he claims. In practice, the best one can hope for is to live in a decent society—one that foregoes the temptation to terrorize its citizens in order to make them reform their ways. Such a regime is a compromise between the ideals one hopes to attain and the traditions and habits people are reluctant to surrender. Only the foolish or the ruthless, he reasons, would attempt to build the future without giving the past its due.[59] There are, furthermore, more important things than the right form of political association, such as the opportunity to acquire friends.[60] And "there is nothing more precious than the development of a man's soul."[61]

Although he is known as a proponent of conservatism, Solzhenitsyn would not have us become slaves of the past. He ridicules the suggestion that his ideas propose a reintroduction of "a patriarchal way of life," or the foundation of "a theocratic state." He explains that a careful reading of his "Letter to the Soviet Leaders" would show, not that the state should give itself over to religion, but only that religion ought to make "an appropriate contribution to the spiritual life of the community."[62] In no instances should it be suppressed, as is the case in the Soviet Union and elsewhere in the Communist world.[63]

Solzhenitsyn also rejects a return to the patriarchal way of life, although his attitude towards autocracy, the government that fostered that social order, is a bit more complex. He argues that for centuries people lived tolerable, even fruitful, lives within such societies, free from the turmoil that has so marked the democratic twentieth century. Just as other types of government, autocracy has both its strengths and its weaknesses. Its virtues of stability and continuity must be measured against its vices, which include: "the danger of dishonest authorities, upheld by violence, the danger of arbitrary decisions and the difficulty of correcting them, the danger of sliding into tyranny."[64] But autocracy need not become despotic if its leaders are correctly restrained. He explains that, "authoritarian regimes as such are not frightening—only those which are answerable to no one and nothing. The autocrats of earlier, religious ages, though their power was ostensibly unlimited, felt themselves responsible before God and their own consciences."[65]

Although autocracies have complete power over the lives of their citizens, they rarely use that power to control people's souls. The fearsome dictatorships that Marxism has spawned are not interested in gaining mere compliance from their citizens. The Marxist state demands that people make a positive commitment to the goals of the party. Therefore, it must endeavor to wrest every last shred of freedom and independent spirit from the populace. It forces people to constantly concur in lies, thereby corrupting their personal integrity and leaving them little control over their individual wills.[66]

Solzhenitsyn's admiration for autocracy is partly due to his uneasiness about democracy. In many nations with no tradition of self-rule, democracy has led first to anarchy and then to tyranny. In fact, weak democracies have been the breeding ground for four totalitarian states—"the February Revolution in Russia, the Weimar and Italian republics, and Chiang Kai-shek's China."[67] Other weaknesses of democracy include: its tendency to produce politicians who pander to the masses instead of leading them, its feebleness in dealing with the violence of terrorists and criminals, its difficulty in raising people above mass culture, and its inability "to check unrestrained profiteering at the expense of public morality."[68]

Despite his criticism of democracy, he has a certain admiration for that form of government. He claims to be a critic only of democracy's weaknesses and does not oppose "good democracies." He goes so far as to encourage autocratic and totalitarian states to emulate some of the positive aspects of representative government. He calls for the separation of powers, complete freedom of speech and the press, government powers that are responsible to public opinion, and a decision-making process that promotes compromise and, above all, deliberation. The thrust of Solzhenitsyn's suggestions leads one to believe that whatever the ultimate source of sovereignty within a nation, be it the people or some ruling class, it ought to be checked by institutions, laws, and moral restraints—preferably all three.[69]

Solzhenitsyn's reluctance to present an ideal state does not keep him from showing his preference for small, inward-looking communities, in which relations between citizens rest on mutual friendship and respect. While he recognizes that the requirements of the modern age, and especially the challenges of foreign affairs, make the ideal of the small community impractical, he still wonders whether decentralization may not be a remedy for the impersonality and crassness that are so much a part of contemporary life. He restates the argument in favor of a society drawn together by patriotism and a dedication to the common good, and of a government as committed to the inculcation of duties as it is to the protection of rights.[70]

Because he places such importance on the common good, he questions the need for political parties. They represent, he says, the particular, rather than the general, interest and reflect material, rather than spiritual, concerns. He asks—without giving a conclusive answer—if there are no "non-party paths to national development."[71]

For those schooled in the virtues of representative government it is difficult to answer that question in the affirmative. After all, parties have existed in one form or another almost since the dawn of political life. As James Madison explains, to rid society of the "spirit of faction" it would be necessary to do away with liberty or to give everyone the same opinion. Since, under a decent government, the likelihood of taking either step is remote, it is safe to assume that parties will remain an important aspect of political life.[72]

It is important to note that Solzhenitsyn's proposal for a nonparty state is left as a question. It is likely that he stated the proposition as he did because he is aware of the difficulty of such an approach. In fact, the real issue is, not whether parties should be abolished, but whether the spokesmen of those parties can rise above the parochial and material interests that they represent.

The answer to that question depends, to a large extent, on whether a moral revival actually is plausible. Solzhenitsyn's optimistic remark that such a transformation of Western culture is in the offing may be more rhetorical than real. His analysis of modernity, detailed above in chapter 6, makes one wonder whether a change of this sort is conceivable. Indeed, he has come to doubt whether people actually can learn from experience. Does this mean that the West is destined to reenact the errors of the East by throwing itself into an all-consuming materialism?[73]

Whether a moral revival is likely or not, Solzhenitsyn's grim account of Marxism makes us believe that Western culture is confronted with a great challenge. While it is promising that the East may be moving away from a strict adherence to Marxist doctrine, the principles of Marx remain attractive in the West. For many in the developing world, Marxism seems to provide a ready-made solution to the poverty and inequity of the social situation. It continues to inspire a revolutionary fervor, for it promises equality, community, and liberation.

In the advanced nations of the West, only a segment of the intellectuals embraces doctrinaire Marxism. Yet a wider group of the educated class, while rejecting the harsh political measures of revolutionary ideology, avows an affinity for the goals of Marxism: full social, economic, and political equality; communitarianism; and a liberation from all socially enforced moral dictates. Such people are opinion leaders, and their views always come to play an important role in the making of public policy.

Indeed, the effect of this intellectual opinion has given rise to the most onerous predicament facing the West, relativism. This view, now widely accepted in the popular culture, poses great risks to the health and stability of the Western way of life. Relativism holds that there are no commonly shared moral standards, or, to put it in the vernacular of the day, no one has a right to judge the values of another. As Solzhenitsyn argues, the loss of a higher moral purpose makes it difficult for people to defend their way of life. They come to accept that all opinions and life-styles are of equal merit. Without a moral bulwark to keep the lower passions in check, many come to seek gratification in the most convenient manner possible; crime and drug use are on the rise. Without a commitment to spiritual principles, human life becomes little more than the pursuit of physical well-being. People imbued with such a doctrine are easy prey to a political system that, though more beneficent than past dictatorships, claims all power unto itself in order to equally dispense the material needs of its citizens. Such people are tempted to seek a political doctrine that offers what religion once supplied to man—a hope of perfection. A regime based on such principles might be less fearsome than a Marxist totalitarian state, yet it would be dispiriting nonetheless. It would hinder the full development of character and the pursuit of human excellence.

Within the Communist world the 1980s brought unexpected changes that have moved those nations away from totalitarianism. This development partly refutes Solzhenitsyn's criticism of the East. Yet, despite the optimism that *glasnost* has justly raised, it should not be forgotten that Gorbachev and other Communist leaders have been able to improve their societies only by abandoning Marxist principles. In essence, they have come to accept the position espoused by Solzhenitsyn: human nature cannot be altered to fit the ideals of Marx. The current reforms accentuate the continuing relevance and depth of Solzhenitsyn's evaluation of Marxism. Marxism has been tried and has failed because there are limits to the malleability of human nature, and to discard those limits, even with the best of intentions, may bring about truly horrendous consequences. Insofar as Communist leaders have altered their systems, they have done so by adopting non-Marxist policies, for, when put into practice, the principles of Marxism are as dangerous as they were in the time of Stalin. Further, Solzhenitsyn's judgment that a commitment to Marxist ideology, not Russian or Chinese nationalism, has been the source of the antagonism between East and West has also been borne out. As the major Communist powers have moved away from Marxism, they have moderated their international stances.

Finally, the rulers of Communist states are restricted in how far they can foster change. In order to transform the brutal and inefficient political system established as the result of adherence to Communism, they must deviate from the ideals of Marx. But if they jettison Marxism entirely, they undermine their own legitimacy. What claim do Communists have to rule if they are not Communists? The danger that this dilemma poses to the power of the party hierarchy may very well inspire it to revert to the old ways. If once again Communist rulers attempt to implement the principles of Marx, the West will have to muster its fortitude to forestall the encroachments of barbarism. In its state of moral confusion, that task may be more difficult than in the past.

The writings of Solzhenitsyn, perhaps more than any others of his generation, remind their readers of the bitter truth revealed by Tocqueville more than a century ago, mankind faces a choice between freedom and universal tyranny.[74] Either the human race lifts itself on the upward currents of the spirit or it may sink into the crushing burden of matter.

Notes
Selected Bibliography
Index

Notes

Introduction

[1] Ronald Berman, "Through Western Eyes," in *Solzhenitsyn at Harvard: The Address, Twelve Early Responses, and Six Later Reflections,* ed. Ronald Berman (Washington, D.C.: Ethics and Public Policy Center, 1980), p. 75.

[2] Alexander Solzhenitsyn, "The Nobel Lecture on Literature," in *East and West,* trans. Alexis Klimoff (New York: Harper and Row, 1980), pp. 7–8 (hereafter cited as *East*). For Solzhenitsyn's remarks on the inability of many in the West to make judgments concerning "good and evil," see Alexander Solzhenitsyn, *Warning to the West,* trans. Harris Coulter, Nataly Martin, and Alexis Klimoff (New York: Farrar, Straus, and Giroux, 1976), p. 46 (hereafter cited as *Warning*).

[3] "Interview with BBC," in *East,* p. 147. See also, Michael Scammell, *Solzhenitsyn: A Biography* (New York: Norton, 1984), p. 878.

[4] James Allen, "Solzhenitsyn's Vision of the Reconstruction of East and West," B.A. honors thesis, Kenyon College, 1982, pp. 112–13.

[5] Alexander Solzhenitsyn, *August 1914,* trans. Michael Glenny (New York: Bantam Books, 1974), p. 475.

[6] Alexander Solzhenitsyn, *The Gulag Archipelago,* trans. Thomas P. Whitney (New York: Harper and Row, 1973), p. vi (hereafter cited as *Gulag* I).

[7] Both cruelty and secrecy are intrinsic not just to the Soviet Union, he says, but to all Communist societies. He explains, "If we know next to nothing about forced labor camps in China, North Korea, or Vietnam this means only that people are held there in even harsher conditions than in Soviet camps: no individual and no information has been allowed to slip out" (Alexander Solzhenitsyn,

"Communism at the End of the Brezhnev Era," trans. Alexis Klimoff, *National Review*, 21 January 1983, p. 34). See also, Scammell, *Solzhenitsyn*, p. 15.

⁸Alexander Solzhenitsyn, "The Artist as Witness," trans. Michael Glenny, *Times Literary Supplement*, 23 May 1975, pp. 558, 561.

⁹*Gulag* I, pp. xi, xii. Gorky once described those who built the White Sea Canal as happy, free workers, when in truth they were slave laborers.

¹⁰See Alexander Solzhenitsyn, "Our Pluralists," *Survey* 29, no. 2 (Summer 1985): 1–28.

¹¹For example, see James Allen, *No Citation* (London: Angus & Robertson, 1955); Andrei Amalrik, *Notes of a Revolutionary*, trans. Guy Daniels (New York: Alfred Knopf, 1982); Andrei Amalrik, *Will the Soviet Union Survive until 1984?* trans. Peter Reddaway (London: Pelican Books, 1980); Vladimir Bukovsky, *To Build a Castle*, trans. Michael Scammell (New York: Viking Press, 1978); Efim Etkind, *Notes of a Non-Conspirator*, trans. Peter France (Oxford: Oxford University Press, 1978); Euginia Ginzburg, *Journey into the Whirlwind* (New York: Harcourt, Brace & World, 1967); Max Hayward, ed. and trans. *On Trial* (New York: Harper & Row, 1967); Edward Kuznetsov, *Prison Diaries*, trans. Howard Spier (New York: Stein & Day, 1975); Nadezhda Mandelstam, *Hope against Hope*, trans. Max Hayward (New York: Atheneum, 1983); Anatoly Marchenko, *My Testimony*, trans. Michael Scammell (New York: E. P. Dutton, 1969); Czeslaw Milosz, *The Captive Mind*, trans. Jane Zielonko (New York: Vintage Books, 1953); Varlam Shalamov, *Kolyma Tales*, trans. John Glad (New York: W. W. Norton, 1980); Armando Valladares, *Against All Hope* (New York: Alfred Knopf, 1985).

See also, Helmut Andies, *Rule of Terror*, trans. A. Lieven (New York: Holt, Rinehart & Winston, 1969); Hannah Arendt, *The Origins of Totalitarianism* (New York: Harcourt, Brace & World, 1968); R. Beck and W. Godin, *Russian Purge* (London: Hurst & Balckett, 1951); Zbigniew Brzezinski, *The Permanent Purge* (Cambridge: Harvard University Press, 1956); Robert Conquest, *The Great Terror* (New York: Macmillan, 1968); Robert Conquest, *Kolyma: The Arctic Death* (New York: Viking Press, 1976); Alexander Dallin and W. Breslauer, *Political Terror in Communist Systems* (Stanford: Stanford University Press, 1970); Merle Fainsod, *Smolensk under Soviet Rule* (New York: Vintage Books, 1958); Carl Friedrich and Zbigniew Brzezinski, *Totalitarian Dictatorship and Democracy* (Cambridge: Harvard University Press, 1956); Montgomery Hyde, *Stalin* (London: Rupert, Hart & Davis, 1971); Ivo Lapenna, *Soviet Penal Policy* (London: Bodley Head, 1968); Roy Medvedev, *Let History Judge*, trans. Colleen Taylor (London: Macmillan, 1971); T. H. Rigby, *The Stalin Dictatorship* (Sydney: Sydney University Press, 1960); Peter Reddaway, ed. and trans., *Uncensored Russia* (New York: American Heritage Press, 1972); Joshua Rubenstein, *Soviet Dissidents* (Boston: Beacon Press, 1980); Robert Tucker and S. Cohen, eds., *The Great Purge Trials* (New York: Grosset and Dunlap, 1965); Thaddeus Witten, *Commissar: The Life and Death of Beria* (New York: Macmillan, 1972).

¹²See Jerry Hough, *Soviet Leadership in Transition* (Washington, D.C.: Brookings, 1980); Alex Inkles and Raymond Bauer, *The Soviet Citizen* (New York:

Atheneum, 1968); Chalmers Johnson, *Change in Communist Systems* (Stanford: Stanford University Press, 1970); Isaac Deutscher, *The Unfinished Revolution: Russia, 1917–1967* (Oxford: Oxford University Press, 1975); Frederich Fleron, ed., *Communist Studies and the Social Sciences* (Chicago: Rand McNally, 1969). For some of the controversy surrounding Solzhenitsyn's views, see Scammell, *Solzhenitsyn*, pp. 931–49.

[13] John Muggeridge, review of *Solzhenitsyn: A Biography* by Michael Scammell, in *American Spectator*, 8 August 1985, p. 31; John Dunlop, Richard Haugh, and Michael Nicholson, eds. *Solzhenitsyn in Exile: Critical Essays and Documentary Materials* (Stanford, Calif.: Hoover Institution Press, 1985) pp. 3–142 (hereafter cited as Dunlop, *Solzhenitsyn in Exile*).

[14] David Remnick, "Lenin's Errors Aired in Pages of *Pravda*," *Washington Post*, 30 December 1989, p. A12.

[15] Scammell, *Solzhenitsyn*, p. 916.

[16] Ibid., pp. 969–73. See also Charles Trueheart, "Solzhenitsyn and His Message of Silence," *Washington Post*, 24 November 1987, pp. D1, D4.

Chapter I

[1] *Gulag* I, p. 437.

[2] These figures are much disputed, of course. Roy Medvedev holds that no more than twenty-five to twenty-six million perished, while Robert Conquest projects about thirty million (Medvedev, *Let History Judge*, p. 38; and Conquest, *The Great Terror*, pp. 200–211). The truth may never be established because there are probably no official records. Any of the numbers listed above stagger the imagination and lead one to wonder whether this is not a unique phenomenon in human history. Yet Solzhenitsyn contends that China may have committed even greater atrocities, given its greater population (*East*, p. 106; *Warning* p. 10).

[3] *Gulag* I, pp. 69–70.

[4] Ibid.

[5] Ibid.

[6] Alexander Solzhenitsyn, *The Gulag Archipelago II*, trans. Thomas P. Whitney (New York: Harper & Row, 1975), p. 293 (hereafter cited as *Gulag II*).

[7] Ibid.

[8] Ibid., p. 294.

[9] Ibid., p. 316.

[10] *Gulag* I, p. 200. Perhaps these accusations fell on sympathetic ears. Stalin had left the city himself.

[11] Ibid., p. 247.

[12] *Gulag* I, p. 37.

[13] Ibid., p. 351.

[14] Ibid., p. 435.

[15] Alexander Solzhenitsyn, *The Gulag Archipelago III*, trans. Harry Willetts (New York: Harper and Row, 1976), p. 511 (hereafter cited as *Gulag III*).

[16] Solzhenitsyn comments concerning the deaths of 2 June 1962: "Rather fewer than before the Winter Palace, yet all Russia was outraged by January 9 and observed its anniversary yearly. When shall we begin commemorating June 2?" (*Gulag III*, p. 510n; see also pp. 511–14).

[17] *Socialist* is used here and throughout as the Soviets and Solzhenitsyn use it—as a term interchangeable with Communism and one denoting that regime founded by the Russian Revolution.

[18] *Gulag* I, p. 353; see also p. 28.

[19] Ibid., p. 27; see also p. 34.

[20] Ibid., pp. 24–91. Solzhenitsyn explains that, "executions were carried out . . . on the basis of lists—in other words, free people were simply arrested and executed immediately. . . . [Singled out were] all scientific circles, all university circles, all artistic, literary . . . and engineering circles" (*Gulag* I, p. 31).

[21] *Gulag* II, p. 393.

[22] *Gulag* I, pp. 11, 378; *Warning*, pp. 32–33.

[23] *Gulag* I, pp. 103–16.

[24] Ibid., pp. 101–5, 133.

[25] Ibid., p. 307; see also pp. 287, 298–311, 431.

[26] Ibid., pp. 307–8.

[27] Ibid., p. 308. See also Stephen Carter, *The Politics of Solzhenitsyn* (New York: Holmes and Meier, 1977), p. 37.

[28] *Gulag* I, pp. 308–9. Solzhenitsyn comments that, "people lived and breathed and suddenly found out their existence was inexpedient" (*Gulag* I, p. 309).

[29] Solzhenitsyn quotes lines from Faust: "The whole world changes and everything moves forward, And why should I be afraid to break my word?" (ibid., p. 290).

[30] *Gulag* II, p. 147; *Gulag III*, p. 496; Nerzhin, the leading character of the novel *The First Circle*, loves to make prison guards live by the letter of the law. See Alexander Solzhenitsyn, *The First Circle*, trans. Thomas P. Whitney (New York: Harper and Row, 1968), p. 147.

[31] *Gulag* I, p. 60.

[32] Ibid., p. 284. Solzhenitsyn comments, "Hand me St. Augustine and in a trice I can find room in that article for him too" (ibid., p. 354).

[33] Ibid., p. 364.

[34] One prisoner noted concerning his sentence, " 'It is strange. I was condemned for lack of faith in the victory of socialism in our country. But, can Kalinin [then president of the Soviet Union] himself believe in it if he thinks camps will still be needed in our country twenty years from now?' " (ibid., p. 455).

[35] Ibid., p. 438.

[36] It is somewhat mystifying, however, as Solzhenitsyn points out, how people arrested for their bourgeois social origins could be reforged. Is not consciousness determined by class origin? Even labor cannot change one's parents. See *Gulag* II, pp. 13, 67, 86, 103, 502–3.

[37] One former prisoner described the transit sites, where prisoners were assigned to labor camps, as follows:

People were stuck there for several months at a time. The bedbugs infested the board bunks like locusts. Half a mug of water
a day; there wasn't any more!—no one to haul it. There was a
whole compound of Koreans, and they all died from dysentery,
every last one of them. They took a hundred corpses out of the
compound every morning. They were building a morgue, so
they hitched the zeks to the carts and hauled the stone that way.
Today you do the hauling and tomorrow they haul you there
yourself. And in the autumn the typhus arrived. And we did the
same thing; we didn't hand over the corpses till they stank—and
took the extra rations. No medication whatever. We crawled to
the fences and begged: "Give us medicine." And the guards fired
a volley from the watchtowers. Then they assembled those with
typhus in separate barracks. Some didn't make it there, and only
a few came back. The bunks there had two stories. And anyone
on an upper who was sick and running a fever wasn't able to
clamber down to go to the toilet—and so it would all pour
down on the people underneath. There were fifteen hundred sick
there. And all the orderlies were thieves. They'd pull out the
gold teeth from the corpses. And not only from the corpses.

(*Gulag* I, p. 536.)

[38] *Gulag II*, p. 14.
[39] Ibid., p. 198; see also pp. 113, 155–56, 209.
[40] Solzhenitsyn explains, "Those who increase work norms in industry can still
deceive themselves into thinking that such are the successes of the technology of
production. But those who increase the norms of physical labor are executioners
par excellence! They cannot seriously believe that under socialism the human
being is twice as big and twice as muscular. They are the ones . . . who should be
tried! They are the ones who should be sent out to fulfill those work norms!"
(ibid., p. 201).
[41] Ibid., pp. 78, 158; Carter, *Politics of Solzhenitsyn*, pp. 37–38.
[42] *Gulag II*, p. 620, Solzhenitsyn's emphasis.
[43] *Gulag* I, p. 468.
[44] *Gulag II*, pp. 355–59.
[45] Ibid., p. 159.
[46] Their code was, "1. I want to live and enjoy myself; and f—— the rest!
2. Whoever is strongest is right! 3. If they aren't (beat)ing you, then don't ask
for it. (In other words: as long as they're beating up someone else, don't stick up
for the ones being beaten. Wait your turn)" (ibid., p. 428). See also Meyer Galler,
Soviet Prison Camp Speech: A Survivor's Glossary Supplement (Madison: University of Wisconsin Press, 1972).
[47] Solzhenitsyn calls Stalin *pakhan*, or ringleader of a band of thieves (*Gulag* I,
p. 134; see also pp. 502, 506–7, and *Gulag II*, pp. 44, 440).
[48] *Gulag II*, pp. 307, 428.

⁴⁹Ibid., pp. 602–3; see also Carter, *Politics of Solzhenitsyn,* p. 37.
⁵⁰ *Gulag II,* p. 626; see also pp. 603–5.
⁵¹ *Gulag III,* p. 445. Which, Solzhenitsyn surmises, is not to say that the heirs of Stalin who became the rulers of the Soviet Union did not have their slaves.
⁵² *Gulag II,* pp. 564–65.
⁵³ *Gulag I,* p. 431n. See also Carter, *Politics of Solzhenitsyn,* p. 16, where he wonders if there was any place in the Soviet Union that could be considered the outside. He notes:

> as Solzhenitsyn points out, practically no one in the prison camps is either guilty of a crime or any sort of threat to society. This is contrary to any theories of reasonably wide currency about the justification of punishment or imprisonment. . . . In fact, in such a situation, one can make no distinction between those in prison and the rest of society. Hence, prison and normal society seem in this sense to have no dividing lines between them, although of course prison life does have some appalling restrictions which are not directly encountered elsewhere.

⁵⁴ *Warning,* pp. 14–17. See also *Gulag III,* p. 363, where Solzhenitsyn explains, "No Genghis Khan ever destroyed so many peasants as our glorious Organs, under the leadership of the Party."
⁵⁵ *Warning,* p. 12.
⁵⁶ *Gulag II,* p. 633; see also *Gulag I,* p. 17.
⁵⁷ *Gulag II,* p. 635.
⁵⁸ Ibid., p. 640.
⁵⁹ Quoted ibid., p. 646.
⁶⁰ Ibid., pp. 646–47.
⁶¹ Ibid., pp. 632–55; *Gulag I,* pp. 106, 335; *First Circle,* pp. 138, 636; *Warning,* p. 82; Alexander Solzhenitsyn, Mikhail Agursky, A. B., Evgeny Barabanov, Vadim Borisov, F. Korsakov, and Igor Shafarevich, *From under the Rubble,* trans. A. M. Brock, Milada Haigh, Marita Sapiets, Hilary Sternberg, and Harry Willetts under the direction of Michael Scammell (Boston: Little, Brown, 1975), pp. 2, 7 (hereafter cited as *Rubble*); Alexander Solzhenitsyn, *The Oak and the Calf,* trans. Harry Willetts (New York: Harper and Row, 1979), p. 171 (hereafter cited as *Oak*); Carter, *Politics of Solzhenitsyn,* p. 55.
⁶² *Gulag I,* pp. 11–12, 35–37, 188, 262; *Gulag II,* pp. 304, 382n, 393–94; *Gulag III,* pp. 92–93; Alexander Solzhenitsyn, *Lenin in Zurich,* trans. Harry Willetts (New York: Farrar, Straus, and Giroux, 1976), p. 215 (hereafter cited as *Zurich*).
⁶³ *Gulag I,* p. 13. Solzhenitsyn explains his idea of civil valor as follows:

> And how we burned in the camps later, thinking: What would things have been like if every Security operative, when he went out at night to an arrest, had been uncertain whether he would

return alive and had to say good-bye to his family? Or if, during periods of mass arrests, as for example in Leningrad, when they arrested a quarter of the entire city, people had not simply sat there in their lairs, paling with terror at every bang of the downstairs door and at every step on the stair case, but had understood they had nothing left to lose and had boldly set up in the downstairs hall an ambush of half a dozen people with axes, hammers, poles, or whatever else was at hand? After all, you know ahead of time that those [police] were out at night for no good purpose. and you could be sure ahead of time that you'd be cracking the skull of a cutthroat. Or what about the Black Maria sitting out there on the street with one lonely chauffeur—what if it had been driven off or its tires spiked? The Organs would quickly have suffered a shortage of officers and transport and, notwithstanding all Stalin's thirst, the cursed machine would have ground to a halt!

Chapter II

[1] Maurice Merleau-Ponty, *Humanism and Terror*, trans. John O'Neill (Boston: Beacon Press, 1969), pp. 1–24, 70.

[2] *Gulag II*, p. 330.

[3] *Gulag I*, pp. 237–76; *Gulag III*, pp. 22–28.

[4] Stalin's nicknames abound. Besides *pakham*—incorrectly translated as plowman in *The First Circle*—Solzhenitsyn gives Stalin many titles, but not so many as were accorded him during his life. Solzhenitsyn's list includes: Leader of Nations, Father of Western and Eastern People, Father of Peoples, Best Friend of Communications Workers, Greatest Genius of Geniuses, Great Generalissimo, Most Brilliant Strategist of All Times and People, Best Friend of Counter-Intelligence Operatives, Most Humane Statesman, etc. It is obvious that Solzhenitsyn wants his readers to recall just how far the idolization of Stalin had gone. See *The First Circle*.

[5] *First Circle*, p. 122.

[6] *Gulag I*, p. 240.

[7] Ibid., p. 253n. After the invasion and after most of European Russia had been conquered, Stalin recovered and pursued the war vigorously, Solzhenitsyn acknowledges.

[8] Ibid., p. 129. See also Carter, *Politics of Solzhenitsyn*, pp. 26, 31. Carter states, "Solzhenitsyn makes the point that those who defend illegality, even if their reasoning is based on impeccable Marxist principles, cannot expect legal principles themselves. . . . justice and legality are indivisible, those who participate in injustice have no claim on justice themselves."

[9] *Gulag II*, pp. 322–52. Again one must raise the question of whether Stalin believed there to be serious splits within the party. Solzhenitsyn merely makes the

point that there was no objective evidence of resistance to Stalin. Any opposition
that might have existed was in Stalin's imagination. As we shall see, Solzhenitsyn's
depiction of Stalin endeavors to show that Stalin was paranoid.

¹⁰Solzhenitsyn's memoirs are not kind to Communists imprisoned in the
camps. Many broke immediately. They humbled themselves before their interrogators, admitted to crimes they had not committed, and implicated friends and
associates in their fictitious crimes. In the camps they became stoolies, and, in
trustee jobs, they stole food from the rations of others. See *Gulag* I, pp. 129–32,
201; *Gulag II*, pp. 346, 351.

¹¹Solzhenitsyn takes the same position as Arthur Koestler in *Darkness at
Noon*, trans. Daphne Hardy (New York: Bantam, 1966); see *Gulag* I, p. 409. See
also *Gulag* I, pp. 405–9, 412, 418, 477.

¹²*Gulag II*, pp. 317–18.

¹³*Gulag* I, pp. 6, 106, 116, 131–33, 145, 190n, 191, 226, 242, 352, 409,
432–35, 440, 460, 462, 465–67, 500; *Gulag II*, pp. 203–4, 222–23, 317,
339n; *Gulag III*, pp. 36, 62, 77, 80–82, 110, 329, 384, 397, 514, 635; *Oak*,
pp. 1–2; *Zurich*, p. 73.

¹⁴Richard Pipes, *Russia Under the Old Regime* (New York: Charles Scribner's
Sons, 1974); Robert C. Tucker, "Stalin, the Last Bolshevik," *New York Times*,
21 December 1979, p. 35.

¹⁵Alexander Solzhenitsyn, "How Misconceptions about Russia Are a Threat to
America," *Foreign Affairs* 58, no. 4 (Spring 1980): 797–834; reprinted as *The
Mortal Danger*, trans. Michael Nicholson and Alexis Klimoff (New York: Harper
& Row, 1980), pp. 14–15 (hereafter cited as *Mortal*).

¹⁶Ibid., pp. 15–16. See also James Y. Simms, "The Crisis in Russian Agriculture at the End of the Nineteenth Century: A Different View," *Slavic Review* 36,
no. 3 (September 1977): 377–93

¹⁷*Mortal*, p. 16. Two well-researched works on this topic seem to bear out
Solzhenitsyn's own research: W. Bruce Lincoln, *Passage through Armageddon:
The Russians in War, 1914–1918* (New York: Simon and Schuster, 1987); Mi-
khail Heller and Alexandr Nekrich, *Utopia in Power: The History of the Soviet
Union from 1917 to the Present* (New York: Summit, 1987).

¹⁸He was Georgian.

¹⁹*Mortal*, p. 14. Solzhenitsyn's own connection to Russian nationalism has
been an important topic of conversation among his critics. Some suggest that he
is a Slavophile. See the essay by Ronald Berman, "Through Western Eyes," in
Berman, *Solzhenitsyn at Harvard*. Berman seems to argue that Solzhenitsyn's defense of the old regime is, in reality, a call for a return to tsarism, or rather, to a
Russian theocracy. In other words, Solzhenitsyn has no standard of judgment
other than that supplied him by Russian tradition.

One could remark that love of one's country—its people and culture—was not
always perceived as an ignoble sentiment. Be that as it may, Solzhenitsyn never
once calls for a return to the old regime or for the founding of a theocracy. He
merely compares the tsarist government to the one that came after it. If the facts
prove life to have been superior before the revolution, that does not make Solzhe-

nitsyn a Slavophile. Indeed, he is well acquainted with the defects of autocracy (see *August 1914; Gulag III,* p. 15). At one point he even says that the old Russia experienced "Asiatic Slavery" (*Gulag II,* pp. 152, 154). Yet he is still able to judge one government superior, the other inferior; one generally good, the other mostly bad. The ability to make such decisions is not rooted in an attachment to Mother Russia, but rests on the human capacity to make rational valuations based on a careful examination of the empirical evidence.

²⁰ *Oak,* p. 78. In order to distinguish Solzhenitsyn's fictional account from the facts of Stalin's rule as Solzhenitsyn represents them, the present tense is used in this section.

²¹ Stephen Allaback, *Alexander Solzhenitsyn* (New York: Taplinger Publishing, 1978), p. 86.

²² Andrej Kodjak, *Alexander Solzhenitsyn* (Boston: G. K. Hall and Co., 1978), p. 8.

²³ Allaback, *Alexander Solzhenitsyn,* p. 86.

²⁴ *First Circle,* pp. 100, 122. Xenophon's *Heiro,* or *On Tyranny,* explains the desires of tyrants in much the same way.

²⁵ Ibid., p. 102. On his birthday, "the works of thousands upon thousands of master craftsmen, the finest gifts of the earth stood, lay, and hung before him. But there, too, he felt that same indifference, that same fading interest. He quickly became bored."

²⁶ Ibid., pp. 121, 118.

²⁷ Ibid., p. 99.

²⁸ Ibid., pp. 100, 120.

²⁹ Ibid., p. 130.

³⁰ Ibid., p. 112.

³¹ Aristotle, *Nichmachean Ethics,* trans. J. A. K. Thompson (Middlesex, England: Penguin Books, 1955): bk. 2, chap. 3.

³² *First Circle,* p. 123.

³³ Ibid., pp. 104, 106.

³⁴ Ibid., p. 102.

³⁵ Ibid., p. 103.

³⁶ Ibid., p. 109.

³⁷ Ibid., pp. 107, 104.

³⁸ Ibid., p. 117.

³⁹ *Gulag III,* p. 431.

⁴⁰ *First Circle,* p. 113.

⁴¹ *Gulag I,* p. 412.

⁴² *Gulag II,* p. 332; see also Carter, *Politics of Solzhenitsyn,* pp. 26, 31.

⁴³ *First Circle,* p. 129.

⁴⁴ Ibid., pp. 124–25.

⁴⁵ Ibid., p. 126.

⁴⁶ Ibid., p. 134.

⁴⁷ Koestler, *Darkness at Noon.* See also Barrington Moore, *The Social Origins of Dictatorship and Democracy* (Boston: Beacon Press, 1966).

⁴⁸ *Gulag III*, p. 353.
⁴⁹ Ibid., pp. 350–68.
⁵⁰ Solzhenitsyn makes a great deal of the destruction of the peasant way of life, its language, its customs, and, most peculiar of all, its animals. For example, he points out that the party was "pitiless to horses . . . because horses were a kulaks' animal and also destined to die." By eliminating the farmers' means of production, the party was successful in changing the way farmers lived. For one thing, they became dependent on industrialization, particularly as it applied to tractor factories.

Not only were horses killed, but dogs were also singled out for extermination. They were rounded up, hauled off, or shot on the spot, Solzhenitsyn explains, as a means of attacking the individuality of their masters. Dogs, unlike Stalin, never lose sight of a most ancient verity of social life: one should help one's friends and hurt one's enemies. No matter how much propaganda the party broadcast over the radio or printed in the newspapers, dogs just could not be convinced that their masters had become enemies of the people, to be dragged off in the middle of the night by strangers. Because dogs were beyond the control of the state, they had to be eliminated.

Solzhenitsyn implies that the party's loathing for these pets originated in Marxist principles. The Progressive Doctrine states that man becomes human through labor. His relationship to nature is instrumental and exploitive. If all life is bound up in productive forces, surely animals are too. They are useful or harmful according to whether they are necessary to a certain historical epoch.

If one makes an animal a pet, however, one quickly learns, mostly from the animal, that although our species may be the crowning achievement of nature, still, we are only one of its parts—the so-called chain of being. Friendship between man and beast teaches us that our relationship with nature need not always be exploitive, but may be communal (*Gulag II*, pp. 429–30n). Perhaps this is reading too much into it, but Solzhenitsyn's point seems to be that Marx had it wrong from the start.

Marx writes, "Where a relationship does exist, it exists for me. The animal has no 'relationship' with anything, no relations at all. Its relations to others do not exist as relations. Consciousness is thus from the very beginning a social product and will remain so long as men exist" (Lloyd Easton and Kurt Guddat, eds. and trans., *Writings of the Young Marx on Philosophy and History* [Garden City, N.Y.: Doubleday, 1976], p. 422 [hereafter cited as *Writings of the Young Marx*]; see also pp. 293, 308). For a good discussion of the issue, see Oliver Clement, *The Spirit of Solzhenitsyn*, trans. Sarah Fawcett and Paul Burns (London: Search Press Ltd., 1976), pp. 104–5.
⁵¹ *Gulag II*, p. 78.
⁵² Ibid., pp. 578–79.
⁵³ Ibid., p. 102.
⁵⁴ For a partial list see ibid., pp. 591–93.
⁵⁵ Ibid., pp. 122, 198, 577–78; *Gulag III*, pp. 394, 493, 505.
⁵⁶ *Rubble*, pp. 8–9. In *Gulag I*, Solzhenitsyn comments: "Was not the land

given to the peasants during the revolution only to be taken into state ownership soon afterward? . . . Were not the factories promised to the workers, but brought under central administration in a matter of weeks? When did the trade unions begin to serve not the masses but the state? . . . What of the concentration camps (1918–1921)? . . . None of this was Stalin . . . [and even rapid industrialization] . . . again was not his invention" (p. 613n).

57 *Rubble*, pp. 9–10. Whether Lenin changed the ideas of Marx will be considered in the next chapter.

58 Ibid., p. 10. Of his dawning personal awareness that Stalin alone was not the cause of the Soviet Union's problems, Solzhenitsyn explains, "In my pre-prison and prison years I, too, had long ago come to the conclusion that Stalin had set the course of the Soviet state. But then Stalin died quietly—and did the ship of state change course very noticeably? [A]ll followed the beaten path exactly as it had been signposted, step by step." Solzhenitsyn recognizes elsewhere that the government did change after Stalin's demise (*Gulag III*, p. 445).

59 Alexander Solzhenitsyn, "Solzhenitsyn Speaks Out," trans. Albert and Tanya Schmidt, *National Review* 27 (6 June 1975): 606.

Chapter III

1 *Zurich*, p. 270.

2 *Warning*, p. 113. Whether Solzhenitsyn is accurate about Lenin is a matter of debate. To judge the matter fairly one would have to recreate Solzhenitsyn's research, attempting to find not only Lenin's personality but his place within the long tradition of revolutionary activity in Russia. That task is beyond the scope of this book. Various views of Lenin can be found in *Zurich*, pp. 269–70; Adam Ulam, *Lenin and the Bolsheviks* (New York: Fontana, 1966); B. Wolfe, *Three Who Made a Revolution* (New York: Pelican, 1966); R. Payne, *The Life and Death of Lenin* (New York: Pan, 1964). See also Vladimir I. Lenin, *Collected Works*, 45 vols. (London: Lawrence & Wisehart, 1960). Carter makes the same criticism as he did of Solzhenitsyn's Stalin: it is as if the author were inside Lenin's head and knew his thoughts (Carter, *Politics of Solzhenitsyn*, p. 110). See Solzhenitsyn's remarks on his characterization of Lenin in Dunlop, *Solzhenitsyn in Exile*, pp. 329–40. See also Scammell, *Solzhenitsyn*, pp. 944–45.

3 Lenin's mother, who provided him money until her death, received a government pension from the benefits of her deceased husband. *Gulag III*, p. 89. See also *Gulag III*, pp. 79–85, 89–91.

4 *Zurich*, p. 73; *Gulag III*, pp. 81–83.

5 *Warning*, p. 114. In January 1917 Lenin stated that he doubted whether he would "live to see the decisive battles of the upcoming revolution" (quoted in Edward H. Carr, *The Bolshevik Revolution: 1917–1923* [New York: Macmillan, 1951], p. 69.

6 *Zurich*, p. 55.

7 *Oak*, p. 140.

[8] *Zurich*, pp. 21, 47, 198, 250.
[9] Ibid., p. 37.
[10] *Mortal*, p. 16.
[11] *East*, p. 150.
[12] Solzhenitsyn has been accused of opposing modern science, a charge that he denies (*Mortal*, p. 64). He does seem to worry, however, that the discoveries of science are invariably turned into the weapons of war. As long as separate nations remain, each state will have a compelling interest in converting knowledge into the means of destruction. See, for example, Solzhenitsyn's remarks on how a "disarmed" Russia still might have to arm itself against China (*East*, p. 113; see also *Warning*, pp. 120–21). On the whole, Solzhenitsyn seems sympathetic to premodern scientists who, fearing mankind's capacity for brutality and greed, refused to make their discoveries public (*Rubble*, p. 15).
[13] Mary McCarthy sees as a "debatable proposition" the assertion that the Russian defeat could "'cause' Stalin" ("The Tolstoy Connection," in John Dunlop, Richard Haugh, and Alexis Klimoff, eds., *Alexander Solzhenitsyn: Critical Essays and Documentary Materials* [Belmont, Mass.: Nordland, 1975], p. 336 [hereafter cited as Dunlop, *Critical Essays*]). A cause can be necessary without being sufficient. According to Solzhenitsyn the Stalinist era need not have occurred as the result of losing the war, but it could not have happened had that defeat never taken place.
[14] Dorothy Atkins, "*August 1914*: Historical Novel or Novel History," ibid., p. 411.
[15] *Zurich*, pp. 285–87.
[16] See, for example, ibid., pp. 267–68, where he cites the following dispatch:

> (Count Brockdorff-Rantzau, German ambassador in Copenhagen, to the Ministry of Foreign Affairs. Top secret). . . . We must now definitely try to create the utmost chaos in Russia. To this end we must avoid any discernible interference in the course of the Russian revolution. But we must secretly do all we can to aggravate the contradictions between moderate and extreme parties, since we are extremely interested in the victory of the latter, for another upheaval will then be inevitable, and will shake the Russian state to its foundations. . . .
> Support by us of the extreme elements is preferable, because in this way the work is done more thoroughly.

See also, Scammell, *Solzhenitsyn*, p. 942.
[17] *Gulag* I, p. 458.
[18] *Gulag* III, pp. 79–97; *Mortal*, pp. 14–15; *Rubble*, pp. 237–39.
[19] *Rubble*, p. 238.
[20] Ibid. Published in 1909, *Vehki* (Landmarks) attacked the ideas of left-leaning intellectuals. It challenged the theories of positivism, materialism, atheism, and scientific socialism. Among the contributors were Nikolai Berdyayev, Sergei Bulgakov, and Peter Struve (*Rubble*, pp. v–viii).

[21] *Rubble*, p. 235.

[22] Ibid., p. 236. Solzhenitsyn explains that the virtues of the old intelligentsia included:

> A universal search for an integral world view, a thirst for faith (albeit secular), and an urge to subordinate one's life to this faith. . . . Social compunction, a sense of guilt with regard to the people. . . . Moral judgments and moral considerations occupy an exceptional position in the soul of the Russian intellectual: all thought of himself is egoism; his personal interests and very existence must be unconditionally subordinated to service to society; puritanism, personal asceticism, total selflessness, even abhorrence and fear of personal wealth as a burden and a temptation. . . . A fanatical willingness to sacrifice oneself—even an active quest for such sacrifice; although this path is trodden by only a handful of individuals, it is nevertheless the obligatory and only worthy ideal aspired to by all.
>
> (Ibid., pp. 230–31)

[23] *Gulag III*, p. 91.

[24] Among the faults of the old intelligentsia Solzhenitsyn names:

> Clannishness, unnatural disengagement from the general life of the nation. . . . Intense opposition to the state as a matter of principle. . . . Individual moral cowardice in the face of "public opinion," mental mediocrity. . . . Love of egalitarian justice, the social good and the material well-being of the people, which paralyzed its love of and interest in the truth; "the temptation of the Grand Inquisitor": let the truth perish if people will be the happier for it. . . . ideological intolerance of any other. . . . Fanaticism that made the intelligentsia deaf to the voice of life. . . . Daydreaming, a naïve idealism, an inadequate sense of reality. . . . A strenuous, unanimous atheism which uncritically accepted the competence of science to decide even matters of religion—. . . of course negatively; dogmatic idolatry of man and mankind. . . . and even hostility to autonomous spiritual claims.
>
> (*Rubble*, pp. 230–31)

To which Winthrop comments, "In sum, a misunderstanding of what political philosophy is and how it relates to politics and to man's place in the whole" (Delba Winthrop, "Solzhenitsyn: Emerging from under the Rubble," paper delivered at the American Political Science Association Annual Meeting, New York, September 1978, p. 6 [hereafter cited as Winthrop, "Solzhenitsyn: Emerging"]).

[25] Winthrop adds that the intellectuals went astray because they lost sight of the fact that a life of the mind has a value all its own and cannot have as its end material well-being or fame ("Solzhenitsyn: Emerging," p. 7).

²⁶Tolstoy's love commandment was more in line with Kant's categorical imperative than with traditional Christian doctrine.

²⁷Kathryn Feuer, ed., *Solzhenitsyn: A Collection of Critical Essays* (Englewood Cliffs, N.J.: Prentice Hall, 1976), pp. 13, 22, 86. Compare, for example, the harsh realism of Marxists to the idealism of the followers of Tolstoy in Alexander Solzhenitsyn, *Cancer Ward*, trans. Nicholas Bethell and David Burg (New York: Bantam, 1969), pp. 104–5.

²⁸*Gulag I*, pp. 303–5, 613; *Gulag III*, p. 89.

²⁹McCarthy ("The Tolstoy Connection," p. 339) argues that American liberals will not like Solzhenitsyn's ethics of duty to country. Her point is well taken. Many spokespeople of American liberalism attacked Solzhenitsyn's views. But why should liberals find duty to country something to criticize? Surely it was not always so. One need only look at President Kennedy's inaugural address.

³⁰That he understands the desire for absolute social equality to be a serious problem can be seen in his speech to the AFL-CIO, where he warned against attempting to establish "fine degrees of justice and even finer legal shades of equality" (*Warning*, p. 49). See also *Zurich*, pp. 49, 52, 65, 196.

³¹Solzhenitsyn and Tocqueville both leave the meaning of *equality* vague. To be more rigorous one must say that both favor equality of opportunity (means), but are opposed to equality of results (ends), especially if government is empowered to enforce those ends. Marx, on the other hand, considered equality of results possible and desirable, once the economic arrangement is transformed. (Alexis de Tocqueville, *Democracy in America*, trans. George Lawrence [Garden City, N.Y.: Doubleday, 1969]).

³²Carter, *Politics of Solzhenitsyn*, pp. 70–71; Feuer, *Solzhenitsyn*, p. 13; Tocqueville, *Democracy*, pp. 9–20, 56–57, 546–47. Compare *Rubble*, pp. 269–70.

³³*Rubble*, pp. 236–37.

³⁴*Liberal* can be used in the traditional sense to mean one who favors a limited, representative government established to protect natural rights. Solzhenitsyn seems to use the term here to describe those who favored progressive ideas. Our own experience with the New Deal shows how the idea of *liberal* has changed.

³⁵*East*, pp. 150–51.

³⁶Ibid., pp. 151–53. He continues, "The way in which our Russian liberals and socialists gave way to Communists has been repeated on a worldwide scale since those days" (ibid., p. 154). See also *Rubble*, p. 127.

³⁷Historians argue among themselves about who were the greatest presidents. The choice made here is based on the extraordinary crises Washington and Lincoln succeeded in overcoming: founding the country and saving it during the civil war.

³⁸*Gulag III*, p. 91.

³⁹*Zurich*, pp. 65, 212; see also "Solzhenitsyn Speaks Out," p. 606.

⁴⁰*Gulag I*, p. 353. Trotsky proclaimed, "Terror is a powerful means of policy and one would have to be a hypocrite not to understand this" (*Gulag I*, p. 300n).

⁴¹*East*, pp. 151, 153.

[42] *Oak*, pp. 212, 220, 540.

[43] *Zurich*, pp. 69, 79, 146–47.

[44] Ibid., pp. 20, 57.

[45] Ibid., pp. 9, 12, 25, 30, 32, 43, 51, 73.

[46] Ibid., pp. 15, 140.

[47] *Oak*, p. 140.

[48] *Zurich*, pp. 20, 51, 77–78, 93.

[49] Ibid., pp. 13, 22.

[50] Ibid., pp. 31, 56, 73, 76, 79, 112, 126, 174–75, 214.

[51] Ibid., p. 143.

[52] For examples of socialist self-abnegation, see Scammell, *Solzhenitsyn*, p. 93.

[53] *Zurich*, pp. 20, 80.

[54] Ibid., pp. 77, 96–97, 99. Solzhenitsyn gleefully reminds his readers that his hated adversary, Stalin, was introduced to the central committee by Malinovsky. Who knows, perhaps Stalin was cynical enough to have been a double agent for the tsar at one time.

[55] Ibid., pp. 68–69.

[56] Ibid., pp. 55, 90.

[57] Ibid., p. 91.

[58] Ibid., pp. 76, 94.

[59] Ibid., pp. 56, 59.

[60] Ibid., pp. 42, 56, 60, 71, 215.

[61] Ibid., p. 87; see also 45–46, 51, 53, 58–61, 71, 81, 215.

[62] Ibid., pp. 80, 234.

[63] Ibid., pp. 34–37. Lenin wrote in 1915, "To reject war in principle is un-Marxist. Who objectively stands to gain from the slogan 'peace'? In any case, not the revolutionary proletariat" (quoted in *Warning*, p. 70).

[64] *Zurich*, pp. 52, 101–4.

[65] Ibid., pp. 103–4. Lenin also hated the Swiss nation and culture, Solzhenitsyn argues. See also ibid., pp. 50, 214.

[66] *East*, p. 20.

[67] *Zurich*, pp. 70, 214.

[68] One critic argues that Solzhenitsyn can find no evidence of Lenin's use of terror in the first few months after the revolution. This, he claims, exonerates Lenin; he was merely reacting to the "White Terror" (Francis Barker, *Solzhenitsyn: Politics and Form* [London: MacMillan, 1977], p. 89). Solzhenitsyn claims that the terror was begun immediately after the revolution. But perhaps it did take the Bolsheviks a few months to put the terror in place. One should not forget, however, that the suppression intensified after the White partisans were dead or defeated.

[69] *Warning*, p. 63; "Solzhenitsyn Speaks Out," p. 607.

[70] "Solzhenitsyn Speaks Out," p. 606. The law was so broad that anything either done or not done could be considered a crime. Lenin was the person who constructed the far-reaching article 58.

[71] *Gulag* I, p. 328.

72 Ibid., p. 332.
73 Ibid., pp. 329, 371–72, 399. Solzhenitsyn may have had his political differences with the old intelligentsia, but that does not hinder him from admiring its strengths or grieving over its loss. He recognizes that within it was a stratum of thoughtful people who reached fervently for the sublime. See especially ibid., pp. 188–89.
74 "Solzhenitsyn Speaks Out," p. 606.
75 Warning, pp. 61–62.

Chapter IV

1 Paul Johnson, "Solzhenitsyn: Hero of Our Time," Washington Post Book World, 2 September 1984, pp. 1, 11. The influence of Solzhenitsyn's Gulag Archipelago was especially strong in France. Georges Suffert, the editor of Le Point, remarked that it had "forever eclipsed the beacon of communism" (quoted in Scammell, Solzhenitsyn, p. 877n).
2 Although he may not have been entirely systematic in presenting his differences with the ideas of Marx, Solzhenitsyn is well acquainted with Marx's views. (See Scammell, Solzhenitsyn, pp. 87, 94, 104–5). He seems to have read the many volumes of Marx's Collected Works; at least he derives all his citations from that source. For the convenience of my readers I have used the most readily available contemporary editions of Marx's works wherever possible.
3 Raymond Aron, Marxism and the Existentialists, trans. Helen Weaver, Robert Addis, and John Weightman. (New York: Simon and Schuster, 1970), pp. 4–5. See also Herbert Marcuse, Reason and Revolution (Boston: Beacon Press, 1969), p. 317.
4 Compare Lenin, Collected Works, with Marcuse, Reason and Revolution, and Erich Fromm, Marx's Concept of Man (New York: Ungar, 1961).
5 Shlomo Avineri, The Social and Political Thought of Karl Marx (Cambridge: Cambridge University Press, 1968), pp. vii, 258. Two points can be raised against Avineri's interpretation. First, Engels graciously and rightly conceded that he was not the leading member of the partnership with Marx. If Engels was saying something wrong about Marx's ideas, one can only wonder why, in a collaboration that lasted nearly forty years, Marx did not find the time to straighten him out. Second, if Marx's closest friend and confidant (their exchange of letters is voluminous) could not rightly understand his mentor, one is left to wonder whether Marx wrote too incautiously. Perhaps he wanted to be misunderstood, if that would help bring an end to capitalism. If, after all, the humanist interpreters of Marx are correct and human beings are free, then there is nothing certain about the victory of socialism. Marx may have wanted to give the enemies of capitalism the assurance that their cause would ultimately triumph. What surer way is there of turning philosophy into praxis?
6 Warning, pp. 56–57. See also Aron, Marxism, p. 6.
7 See Solzhenitsyn's "Letter to the Soviet Leaders" in East, pp. 75–142. Some

have argued that the writings of the early Marx are particularly embarrassing to the Soviet authorities. In a very real sense all of Marx's writings have been an embarrassment to Communist rulers. So little has worked out as planned. Yet for seventy years the Soviets doggedly held to Marxism as an explanation of life; even under Gorbachev, it has continued to shape the behavior of many within the ruling elite.

⁸Compare *East*, pp. 89–90, and Karl Marx, *Critique of Political Economy* (Moscow: Progress Press, 1976), Preface. See also Aron, *Marxism*, p. 8.

⁹Marx argues that capitalism "rivets" workers to the "agony of toil, slavery, ignorance, brutality [and] mental degradation . . . more firmly than the wedges of Vulcan did Prometheus to the rock" (*Capital* [New York: Modern Library, n.d.], p. 45). Compare *East*, p. 121; *Rubble*, p. 4.

¹⁰See, for example, his defense of moving the international socialist movement headquarters to New York. (Robert C. Tucker, ed., *Marx-Engels Reader*, [New York: W. W. Norton, 1978], p. 523; hereafter cited as Tucker, *Marx Reader*).

¹¹*East*, 121–22; *Warning*, 56.

¹²Robert C. Tucker, *The Marxian Revolutionary Idea* (New York: W. W. Norton, 1970), p. 3. Avineri (*Social and Political Thought*, p. 258) argues that because Marx rejected "Jacobin subjectivism," the picture of him as a revolutionary is overblown. Perhaps he did reject it, but before deciding the question it is important to know exactly what is meant by *Jacobin subjectivism*. How, for example, does the term differ from the generic word, *Jacobinism*—a term coined during the French revolution and defined as the irrational use of violence? More importantly, how does it differ from *Jacobin objectivism*, which, given Marxist terminology, means that if objective conditions are correct, the use of Jacobin violence (*Jacobinism*) is justified? Avineri proves too much and too little by his assertion. Marx never disclaimed violence; he only objected to its uses when history had not provided the proper opportunity for it to advance the cause of the proletariat victory.

To paraphrase Lenin, Avineri takes the revolutionary heart out of Marx. On this point Lenin's scholarship seems superior. See Arthur Mendel, ed., *Essential Works of Marxism* (New York: Bantam, 1965), pp. 103–5, 115, 117, 121, 126, 129, 131 (hereafter cited as Mendel, *Essential Works*). See also Tucker, *Marxian Revolutionary Idea*, pp. 3–48; Marcuse, *Reason*, p. 288.

¹³*Writings of the Young Marx*, pp. 253, 357; Tucker, *Marx Reader*, pp. 219, 543. On rare occasions Marx did admit the possibility of peaceful change. He saw peaceful change as an exception rather than a rule. For most of his life he fought against the idea of a "peaceful process of dissolution," thinking the nonrevolutionary route sapped the movement of its strength. Compare Tucker, *Marx Reader*, p. 522, with p. 553. In his speech before the International he may have toned down his remarks because he faced an audience of workers less than imbued with revolutionary fervor.

¹⁴"Solzhenitsyn Speaks Out," p. 606; *Warning*, p. 57.

¹⁵*Gulag* I, p. 355.

¹⁶In the *Discourses*, Machiavelli argues that people must occasionally be

thrown back to the origin of political foundations to remind them of the need for virtue (Niccolo Machiavelli, *The Prince and the Discourses* [New York: Random House, 1950], pp. 166, 400, 478, 480. Compare Solzhenitsyn's discussion of sexual restraint during the camp uprisings at Kengir (*Gulag III*, p. 306).

[17] He makes this assertion despite his own—implied—use of violence at Kengir. Compare *Oak*, p. 222, where he hopes to "start something" in his own country.

[18] *Gulag I*, pp. 335, 338, 382; *Gulag II*, p. 51.

[19] *Rubble*, p. 5; *East*, p. 29, also pp. 25, 130–31; *Gulag I*, p. 33; *Gulag II*, pp. 427–28. One is led to wonder if this lawlessness does not contradict Machiavelli's point (see note 16, above). However, since these crimes were committed before power had been solidified, there would be no force capable of sufficiently frightening people into probity.

[20] *Gulag III*, pp. 240n, 315. Marxist theory does distinguish between the final stage of Communism, in which all political and economic differences are abolished, and the temporary era of the dictatorship of the proletariat, in which the workers use the power of the state to sweep aside the vestiges of the old class system. Thus, Solzhenitsyn's criticism of the revolutionary phase of a Marxist struggle is only partly justified. Still, his practical critique of Communist revolutions is quite apt, for until 1989 no Communist revolutionaries gave up power voluntarily to the people. Even in Eastern Europe, the Communists were forced from power by mass protests. Communists traditionally have used whatever methods were available, from intimidation to propaganda, as ways of maintaining their position of dominance over the ordinary people. Only after there were no enemies of Communism left in the world, they claimed, would the party safely be able to relinquish its power.

[21] *Gulag II*, p. 88, where Solzhenitsyn says of one of them: "It is evident from his face how he brimmed with vicious, human hating animus." See also *Gulag II*, p. 319.

[22] *Mortal*, p. 14. As Carter (*Politics of Solzhenitsyn*, p. 93) points out, Solzhenitsyn's views are somewhat heretical even in the United States, which is itself steeped in a revolutionary tradition. Solzhenitsyn is remarkably silent on the American Revolution, perhaps because he knows that in its name some Americans feel a certain sympathy for struggles of national liberation. Or perhaps he reasons that in America the conflict was over independence, not social transformation.

[23] Marx proclaimed that "a revolution . . . can succeed . . . only . . . in getting rid of all the traditional muck and . . . [in] establishing society anew" (*Writings of the Young Marx*, p. 431).

[24] *Gulag I*, pp. 137, 188, 262; *Zurich*, p. 215; see also Solzhenitsyn's prose poems "Easter Procession," "A Journey along the Oka," and "City of Neva" and his short story "Zahkar-the-Pouch" in *Stories and Prose Poems*, trans. Michael Glenny (New York: Bantam, 1973); and "The Nobel Lecture" in *East*, pp. 3–38. For a discussion see Clement, *The Spirit of Solzhenitsyn*, p. 186; Dunlop, *Critical Essays*, pp. 102, 252.

[25] Tucker, *Marxian Revolutionary Idea*, pp. 53, 136; Mendel, *Essential Works*, p. 104; *Writings of the Young Marx*, pp. 19, 149, 409, 458.

[26] *Gulag* I, p. 96; see also *Gulag* II, pp. 46, 282; *Gulag* III, pp. 350–55; *Rubble*, p. 241.

[27] *Gulag* II, p. 46.

[28] Ibid., pp. 502–33.

[29] *Gulag* I, p. 325n. Usually the Bolsheviks did not accept the idea that people could convert. In at least one instance they did. A young fellow killed his father, a priest, out of class hatred. He was punished, but later rose quickly through the ranks (*Gulag* II, pp. 64–65).

[30] Krylenko discovered this fact, much to his chagrin, while questioning some high-ranking engineers on trial for wrecking the economy (Promparty Trial, 1930). In man's eternal quest to make reality fit theory, Krylenko felt compelled to uncover the motivation for the engineers' dastardly acts in their social origins. But Solzhenitsyn comments that he dug too deep. It turned out that all eight on trial had worked their way up from poor families (*Gulag* II, pp. 387–88).

[31] *Writings of the Young Marx*, p. 175.

[32] Dante Germino, *Beyond Ideology* (Chicago: University of Chicago Press, 1976), p. 58.

[33] Tucker, *Marx Reader*, p. 521; *East*, p. 135; *Gulag* I, p. 101; *Warning*, p. 80; *Gulag* II, p. 375.

[34] Mandel, *Essential Works*, p. 32. See also *Writings of the Young Marx*, pp. 460–61; Marcuse, *Reason*, p. 288.

[35] Solzhenitsyn himself was not uncorrupted by power. (See *Gulag* I, pp. 1–23, 147, 160–64.) One of the reasons the Organs were always inventing cases against innocent people was to justify their privilege and high pay. During World War II it was particularly attractive to uncover plots. It meant that the Organs were vigilant in the battle against a fifth column, and, of course, it kept them from the front (*Gulag* II, pp. 377–78).

[36] *Gulag* I, pp. 146–52.

[37] Ibid., p. 562; see also pp. 511–12, 539–63; *Gulag* II, p. 553. Solzhenitsyn mentions Dostoyevsky when speaking of the human propensity to enjoy cruelty and seems to take him as an authority on the darker side of the human soul. See Fyodor Dostoyevsky, *House of the Dead*, trans. Constance Garnett (New York: Dell, 1959), pp. 240–41.

[38] *Rubble*, pp. 15–16; *First Circle*, pp. 394–96, 402, 426–29. Marx was warned that this phenomenon would occur. The anarchist Mikail Bakunin in *Statehood and Anarchy* (1873) held that the ruling members of the proletariat would "start looking down on all ordinary workers from the heights of the state. . . . He who doubts this simply doesn't know human nature." Marx's point by point rebuttal is fascinating. It shows that Marx was oblivious to the possibility of an entrenched workers' dictatorship. He really did expect that a change in the economic foundations would make prudence unnecessary. (Quoted in Tucker, *Marx Reader*, pp. 542–48.)

[39] Tucker, *Marxian Revolutionary Idea*, p. 15; Aron, *Marxism*, p. 13; *Writings of the Young Marx*, pp. 409, 412, 432; *Capital*, p. 177. See also Tucker, *Marx Reader*, pp. 144, 170; letter from Marx to P. V. Annenkov, 12 December 1848, quoted in Leo Strauss and Joseph Cropsey, eds. *History of Political Philosophy* (New York: Rand McNally, 1972), p. 757; Karl Marx, *The Poverty of Philosophy* (Moscow: International Publishers, n.d.), p. 127.

[40] *Writings of the Young Marx*, p. 438. For example, he states, "The ideas of religious liberty and freedom of conscience merely give expression to the sway of free competition" (Mendel, *Essential Works*, p. 31). A fuller discussion of natural rights is found in *Writings of the Young Marx*, pp. 233–41.

[41] Tucker, *Marx Reader*, pp. 726–27.

[42] Aron, *Marxism*, p. 13. In *Gulag II* (p. 345n) Solzhenitsyn explains, "Principles are principles, but sometimes it is necessary to be elastic. There was a period when Ulbright and Dimitrov instructed their Communist Parties to make peace with Nazis and even support them. Well, we have nothing to top that; that's dialectics!" Taken to its logical conclusion Marx's position leads to the assertion that truth itself is impossible to establish. The human capacity to comprehend the reality perceived all around may be questioned, as it was by Vyshinsky. See also *Gulag I*, pp. 100–101, 433; *First Circle*, pp. 108, 226–27.

[43] *Gulag II*, pp. 58, 331–38. According to Marxist doctrine the party could bring about only progressive change. When, in reality, Communist rule all but ruined the economy and worsened most people's standard of living, blame for this regressive fact had to be placed elsewhere. Thus, Soviet society suddenly became infected with "wreckers." See also *Gulag I*, pp. 402–18.

[44] *Gulag I*, pp. 322–41; *Gulag II*, pp. 22, 78–80, 418; see especially *Gulag III*, p. 224, where Solzhenitsyn laments the loss of immutable notions of good and evil. Why else would people of the twentieth century, more than people of previous ages, be willing to carry out every order—no matter how inhumane?

[45] *Gulag II*, p. 344; *Gulag III*, pp. 279, 421–22.

[46] Marx suggests language does change (see *Writings of the Young Marx*, p. 421; compare *Gulag I*, p. 188, and *First Circle*, p. 112). Solzhenitsyn is trying to enhance his people's consciousness by restoring the Russian language using an intricate style and an enriched vocabulary. See also Carter, *Politics of Solzhenitsyn*, p. 50.

[47] *Writings of the Young Marx*, pp. 414–15. Marx argues, "Man is distinguished from the animals by consciousness, religion, or anything else you please. He begins to distinguish himself from the animals the moment he begins to produce his means of subsistence" (*Writings of the Young Marx*, p. 409; see also pp. 295, 419). Marx does say at one point that human beings create according to the laws of beauty, implying that there are some concepts independent of the productive forces. However, he never explains what these laws are or whether they change from one historical epoch to another. Elsewhere Marx rejects Hegel's assertion that ideas have an independent life of their own.

[48] *Gulag I*, p. 319; *Gulag II*, p. 149.

⁴⁹ A theory widely circulated by Frantz Fanon in *Wretched of the Earth*, trans. Constance Farrington (New York: Grove Press, 1968).
⁵⁰ *Gulag II*, pp. 68, 74, 144–45, 431–34; *Cancer Ward*, pp. 506–7; Kodjak, *Alexander Solzhenitsyn*, pp. 69–70.
⁵¹ *Gulag II*, pp. 412, 539, 627. In *Gulag* I (pp. 553–54), for example, Solzhenitsyn tells of one, Aric Arvid Anderson, a British officer of Swedish nationality, who sympathized with the ideals of Marx. He was kidnapped after World War II and brought to the Soviet Union in hopes of making him an outspoken defector. He refused, however, even when he came face-to-face with Gromyko. He was kept in solitary confinement for a year, but still refused to advertise the virtues of socialism. In doing so, Solzhenitsyn comments, "he made existence contingent on consciousness." Finally, Anderson was given a twenty-year sentence in the Gulag. He expected to be released in a few years. He never was. Solzhenitsyn says he misunderstood the strength of the East, a common mistake among Westerners.
⁵² Marx writes, "For the starving man food does not exist in its human form but only in its abstract character as food. It could be available in its crudest form and one could not say where the starving man's eating differs from that of animals. The care-laden, needy man has no mind for the most beautiful play" (*Writings of the Young Marx*, p. 310). Compare *Gulag* I, p. 209, where Solzhenitsyn recognizes the power of necessity, but writes, "all your Progressive Doctrine is . . . built on hunger, on the thesis that hungry people will inevitably revolt against the well-fed." See also Alexander Solzhenitsyn, *One Day in the Life of Ivan Denisovich*, trans. Ronald Hingley and Max Hayward (New York: Bantam, 1963), pp. 2, 16–17, 54, 86–87, 168–72, 200, 202 (hereafter cited as *Ivan Denisovich*); and *Gulag* I, p. 540n.
⁵³ *Gulag II*, pp. 336, 503–22; *Gulag III*, pp. 17–19, 78.
⁵⁴ Tucker, *Marxian Revolutionary Idea*, p. 5; Tucker, *Marx Reader*, p. 193. See also *Writings of the Young Marx*, pp. 240–41, where Marx quotes Rousseau approvingly.
⁵⁵ *Gulag III*, pp. 292–93, 422.
⁵⁶ *Gulag II*, pp. 47, 563; *Warning*, p. 125. See also *First Circle*, pp. 296–98. It is not surprising that Solzhenitsyn most clearly gives us a glimpse into the riddle of human nature in a work of art—*The First Circle*.
⁵⁷ Tucker, *Marx Reader*, p. xxxi; *Writings of the Young Marx*, pp. 293, 410–12.
⁵⁸ See Marx's statements about "the laws of surplus value" (*Capital*, pp. 708–9).
⁵⁹ *East*, p. 120; *Warning*, p. 54.
⁶⁰ *Ivan Denisovich*, p. 54.
⁶¹ *Gulag II*, pp. 259, 331, 336–37, 610, and *First Circle*, p. 40, where the zeks "were so wrapped up in their work, which brought them no return."
⁶² *Rubble*, pp. 12–13, 21. Solzhenitsyn also compares the artistic creations of the past, as expressed in Bach, Rembrandt, and Dante, to contemporary pop culture. He wonders whether a listener from outer space, upon hearing the former, would ever imagine that the same species had produced the latter. His prose

poem "The City of Neva" compresses the quest for the sublime into artistic form (*Stories*, p. 205).

[63] Compare *Ivan Denisovich*, pp. 106–7, 110, 114, and *Gulag II*, pp. 265–66, with *Writings of the Young Marx*, pp. 424–25.

[64] Compare *Writings of the Young Marx*, p. 424, with *First Circle*, p. 236, where he writes, "Once a single great passion occupies the soul, it displaces everything else." Some of Solzhenitsyn's other characters: Dr. Oreschenko in *Cancer Ward*, Sologdin in *First Circle*, and Captain Vorotyntsev in *August 1914*, do one thing well. They might be compared to Rusanov in *Cancer Ward* and Yakanov in *First Circle*, who do more than one thing, but not well. For a discussion of Solzhenitsyn's criticism of Marx's ideas on labor see Clement, *Spirit of Solzhenitsyn*, pp. 49–54.

[65] *Writings of the Young Marx*, p. 314.

[66] *Oak*, p. 494.

[67] *Gulag II*, p. 143. "the paper did not resist." Perhaps I am reading too much into it, but I interpret this remark to mean that Marx was not a materialist at all and that he did not ground his theory in praxis, as he had insisted. Thought, unlike action, meets no resistance in nature. One can think, thus write, anything at all, no matter how incorrect. Practical reality will not contradict thought until, of course, one tries to apply it. That Marx's ideas were used in a way he would never have intended shows the power of thought, thought's independence from praxis, and the danger of attempting to bring theoretical speculation into being.

[68] *Gulag II*, pp. 254–55. This argument does not necessarily contradict the one supporting Ivan Denisovich's enjoyment of labor. Solzhenitsyn is simply reporting that the type of labor that Marx argues created man may have been so burdensome as to make "conscious production" impossible. People had to be conscious before they could be producers. Whatever the origins of the species, the labor intended to reforge criminals was so grueling that it became deadly. Compare Marx's statement on exploitation in *Writings of the Young Marx*, p. 459.

[69] *Gulag II*, pp. 113, 149, 155, 201n, 209.

[70] Ibid., p. 260; see also p. 187.

[71] Compare Tucker, *Marxian Revolutionary Idea*, pp. 74, 78; Mendel, *Essential Works*, pp. 83–100, 199–206; Marcuse, *Reason*, p. 292; *Writings of the Young Marx*, p. 281, with *Rubble*, p. 137; *East*, pp. 95–101. In *Gulag II* (p. 39) Solzhenitsyn reports that exotic tropical trees were once planted at the Solovetsky Islands on the Arctic Circle in an effort to exhibit to the world that the "Soviet Republic was remaking the world and building a new life." For an example of Solzhenitsyn's point see Michael Weisskopf, "Spring in Peking Is Birdless, Shrubless," *Washington Post*, 26 April 1982, p. A24. In accordance with the spirit of Marx, the Chinese made an effort to overcome nature. During the Cultural Revolution of the 1960s, it was decided that the local crop yields around Peking could be increased if the birds were kept from eating the newly sown seeds. The birds were ordered killed, and the deed was done by incessantly stirring up the animals and not letting them sleep. No sooner was this progressive feat of natural engineering accomplished, than the city was inundated by insects. Without natural

predators, they had multiplied geometrically. Reacting decisively to rid the city of this new vermin, the party sent out Peking's nine million citizens to yank up every shrub, tree, and blade of grass in sight. With nothing to eat, it was reasoned, the insects would soon starve. At last nature was brought under control. There were no birds, no insects, and no vegetation. A dusty, barren landscape remained. Without flora to clean the air Peking's air pollution became seven times worse than that of Los Angeles. With the change in leadership came the replanting of trees. Insects reappeared, along, of course, with the birds.

[72] Tucker, *Marxian Revolutionary Idea*, p. 67. *Writings of the Young Marx*, p. 312. See also Solzhenitsyn's prose poem, "The Duckling" in *Stories*, p. 200; and "We Will Never Die" in *Stories*, pp. 217–18. Clement, *Spirit of Solzhenitsyn*, p. 26; Kodjak, *Alexander Solzhenitsyn*, p. 58.

[73] *Warning*, p. 54. Today, such reforms as a graduated income tax and a free education are taken for granted. Other proposals, such as the centralization of bank credit, transportation, and communication are more controversial, but still not radical. Labor armies have seen their day during the Great Depression (CCC).

[74] *Rubble*, p. 137. Compare *Writings of the Young Marx*, p. 301; Mendel, *Essential Works*, p. 26.

[75] *Cancer Ward*, p. 424.

[76] *Cancer Ward*, pp. 412–28. See also *Gulag III*, pp. 352–54; Allaback, *Alexander Solzhenitsyn*, p. 145. Marx was aware of the problem, but he insisted that laziness would vanish when private property was abolished, human nature transformed. See Mendel, *Essential Works*, p. 28.

[77] *Rubble*, pp. 19–20. At *Gulag III*, p. 354, Solzhenitsyn tells of a miller who rebuilt the mill he once owned before it was destroyed in the rush to collectivize, simply to make his neighborhood more beautiful. See also *First Circle*, pp. 453–56.

[78] *Gulag I*, p. 343. To this day the Soviet Union, an exporter of food before World War I, must import grain. One wonders whether the economic system was at fault or whether, as the official annual reports suggested, there were seventy years of bad weather.

[79] *Cancer Ward*, pp. 423–24.

[80] Compare *Writings of the Young Marx*, pp. 467–68, with *Gulag I*, p. 149n. See also Aristotle, *Politics*, trans. Carnes Lord (Chicago: University of Chicago Press, 1984), bk. 2, chaps. 5–7.

[81] *Gulag II*, p. 153; *Ivan Denisovich*, p. 61.

[82] *Gulag I*, p. 61.

[83] Ibid., p. 33, where Solzhenitsyn adds, "A peasant keeps grains for sale in the way of business. What else is his business anyway?"

[84] *Gulag II*, pp. 437–42, 570. At p. 437n, Solzhenitsyn tells of a fellow named Krokhalyov who embezzled about 8,000 rubles a month. He notes that this, "should be understood as an amendment to the Marxist thesis that the lumpen proletariat is not a property owner. Of course he isn't! Krokhalyov didn't use his eight thousand to build himself a private home; he drank them or lost them at cards."

[85] *Gulag III*, pp. 357–59. See also *First Circle*, pp. 169, 172.

[86] In *Gulag I* (p. 313), Solzhenitsyn quotes Marx, who calls priests, "leeches on the capitalist structure." In the same category he places lawyers, police, and notaries. See also *Gulag II*, pp. 30–31.

[87] *Gulag I*, pp. 311, 314–16.

[88] Compare *Writings of the Young Marx*, p. 302, with *Gulag II*, p. 335.

[89] *Gulag I*, pp. 10, 22, 95, 129, 138, 146, 152, 154–55, 489; *Gulag II*, pp. 543, 578, 587–88; *Gulag III*, pp. 23, 222, 311, 377. See also *First Circle*, pp. 118, 267–68, 438, 510; and especially p. 173, where Solzhenitsyn explains the role of the security chief in the prison facility where the action of the *First Circle* takes place. He writes, "From the half barren office, in which the only instruments of production were steel cabinets containing the prisoners' files, a half dozen chairs, a telephone and a buzzer, Lieutenant Colonel Klimentiev—without any visible clutch, drive, or gear box—supervised the outward course of 281 lives and the service of 50 guards." So much for the primacy of economics over politics.

[90] *Rubble*, p. 4; *Stories*, pp. 198–99.

[91] *Gulag II*, p. 220, where Solzhenitsyn admits to having a prisoner's bias against the power of money.

[92] Ibid., pp. 92, 113, 259–85, 568n; *Rubble*, p. 13.

[93] *East*, p. 178; *Gulag I*, p. 516.

[94] *Rubble*, p. 12; see also Kodjak, *Alexander Solzhenitsyn*, p. 106.

[95] *Gulag I*, p. 516; *Gulag II*, p. 607.

[96] *Cancer Ward*, pp. 150–51. See also *First Circle*, p. 584, where Rubin "was soaring aloft on the wings of the spirit." I acknowledge a debt to Delba Winthrop for helping me to understand the significance of those mysterious flights.

[97] *Cancer Ward*, p. 443.

[98] *Rubble*, pp. 121–22, 137.

[99] *Cancer Ward*, pp. 427–28.

[100] Mendel, *Essential Works*, p. 29.

[101] Ibid., p. 32.

[102] *Gulag III*, pp. 402–5. See also *First Circle*, p. 225, where Rubin, the good Communist, is said to have "lived the life of all mankind as if it were his own family life." See also *Gulag II*, pp. 238, 242.

[103] *Gulag II*, 327–28. For Solzhenitsyn's views on the relationship of the individual to humanity in general see his statement that Amnesty International is "nobly conceived" ("Solzhenitsyn Speaks Out," p. 605); his sympathetic treatment of Rubin in *First Circle*; and his admission that there were "good communists" in the camps, individuals who genuinely were interested in the welfare of others (*Gulag II*, pp. 323–25).

[104] *Gulag II*, p. 327, where he comments, "that is the price a man pays for entrusting his God-given soul to human dogma."

[105] Ibid., pp. 243, 448–49.

[106] Ibid., pp. 457, 459–60.

[107] *Cancer Ward*, pp. 396–411. Solzhenitsyn claims that love of one's family is

not necessarily a sign of goodness if, in other things, one acts despicably (*Gulag I*, p. 172). But paternal love may achieve some good things. He portrays the children of Party members in a surprisingly sympathetic light at times. They seem to be far more humane than their parents. See *Cancer Ward*, pp. 396–411; *First Circle*, chap. 39.

[108] *Rubble*, p. 249; *Gulag I*, pp. 106, 397; *Gulag II*, p. 317; *First Circle*, pp. 636–37; Winthrop, "Solzhenitsyn: Emerging," p. 19.

[109] *Gulag III*, p. 402.

[110] Ibid., p. 405.

[111] Ibid.

[112] *First Circle*, pp. 461, 466.

[113] Mendel, *Essential Works*, p. 30. His statement that "relations between man and woman" would become "natural functions" suggests a certain spontaneity (Tucker, *Marx Reader*, p. 83). This interpretation is given credence by Herbert Marcuse in *Eros and Civilization* (New York: Vintage Books, 1962).

[114] *Gulag II*, p. 233.

[115] *First Circle*, p. 600. Sologdin, who claims to be in complete control of himself, yields to the desires of the flesh. He may not be in as much control of himself as he thinks. His invention may have put him in the same situation as the pliable Colonel Yakanov. See *First Circle*, p. 532.

[116] Tucker, *Marx Reader*, p. 96; Mendel, *Essential Works*, p. 30.

[117] *Gulag I*, p. 199; *Gulag II*, p. 67.

[118] *Gulag I*, pp. 199, 530; *Gulag II*, pp. 53, 67, 231, 247–49. To which he adds, "I hear a choir of angels. It is like the unselfish, pure contemplation of the heavenly bodies. It is too lofty for this age of self-interested calculation and hopping-up-and-down jazz" (*Gulag II*, p. 249). See also Clement, *Spirit of Solzhenitsyn*, pp. 63–97, for a discussion.

[119] *Gulag III*, p. 505.

[120] *Writings of the Young Marx*, pp. 256, 402. He writes, "you cannot transcend philosophy without actualizing it. . . . by the negation of philosophy as philosophy. The philosophers have only interpreted the world in various ways; the point is to change it."

[121] Mendel, *Essential Works*, p. 25. Compare *Gulag II*, p. 414; *Gulag III*, p. 340; *First Circle*, pp. 146–47.

[122] "Solzhenitsyn Speaks Out," p. 609; *Gulag II*, pp. 194, 266; *First Circle*, pp. 31, 108, 574; *Oak*, p. 494.

[123] Karl Marx, *The German Ideology*, ed. R. Pascal (New York: International Publishers, 1933), pp. 14–15; *Writings of the Young Marx*, pp. 313–14. Eric Voegelin writes, "Marx . . . does not permit a rational discussion of his principles—you have to be a Marxist or shut up" (*From Enlightenment to Revolution* [Durham: University of North Carolina Press, 1975], p. 298).

[124] *Cancer Ward*, p. 135; *Warning*, pp. 57, 142.

[125] *Rubble*, p. 124.

[126] *Writings of the Young Marx*, pp. 290, 227, 250–51, 312.

[127] *Gulag I*, pp. 538–39; *Gulag II*, pp. 87, 104, 375.

[128] *Gulag* I, p. 147.

[129] *Warning*, pp. 58–59.

[130] *Writings of the Young Marx*, p. 304. The early writings suggest that Marx thought that Communism would be good for people, thus a worthy goal for them to pursue. The later Marx is more scientific and wishes only to explicate the "laws" by which Communism will come into being. This is one of those vexing points that divide commentators on Marx.

[131] Solzhenitsyn explains, "Thomas More, Campanellas, Winstanlye, Moirelli, Deschamps, Babeuf, Fourier, Marx, and dozens of others" (*Warning*, p. 143).

[132] *Rubble*, p. 136. Compare Karl Marx, *Capital III* (Moscow: Progress Press, 1976), p. 820.

[133] *Rubble*, p. 230; See also "The Puppy," in *Stories*, p. 206.

[134] Compare Tucker, *Marxian Revolutionary Idea*, pp. 18, 20, 27, 31, 50, 85–86; Marcuse, *Reason*, pp. 292–95, with *Rubble*, pp. 16, 20, 23, 137; *Gulag* I, p. 595; *First Circle*, pp. 24, 127; and *Stories*, p. 197.

[135] *First Circle*, pp. 146–47.

[136] Ibid., p. 109. Solzhenitsyn notes that thieves seem to be born to their fate, while he contends that artists have their abilities "breathed" into them at birth (*Gulag* I, p. 516; *East*, p. 22). Of course, he does not reject the idea that conditioning and circumstances play an important role in the development of personality. For a fascinating exposition of the difference between natural and conventional inequality, see *Gulag* II, pp. 489–91n; see also *First Circle*, pp. 61, 569–70. *August 1914* is, in part, an artistic recognition of nature's hierarchy of abilities.

[137] *Gulag* I, pp. 337–38, 388–89, 392; *Gulag* II, pp. 353–56; *Gulag III*, p. 353.

[138] *Gulag* II, pp. 84, 325–26, 329, 343, 435, 574; *First Circle*, p. 25; *Rubble*, pp. 240–43.

[139] *Writings of the Young Marx*, pp. 292–94.

[140] *Gulag III*, p. 344. It is not coincidental that he is talking about the failure of post World War II socialist parties in the West to condemn the horrors of Soviet Communism.

[141] Compare *Writings of the Young Marx*, pp. 307, 313–14, with *Cancer Ward*, p. 137.

[142] Mendel, *Essential Works*, p. 32.

[143] *Stories*, pp. 43–101.

[144] Solzhenitsyn implies that the error was begun by Hobbes (*First Circle*, p. 365).

[145] *Warning*, p. 69.

[146] *Writings of the Young Marx*, p. 457.

[147] *Gulag* II, p. 515; *Warning*, p. 64. For example, compare the creative Sologdin, who "got into a quiet side-stream [at the research institute], was never checked on, had enough free time at his disposal, and [was] without supervision," to the uninventive Rubin, who found loneliness "unbearable" and who "did not

allow his thoughts to mature in his head, but finding even half a thought there
... hastened to share it" (*First Circle*, pp. 191, 198, 216).
[148] "Solzhenitsyn Speaks Out," p. 609.
[149] *First Circle*, p. 267; *Gulag II*, p. 187.
[150] "Matryona's House" in *Stories*, pp. 1–42.
[151] See "The Nobel Lecture," in *East*, pp. 3–36. What ties all humanity together is, not the community of material well-being, but the appreciation of artistic creation. See also *Rubble*, pp. 262–64.
[152] *Gulag III*, p. 365.
[153] *Mortal*, pp. 34, 39–43; *Warning*, pp. 134–35. See also Scammell, *Solzhenitsyn*, p. 132.

Chapter V

[1] *Gulag I*, p. 332; *Gulag II*, p. 348; *Gulag III*, p. 22.
[2] *Gulag II*, p. 347.
[3] Ibid., p. 335; *First Circle*, pp. 41, 481; Allaback, *Alexander Solzhenitsyn*,
p. 78; Dunlop, *Critical Essays*, pp. 142–43. Solzhenitsyn estimates that while
only 2 percent of Russia's land was held privately, it produced almost half of the
U.S.S.R.'s foodstuffs. Despite this seeming success, prior to Gorbachev's reforms,
the state officially continued to discourage private farming and to support the
inefficient collective-farm system. Once again, ideology won out over practicality
("Communism at the End of the Brezhnev Era," p. 29). See also, Scammell, *Solzhenitsyn*, p. 96.
[4] *Warning*, pp. 56–58; *Gulag III*, p. 224.
[5] *East*, p. 23.
[6] *Gulag I*, p. 168. Despite the evil within the human soul, Solzhenitsyn rejects
the notion that it is impossible to judge between right and wrong, or that people
should not be held responsible for their actions.
[7] See ibid., p. 173, where Solzhenitsyn comments on the motives of Shakespeare's Iago.
[8] Ibid., pp. 172–75.
[9] *Gulag II*, p. 615.
[10] Ibid., pp. 615–16.
[11] Jerry F. Hough, *Soviet Leadership in Transition* (Washington, D.C.: Brookings Institution, 1980), p. 4.
[12] Ibid., pp. 37–77.
[13] Compare the classic study of totalitarianism by Friedrich and Brzezinski.
They offer six fundamental attributes of totalitarian societies that, taken together,
differentiate them from autocracies and tyrannies. The criteria are: (1) an official ideology or doctrine that claims to cover all vital aspects of human existence; (2) a single mass party, usually headed by one person; (3) a system of
terroristic police control; (4) monopoly control of all means of communica-

tion; (5) monopoly control of all means of effective armed combat; (6) a centrally managed and directed economy. The authors acknowledge that this list may not be complete. In fact, they also seem to suggest that totalitarian governments keep their citizens stirred up and ready for action, "continually on the march," as it were. Friedrich and Brzezinski, *Totalitarian Dictatorship and Autocracy*, pp. 11–12, 40.

[14] Hannah Arendt, *The Origins of Totalitarianism* (New York: Harcourt, Brace & World, 1951), p. 378.

[15] *Warning*, pp. 62–64; *Gulag* I, p. 68n.

[16] "Communism at the End of the Brezhnev Era," p. 33. *East*, p. 126.

[17] Alexander Solzhenitsyn, "Sakharov i kritika 'Pisma vozhdyam,'" *Kontinent* 2 (1975): 352–53, quoted in John Dunlop, "Solzhenitsyn in Exile," *Survey* 21 (Summer 1975): 135–36 (hereafter cited as Dunlop, "Exile").

[18] Alexander Solzhenitsyn, "Live Not by Lies," *Washington Post*, 18 February 1974, p. A26 (hereafter cited as "Live Not by Lies").

[19] Ibid.

[20] "Solzhenitsyn Speaks Out," p. 609; *Rubble*, pp. 23, 117, 275, 278; *East*, pp. 34, 129; *Warning*, p. 7.

[21] *Mortal*, p. 22. See also *Warning*, pp. 36–37; *Gulag* III, pp. 477, 518, 525; *First Circle*, p. 84.

[22] *Warning*, p. 36.

[23] *Mortal*, pp. 32–33.

[24] See especially, "The Easter Procession" in *Stories*, pp. 102–6. See also *Oak*, p. 209; *East*, pp. 117, 223; Carter, *Politics of Solzhenitsyn*, p. 53; Kodjak, *Alexander Solzhenitsyn*, pp. 121–22.

[25] *Gulag* III, p. 494.

[26] *Gulag* III, p. 492; *Oak*, p. 42; *East*, pp. 76–77.

[27] Truehart, "Solzhenitsyn and His Message of Silence"; Paul Grey, "Russia's Prophet in Exile," *Time*, 24 July 1989, pp. 56–60. David Remnick, "Solzhenitsyn—A New Day in the Life," *Washington Post*, 7 January 1990, p. B3.

[28] David Remnick, "Solzhenitsyn Denies Talking with Soviets," *Washington Post*, 28 June 1988, p. A10; Associated Press, "Solzhenitsyn Rejects Invitation," *Washington Post*, 9 September 1988, p. B4; David Remnick, "Soviet Journal to Publish Solzhenitsyn," *Washington Post*, 21 April 1989, pp. C1, C9; David Remnick, "Witness to the Gulag," *Washington Post*, 9 July 1989, p. B7; David Remnick, "'Ivan Denisovich' Returns," *Washington Post*, 21 November 1989, p. D1. Many thanks to John B. Dunlop, America's premier authority on Solzhenitsyn's work, for the insights found in "The Almost Rehabilitation and Re-Anathematization of Alexandr Solzhenitsyn," working paper, Hoover Institution, Stanford University, February 1989.

[29] The enormous difficulty of reforming Communist governments was visible in the crackdown on student protesters in China in June of 1989. It must be recalled that prior to this upheaval, China was thought to be more advanced along the road to reform than the Soviet Union.

[30] James W. Ceaser, *Presidential Selection: Theory and Development* (Princeton: Princeton University Press, 1979).

[31] *Rubble*, p. 3; *Mortal*, pp. 31–32; "Communism at the End of the Brezhnev Era," pp. 28–34.

[32] *Gulag III*, pp. 350–55; *East*, p. 110.

[33] *Warning*, pp. 11–12; *East*, 122–23; *Gulag II*, pp. 165–67.

[34] *Gulag II*, pp. 95, 101, 160–61, 577–78, 583–84; *First Circle*, pp. 97, 151, 521–22.

[35] *East*, pp. 97–101, 118–19; Dunlop, "Exile," p. 142.

[36] Carter, *Politics of Solzhenitsyn*, p. 50.

[37] "We Will Never Die" in *Stories*, pp. 217–18; *Mortal*, pp. 32–33.

[38] *East*, pp. 84, 91, 113, 119–25.

[39] *Warning*, pp. 85, 114.

[40] Ibid., p. 88.

[41] Dunlop, "Exile," p. 146.

[42] *Gulag I*, pp. 133, 145n, 247; *Gulag III*, pp. 359, 386; *Oak*, p. 389.

[43] *Gulag I*, p. 290. See also *Gulag III*, pp. xi, 288n, 373, 385, 516; *Oak*, pp. 112, 149, 332.

[44] Robert Conquest, "Education of an Exile: Gulag Archipelago," in Feuer, *Solzhenitsyn*, p. 94. See also *Gulag III*, pp. 373, 385, where Solzhenitsyn acknowledges the great suffering of black slavery in America. He maintains, however, that because it was not organized by the state, it was milder than the imprisonment of millions of zeks or the deportations of whole nations within the Soviet Union. Still, one could object, it lasted longer.

[45] Carter, *Politics of Solzhenitsyn*, p. 136; Scammell, *Solzhenitsyn*, p. 946.

[46] *Mortal*, pp. 1–2.

[47] *Warning*, p. 64.

[48] Ibid., pp. 63–67.

[49] Ibid., p. 64.

[50] *Mortal*, p. 37.

[51] *Gulag I*, pp. 68n, 398n; *Warning*, pp. 63–64; *East*, pp. 24, 83–84.

[52] *Warning*, pp. 60–61.

Chapter VI

[1] *Mortal*, p. 64.

[2] *Warning*, p. 106. See also *East*, p. 39 and *Warning*, p. 22, where he relates a Russian proverb: "The yes-man is your enemy but your friend will argue with you."

[3] *Warning*, p. 11.

[4] Ibid., pp. 85–86.

[5] Ibid., p. 12. He tells of the greed of Western businessmen who exhibited sophisticated security equipment at a trade fair in Moscow. The devices, used to

catch criminals in the West, became, in the hands of the KGB, the means of spying on people.

⁶Ibid., pp. 12–13.

⁷Ibid., pp. 20–25, 136; *East*, p. 197; *Gulag* I, pp. 259–60n.

⁸Ibid., p. 23.

⁹"The Artist as Witness," p. 561.

¹⁰"Communism at the End of the Brezhnev Era," p. 34.

¹¹*Warning*, p. 38.

¹²Ibid., pp. 39, 117–18, 137, 139; *East*, p. 63.

¹³*Warning*, pp. 38–40, 70–71, 73–74; *Gulag* II, p. 320; *Gulag* III, pp. 270–79.

¹⁴*Warning*, p. 14.

¹⁵Ibid., pp. 39–40, 76–78.

¹⁶"Communism at the End of the Brezhnev Era," pp. 28–33.

¹⁷*Warning*, p. 33; Alexander Solzhenitsyn, "Solzhenitsyn Speaks Out on Poland," *Cleveland Plain Dealer*, 24 January 1982, p. 7AA.

¹⁸See "Communism at the End of the Brezhnev Era," p. 34, where Solzhenitsyn warned that any Communist government is "restrained in its behavior . . . merely because it has not yet gained military strength."

¹⁹Ibid.

²⁰Ibid.

²¹*Mortal*, pp. 20–21.

²²Henry Kissinger, *The White House Years* (Boston: Little, Brown, 1979), pp. 112–62, 215–16, 552–57. Compare Alexsandr I. Solzhenitsyn, "Schlesinger and Kissinger," trans. Raymond H. Anderson, *New York Times*, 1 December 1975, p. 31. See also Scammell, *Solzhenitsyn*, p. 857.

²³*Warning*, p. 87. The practical difficulties of implementing a unified trade embargo were apparent in the Siberian natural-gas pipeline negotiations during the mid-1980s.

²⁴*Mortal*, pp. 20–21, 53, 71. Solzhenitsyn says that at the very least the West ought to be able to distinguish "the enemies of humanity from its friends."

²⁵*Warning*, p. 111; *East*, p. 40. His argument is similar to Lincoln's. The world cannot exist half slave and half free. As long as one island of freedom is left in the world from which the truth about Communist practices can be told, Communist leaders will not be secure. Hence, the aspiration for global conquest.

²⁶*Warning*, pp. 46–47. He explains, "under the cast-iron shell of Communism . . . a liberation of the human spirit is occurring. New generations are growing up, steadfast in their struggle with evil, unwilling to accept unprincipled compromises, preferring to lose everything . . . so as not to sacrifice conscience."

²⁷"Communism at the End of the Brezhnev Era," p. 34.

²⁸*Warning*, pp. 40–44.

²⁹Ibid., pp. 45, 100.

³⁰Ibid., pp. 80–81. See also *East*, p. 59, where Solzhenitsyn makes this point by criticizing the realism of George Kennan. Kennan's argument, that one

"should not apply moral criteria to politics," results in the mixing of "good and evil, right and wrong, and make[s] room for the absolute triumph of absolute evil. . . . Only moral criteria can help the West against communism's well planned strategy. . . . Practical and/or occasional considerations . . . will inevitably be swept aside by strategy. After a certain level is reached, [realism] induces paralysis; it prevents one from seeing the scale and meaning of events."

    [31] *Mortal*, p. 7, where Solzhenitsyn also argues that since certain "topics" are "hidden and carefully hushed-up" by the Soviet government, Western scholars have no choice but to "unwittingly adopt the Procrustean frame-work provided by official Soviet historiography."

Solzhenitsyn capsulizes the ability of Communist governments to manage information in a delightful chapter (chap. 54), entitled "Buddha's Smile," of his novel *The First Circle*. He writes of a visit to a Soviet prison by the activist wife of an American president during World War II. Miraculously, before she arrives, the tattered clothes, the bedbugs, the slop buckets, and the overcrowding are all made to disappear by the quick work of the prison guards. In their place is a clean, well-stocked cell inhabited, the Soviet translator explains, by unusually happy prisoners who are free to observe whatever religious practices they choose. The president's wife is astonished at the humane conditions and returns home believing the Soviet penal system is the most progressive in the world. After her departure, everything, except a forgotten statue of Buddha, reverts to its unsanitary norm.

    [32] *Warning*, pp. 34–36; *Mortal*, pp. 26–27.

    [33] "Artist as Witness," p. 561; "Solzhenitsyn Speaks Out," pp. 604, 607.

    [34] *Mortal*, pp. 11–12, where Solzhenitsyn complains that Richard Pipes attempts to show the defective character of Russian peasants under the old regime by citing a few particularly cruel and cynical folk proverbs. He writes that, "Pipes wrests those half dozen . . . that suit his needs . . . from among some forty thousand proverbs, which in their unity and their inner contradiction make up a dazzling literary and philosophic edifice. . . . This method affects me in much the same way as I imagine Rostropovich would feel if he had to listen to a wolf playing the cello."

    [35] *East*, pp. 171–72.

    [36] "Artist as Witness," p. 561. Solzhenitsyn quotes a Russian proverb: "The man with a full belly cannot understand the hungry man." See also *East*, pp. 16–17; *Warning*, p. 81.

    [37] *Warning*, p. 133, where Solzhenitsyn points out, for example, that George Bernard Shaw, who, while millions starved in the Ukraine, commented from Moscow, "I never dined so well or so sumptuously as when I crossed the Soviet borders." See also *Warning*, p. 35; Dunlop, "Exile," pp. 146, 152; Carter, *Politics of Solzhenitsyn*, p. 38; *East*, p. 172.

    [38] *East*, p. 40.

    [39] Ibid., p. 69. What precisely Solzhenitsyn means by "a Supreme Complete Entity," he does not say. Perhaps, he wishes to convey an idea that is not limited

to the concept of the Judeo-Christian God. Solzhenitsyn seems almost more interested in the effects of Christianity than its verity. See also Scammell, *Solzhenitsyn*, p. 867.

⁴⁰ *East*, p. 65; see also pp. 66–71.

⁴¹ *Warning*, p. 129. Solzhenitsyn does not specify what the excesses were, but one supposes that they were the result of the Church's zealous attempt to enforce strict rules of natural law on all aspects of human life.

⁴² Machiavelli's advice that "imagined republics and principalities" are the source of our misunderstanding of politics (*Prince*, chap. 15), and Hobbes's assertion that there is no *summum bonum* (Thomas Hobbes, *Leviathan* [Cleveland: Meridian Books, 1963], chap. 11) come to mind.

⁴³ Alexander Solzhenitsyn, "Rech pri poluchenii 'Zolotoe klishe' soyuza italianskikh zhurnalistov," in *Mir i Nasilie* (Frankfurt: Possev, 1974), pp. 99–100, quoted in Dunlop, "Exile," p. 145.

⁴⁴ *East*, pp. 64–66, 69–71. See also *Gulag* I, p. 193, for Solzhenitsyn's comments on Descartes's method.

⁴⁵ *Warning*, pp. 127–28.

⁴⁶ *East*, p. 64.

⁴⁷ Ibid., pp. 64–65, 69.

⁴⁸ Ibid., pp. 45–46, 64–71.

⁴⁹ Solzhenitsyn, "Rech pri poluchenii 'Zolotoe klishe' soyuza italianskikh zhurnalistov," pp. 99–100, quoted in Dunlop, "Exile," p. 145.

⁵⁰ *Warning*, pp. 145–46.

⁵¹ *East*, pp. 65–66, 69.

⁵² Ibid., pp. 50–51. See also p. 58, where Solzhenitsyn writes, "The center of your democracy and of your culture is left without electric power for a few hours only, and suddenly crowds of citizens start looting and creating havoc. The smooth surface film must be very thin, then, the social system quite unstable and unhealthy." He seems to be arguing that without internal moral checks, only the law stands in people's way. They will be open to doing most anything as long as they do not get caught. Unless a society is willing to employ sufficient force to continually frighten citizens into compliance—something unlikely under a liberal government—there must be reliance on self-restraint.

⁵³ Ibid., pp. 65–66.

⁵⁴ Ibid., p. 49.

⁵⁵ *First Circle*, pp. 391–400. See also *Warning*, pp. 145–46; *East*, pp. 70–71.

⁵⁶ *Warning*, pp. 132, 141–42.

⁵⁷ *East*, pp. 55–56.

⁵⁸ Ibid., pp. 67–68. Lenin's strategy was always to attack from the left.

⁵⁹ Ibid., pp. 69–70.

⁶⁰ *Warning*, p. 132.

⁶¹ *East*, p. 68.

⁶² Ibid., p. 172.

⁶³ That Solzhenitsyn understands the crisis of the West to be intellectual and not political or military is pointed out by Raymond Aron in his article comparing

Sartre and Solzhenitsyn. Sartre, the "ruler of minds," immersed himself in Leftist politics because he believed Marxism to be the "unsurpassable philosophy of our epoch" (Raymond Aron, "Alexander Solzhenitsyn and European 'Leftism,' " *Survey* 22, no. 3–4 [Summer / Autumn 1976]: 233–41.

Evidently, Solzhenitsyn is less influenced by the fashions of thought in our epoch. See his remarks to Western intellectuals in: *Warning*, p. 119; *Gulag II*, pp. 51n., 57n.; *Gulag III*, pp. xi, 328n; *Oak*, pp. 119n, 332; see also *Rubble*, pp. 229–79.

⁶⁴ For example, one Western intellectual, Melvin Gurtov, in criticizing Solzhenitsyn, proclaims, "Liberation is the critical problem of our time" (Melvin Gurtov, "Return to the Cold War," in Alexandr Solzhenitsyn, *Détente: Prospects for Democracy and Dictatorship* (New Brunswick, N.J.: Transaction Books, 1976), p. 77 (hereafter cited as *Détente*).

⁶⁵ For example, Francis Barker criticizes Solzhenitsyn for losing the "fierce egalitarianism" expressed in his early novels (*Solzhenitsyn: Politics and Form* [London: Macmillan, 1977], p. 1).

⁶⁶ For example, Lynn Turgeon held in 1977 that the Baltic areas were "flourishing" under Soviet rule and "never enjoyed comparable well-being" ("In Defense of Détente" in *Détente*, p. 79).

⁶⁷ *Warning*, pp. 65, 141. "We in the East," Solzhenitsyn says, "never applauded the hangman who appeared in the West. But the Western intelligentsia for decades applauded our hangman" (Alexander Solzhenitsyn, "Excerpts from a Press Conference," in *Posev* 12 [1974]: 2–10, quoted in Dunlop, "Exile," 136).

⁶⁸ *Warning*, p. 88. This trend does not include every intellectual in the West, of course. Solzhenitsyn claims to admire certain academics "who could do much for the renewal and salvation of [their] country." However, because of the "fashions of thinking" that sweep over Western democracies and because the ideas of such people tend to run against the "current" of thought, they are rarely given the opportunity to quietly, if persistently, evoke the light in people's minds. *East*, pp. 54–55.

⁶⁹ *East*, p. 44.

⁷⁰ Ibid., p. 62. See also a somewhat fuller account ibid., p. 46, and in *Warning*, pp. 130–31.

⁷¹ *Warning*, pp. 75–78, 81–84; *East*, p. 63.

⁷² *Mortal*, p. 70.

⁷³ See Immanuel Kant, *Critique of Pure Reason*, trans. F. Max Mueller (New York: Macmillan, 1957), and Immanuel Kant, *Fundamental Principles of the Metaphysics of Morals*, trans. Thomas K. Abbott (New York: Liberal Arts Press, 1940). Compare Tucker, *Marx Reader*, pp. 76–77, where Marx writes:

> Conscious life-activity directly distinguishes man from animal life-activity. . . . But an animal only produces what it immediately needs for itself or its young. It produces one-sidedly, whilst man produces universally. It produces only under the dominion

of immediate physical need, whilst man produces even when he is free from physical need and only truly produces in freedom therefrom. . . .

. . . in degrading spontaneous activity, free activity, to a means, estranged labor makes man's species life a means to his physical existence.

The consciousness which man has of his species is thus transformed by estrangement in such a way that the species life becomes for him a means.

Compare *August 1914,* chaps. 1–3, 5, 33, 42, 45; *Warning,* pp. 140, 142; *Gulag* I, p. 161; *First Circle,* pp. 396–98.

[74] *Rubble,* pp. 104–5.

[75] Michael Novak, "On God and Man," in Berman, *Solzhenitsyn at Harvard,* p. 135.

[76] *East,* p. 70.

[77] Ibid.

[78] Ibid., p. 71.

[79] Melvin Gurtov, "Return to the Cold War," in *Détente,* pp. 74–78; Richard Lowenthal, "The Prophet's Wrong Message," in *Détente,* pp. 87–88, 93–94; Norman Birnbaum, "Solzhenitsyn as Pseudo-Moralist," in *Détente,* p. 101; Ronald Berman, Introduction, in Berman, *Solzhenitsyn at Harvard,* p. xii; James Reston, "A Russian at Harvard," in Berman, *Solzhenitsyn at Harvard,* p. 39; Joseph Kraft, "Solzhenitsyn's Message," *Washington Post,* 3 July 1975, p. A23; "The Obsession of Solzhenitsyn," *New York Times,* 13 June 1978, editorial, p. A18.

[80] *Warning,* pp. 87–89.

[81] *Mortal,* p. 65.

[82] *Warning,* p. 119.

[83] *East,* pp. 62–63. There has been much debate about whether this generation has the right to decide what principles are worth defending, if that defense entails annihilating the race. Perhaps future generations will not think those principles so important. Solzhenitsyn maintains that the present generation should not sacrifice the spiritual life of their "children" merely to preserve their bodies. See *Rubble,* p. 249.

[84] *Warning,* p. 116; *East,* pp. 79–82.

[85] Henry Kissinger, *Years of Upheaval* (Boston: Little, Brown, 1982), pp. 986–88.

[86] See, for example, the statements of former Viet Cong leaders in Al Santoli, "Why the Viet Cong Flee," *Washington Post, Parade* section, 11 July 1982, pp. 1–6. They claim, among other things, that Vietnamese teenage women were shipped to the Soviet Union to work at forced labor as a repayment for Soviet arms and that Vietnam had its own Gulag of about 500,000 people. See also *Warning,* p. 25.

[87] *Warning,* pp. 28–29; "Artist as Witness," pp. 558, 561.

[88] *Warning,* p. 35.

[89] Delba Winthrop, "Solzhenitsyn Reconsidered II," *American Spectator* 13 (December 1980): 15.

[90] *Mortal*, pp. 33–34.

[91] Ibid., pp. 39, 58.

[92] *Warning*, pp. 26–27.

[93] Ibid., pp. 27, 91–96, 144.

[94] *East*, pp. 40, 42–44.

[95] Norman Podhoretz, "Why Can't You Call a Communist a Communist?" *Washington Post*, 16 March 1986, p. D8.

[96] *Warning*, p. 59.

[97] David Remnik, "Corrupt Soviet Uzbekistan Learns about 'Our Rotten History,'" *Washington Post*, 7 October 1988, pp. A1, A27. One of the most infamous incidents uncovered to date was the exposure of a vast network of corruption in Uzbekistan. During the Brezhnev era, the local party chief and his "mafia" were reported to have extorted and stolen four billion dollars. See also David Remnick, "Lenin's Errors Aired in Pages of *Pravda*," *Washington Post*, 30 December 1989, p. A12.

[98] Alexander Solzhenitsyn, "Three Key Moments in Modern Japanese History," trans. Michael Nicholson and Alexis Klimoff, *National Review* 81 (9 December 1983): 1536–37, 1540, 1544, 1546.

[99] *Warning*, pp. 103, 130. *National Review*, editorial, in Berman, *Solzhenitsyn at Harvard*, pp. 30–32. See also Scammell, *Solzhenitsyn*, p. 933.

[100] *East*, p. 44.

Chapter VII

[1] *Gulag III*, p. 350. As is the case with many of Solzhenitsyn's estimates, the numbers cited here are far higher than those usually given. He claims that the higher figures are more accurate since the true extent of Soviet brutality has never before been revealed. For an example of Solzhenitsyn's association of the spirited with the spiritual, see Alexander Solzhenitsyn, *A Lenten Letter to Pimen, Patriarch of All Russia*, trans. Keith Armes (Minneapolis: Burgess, 1972), and "Live Not by Lies." Scammell reports that Solzhenitsyn regards himself as "a sword" in the "Hand of the Highest" (Scammell, *Solzhenitsyn*, p. 769).

[2] *Gulag I*, p. 473; see also *Gulag III*, p. 49.

[3] *Gulag I*, pp. 49, 462.

[4] Ibid., p. 564; *Gulag III*, pp. 260, 263, 265, 320–23.

[5] *Gulag III*, pp. 119, 125–91, 210–17. Scammell, *Solzhenitsyn*, p. 291.

[6] "Live Not By Lies," p. A26.

[7] *East*, p. 61.

[8] Ibid., pp. 61–63.

[9] Carter, *Politics of Solzhenitsyn*, p. 137.

[10] *Warning*, p. 42.

[11] Ibid., pp. 41–44; *Gulag III*, p. xi; *Oak*, p. 197.

[12] Alexander Solzhenitsyn, "Speech before the AFL-CIO," 30 June 1975, quoted in Dunlop, "Exile," pp. 152–53. See also *Warning*, pp. 41–42.

[13] There is some evidence that Solzhenitsyn places himself in this group. He explains that prison "nourished his soul" (*Gulag II*, pp. 616–17). See also Scammell, *Solzhenitsyn*, p. 291.

[14] Ibid., pp. 310, 372–74.

[15] A student of Socrates, Nerzhin, loves ideas, but not as a means of changing the world. He is dedicated to contemplation (*First Circle*, p. 31).

[16] *Gulag I*, pp. 590–92.

[17] Ibid., p. 591.

[18] *Gulag II*, p. 619. Central to all Solzhenitsyn's novels is an ordeal of conscience. He portrays people, whether in their hospital bed, on the battlefield, or in the camps, at a spiritual juncture. It is as if, for the first time, the distractions and cares of everyday life were suspended and the more serious questions of life's meaning were thrust upon them. See, for example, *First Circle*, pp. 275, 340; *Cancer Ward*, pp. 93–105.

[19] *East*, p. 83.

[20] *Gulag I*, pp. 175–77; *Gulag II*, p. 273; see also *Gulag III*, p. 436.

[21] *Gulag I*, p. 225.

[22] Ibid., pp. 224, 484, 516, 560; *Gulag II*, pp. 522–23; *First Circle*, pp. 38–39, 95–96, 229, 340.

[23] *Gulag II*, pp. 489–91n.

[24] Actually he is quoting Shamalov in *Gulag II*, p. 623. See also Carter, *Politics of Solzhenitsyn*, p. 46.

[25] *Rubble*, p. 137.

[26] Fernand Braudel, *Les Structures du Quotidien: Le Possible et L'Impossible*, (Paris: Librairie Armand Colin, 1979), pp. 23–333.

[27] *Rubble*, pp. 106–7, 123.

[28] Ibid., pp. 106–7, 136–42; *East*, pp. 176–77; *Warning*, pp. 79, 133.

[29] As Solzhenitsyn notes in *Rubble*, p. 106.

[30] Winthrop, "Solzhenitsyn: Emerging," p. 14.

[31] Barker asserts, however, that a small technology would codify existing social and economic inequalities (Barker, *Solzhenitsyn*, pp. 61–62). Barker's prediction may be true enough, but that does not necessarily condemn Solzhenitsyn's proposal. Barker judges political societies on the basis of how egalitarian they are. But if people could lead a satisfying life in which neither scarcity nor pollution threatens them, what need would they have of social equality? Furthermore, since nature has not given us comparable abilities, there can never be equality in the most important sense.

Yet there is a deeper sense in which Solzhenitsyn's desire for a small technology might be criticized. Limitations on technology rest, to a large extent, on a nation's ability to curtail the international arms race. If competition exists to build ever-more-modern armaments, then necessity compels nations to (1) discover new technologies, (2) sustain scientific investigations, and (3) maintain an industrial base capable of supporting arms production. Will not the new inventions of technology and the new discoveries of science be used to establish a consumer society in which those who produce using economies of scale will have an advantage? Given that human beings normally choose the most cost-effective products, large industries seem inevitable.

32 *East*, pp. 95–101.

33 *Rubble*, pp. 107–11.

34 Ibid., p. 128.

35 Ibid., pp. 120, 127.

36 Ibid., pp. 115, 129, 133; Winthrop, "Solzhenitsyn: Emerging," p. 15.

37 *Rubble*, p. 142.

38 Ibid., pp. 120, 127, 137.

39 Ibid., p. 137.

40 Ibid., pp. 113, 128–32.

41 Ibid., p. 104.

42 Alexander Solzhenitsyn, "Letter from Solzhenitsyn to Three Students," in Leopold Labedz, *Solzhenitsyn: A Documentary Record* (London: Penguin Press, 1970), p. 101. Perhaps morality is not so easily derived from simple feelings of conscience. Human hearts are sometimes troubled by irregular rhythms and eventually stop altogether. Nonetheless, the analogy may have been sufficient to satisfy the three students to whom it was addressed.

43 *Rubble*, p. 105.

44 Sidney Hook writes that Solzhenitsyn's "profoundest error" is his insistence that "moral responsibility derive[s] from belief in a Supreme Being, and that erosion of religious faith spells the end of moral decency." Hook reasons that "morality is logically independent of religion as Augustine, Kierkegaard and the authors of *The Book of Job* well knew" (Sidney Hook, "Solzhenitsyn and Secular Humanism: A Response," *Humanist* 38 [November / December 1978]: 5).

Morality may be independent of religion, but what Solzhenitsyn recognizes and Hook fails to consider is the mechanism by which morality is inculcated. How many people will take morality seriously if it rests on a mere supposition concerning the nature of existence? If some people create morality for themselves, others can choose to disregard it. The human race needs firmer ground from which to counteract the evil tendencies within it. Although organized religion has been, at times, the worst offender of its own principles, at the very least it has taught that there are proper limits to human actions. For generations those limits, though often breached in practice, served as a bulwark against our baser instincts. Has rationalistic humanism had any greater success? Its age has been the twentieth century, when, Hook's assertions to the contrary notwithstanding, its ideals have been applied to society. The result has been to undermine the belief that any limits are needed on humanity.

45 "A Journey along the Oka," in *Stories*, pp. 214–15; *Gulag II*, pp. 613–15; Clement, *Spirit of Solzhenitsyn*, pp. 227–28.

46 He talks about religious people in the camps, but he never places himself among them. *Gulag II*, p. 612.

47 Both Winthrop ("Solzhenitsyn: Emerging") and Charles Kesler ("Up from

Modernity," in Berman, *Solzhenitsyn at Harvard*) make strong and often convincing arguments that Solzhenitsyn's ideas show a marked similarity to those of classical philosophy. There is some evidence to the contrary, however. First, Solzhenitsyn claims that only a fool would wish to go backwards. By this I gather he means that the Enlightenment let the jinni of scientific knowledge out of its figurative bottle. Humanity has passed through the modern era, an experience that, at least in part, has enriched it. As if to attest to this enrichment, he accepts what the ancients rejected, technology (compare Aristotle, *Politics*, 1253b 20–23). The development of even a small technology needs an openness to scientific discovery. It also requires the publication of the kind of information that may have cost an ancient his life (Aristophanes, *Clouds*, trans. Thomas G. West and Stacy Starry West [Ithaca, N.Y.: Cornell University Press, 1984]).

Solzhenitsyn's acceptance of technology may be dismissed as a minor, if necessary, concession to contemporary life. There are, however, deeper problems raised by an unqualified alignment of Solzhenitsyn with the camp of classical philosophy. He is, of course, not a philosopher but an artist. "Through art," he writes, "we occasionally receive—indistinctly, briefly—revelations the likes of which cannot be achieved by rational thought" (*East*, p. 6).

Finally, he gives no argument about why life is purposive, no account of the whole, and no cosmological argument, except that which presupposes a "Supreme Complete Entity" (which he unashamedly refers to as God, elsewhere).

Winthrop's claim that the philosophic pursuits and artistic creativity give meaning to Solzhenitsyn's life (if not to life itself) is difficult to dismiss. (Winthrop "Solzhenitsyn: Emerging" p. 23; Winthrop, "Solzhenitsyn Reconsidered II," p. 14. See also *Gulag I*, pp. 145, 181, 193, 225, 271, 444, 595; *Gulag II*, pp. 597, 606–7, 611; *Gulag III*, pp. 66, 104; *First Circle*, pp. 31, 33, 39–43, 47, 78–79, 157, 449; *Oak*, p. 146; *Cancer Ward*, pp. 427–28.) Yet sometimes Solzhenitsyn admits to praying (*Gulag III*, p. 104); and uses his artistic skills to create poems about, and even to, God (*Gulag II*, pp. 614–15; Alexander Solzhenitsyn, "Prayer," *Time*, 3 April 1972, p. 31). Nielson suggests that Solzhenitsyn is not a Christian but a Theist (Niels C. Nielson, Jr., *Solzhenitsyn's Religion* [Nashville: Thomas Nelson, 1975], pp. 25–26, 40–41). See also Roy H. Donald, "Solzhenitsyn's Religious Teaching," *Faith and Reason* 7, no. 4 (1981): 305–19.

Scammell reports that Solzhenitsyn does not attend Orthodox services regularly, despite the fact that the rest of his family does (Scammell, *Solzhenitsyn*, pp. 991–92; also p. 769). Alexander Schmemann calls Solzhenitsyn "a Christian writer." He says this despite the fact that Solzhenitsyn may be a "non-believer." Schmemann "humbly asserts" that the "official declarations" of an author are not "a trustworthy test to qualify his work as essentially Christian" (Schmemann, "On Solzhenitsyn," in Dunlop, *Critical Essays*, pp. 39, 44).

Solzhenitsyn responded to Schmemann's essay. He stated that the article "was very valuable to me. It explained me to myself. . . . It also formulated important traits of Christianity which I could not have otherwise formulated myself." (Solzhenitsyn quoted in Dunlop, *Critical Essays*, p. 44). This from a person who does everything "according to plan" (*Oak*, p. 180).

At one point he writes, "Justice has been the common patrimony of humanity throughout the ages. . . . Obviously it is a concept inherent in man, since it cannot be traced to any other source. . . . The love of justice seems to me to be a different sentiment from the love of people (or at least the two coincide only partially)" (Solzhenitsyn quoted in Labedz, *Solzhenitsyn*, p. 110). Which is of greater worth, love of people or justice? Compare Matt. 5:21–26; Matt. 22:38–40; Mark 12:31–34; Luke 11:24–37; John 13:31–35; 1 John 3:29; 1 John 5:7–21; 2 John 1:5–6.

Solzhenitsyn was asked in an interview to clear up the whole matter. He was asked directly: "Are you a Christian?" Alluding to his earlier remarks in which he stated that he was not a socialist, but, while in the Soviet Union, "had to be careful and express" himself "as indirectly as possible," he chose to respond. "I think that question is even clearer from my books than the one asked here about a socialist world view" ("Solzhenitsyn Speaks Out," p. 609).

Indeed, he may be like Silin (*Gulag III*, 107–9). But also see his argument, in the middle of the central volume of his major work on Marxism, concerning the way in which Christianity can be used as a weapon against Communism (*Gulag II*, 370–74). See also *East*, p. 180; *A Lenten Letter to Pimen, Patriarch of All Russia*, p. 6.

[48] Kesler, "Up from Modernity," in Berman, *Solzhenitsyn at Harvard*, p. 55.

[49] *Warning*, p. 45.

[50] *Gulag I*, p. 226; *Gulag II*, p. 611; *First Circle*, pp. 42, 340, 370; *Rubble*, pp. 22, 109; *Mortal*, p. 61.

[51] *East*, p. 4. Evidently, Solzhenitsyn objects to Nietzsche's philosophy, as well as to that of Marx, although perhaps not as strongly. It seems he rejects Nietzsche's attempt to create a wholly human ground for nobility. For Solzhenitsyn human life has purpose only if that purpose is beyond mere survival. Nietzsche's endeavor to raise man above himself has not always borne the intended fruit.

[52] *Gulag I*, pp. 145, 595; *Gulag II*, pp. 597, 607; *Gulag III*, p. 66, 104; *Oak*, p. 494; *First Circle*, p. 104.

[53] *August 1914*, p. 472.

[54] Ibid., pp. 474–75. Carter (*Politics of Solzhenitsyn*, p. 71) notes that this is an attack on Rousseau. But Hegel and Tolstoy are mentioned in the chapter. Solzhenitsyn seems intent on formulating a notion of history somewhere between the two extremes of complete wisdom (Hegel) and utter ignorance (Tolstoy). See Raymond J. Wilson III, "Solzhenitsyn's *August 1914* and *Lenin in Zurich*: A Question of Historical Determinism," *CLIO* 14, no. 1 (Fall 1984): 15–36.

[55] This is why he claims that Communism attempted to destroy the heart of national cultures.

[56] *August 1914*, pp. 473–74. See also *Gulag III*, p. 477.

[57] For instance, Solzhenitsyn makes a great deal of the wisdom contained in Russian folk proverbs (*Mortal*, pp. 11–12).

[58] In sum, he objects to the historicism implicit in attempting to base a community solely on the traditions of the past. Compare, for example, Solzhenitsyn's

position with that of the English philosopher Edmund Burke, *Reflections on the Revolution in France*. Critics of Solzhenitsyn were surprised to discover that he "was not in the tradition of Milton, Paine, Mill, Jefferson, and 'not even' of Edmund Burke" (Scammell, *Solzhenitsyn*, p. 917).

[59] *Mortal*, pp. 61–62; *Rubble*, p. 274.

[60] *Gulag* I, p. 226; *Gulag* II, p. 611; *First Circle*, pp. 42, 340, 370.

[61] *August 1914*, p. 473.

[62] *Mortal*, p. 64.

[63] The oppression of the church was more difficult in places, such as Poland, where it was very powerful.

[64] *Rubble*, p. 22.

[65] Ibid.

[66] Ibid., p. 23; *East*, pp. 123–24; "Solzhenitsyn Speaks Out," p. 608.

[67] *Mortal*, p. 60.

[68] Ibid.; *Rubble*, pp. 20–21; *East*, pp. 130–34. These objections are particularly difficult to comprehend for those who accept democracy as *the* political standard. Because Solzhenitsyn is guided by a standard higher than any in political life, he is able to criticize every type of existing government.

[69] *East*, pp. 23, 135; *Oak*, p. 460; *Gulag* III, pp. 81, 92–93; "Live Not by Lies"; *Mortal*, p. 62.

[70] "Matryona's House," in *Stories*, pp. 1–42. In his own country he favors: the abandonment of Marxism; the retention of an authoritarian nationalist state; the institution of government by laws, of civil and religious liberties, and of the separation of powers; the development of Siberia instead of the support of client states; and the husbanding of Russia's natural resources (see *East*, pp. 75–142, 181; *Rubble*, pp. 21, 135–41; *Mortal*, pp. 55–62; *Warning*, p. 107. Scammell, *Solzhenitsyn*, pp. 883–84).

[71] *Warning*, p. 17.

[72] Alexander Hamilton, John Jay, and James Madison, *The Federalist Papers* (New York: Modern Library, n.d.), Federalist no. 10, p. 56.

[73] Ibid., p. 101.

[74] Tocqueville, *Democracy in America*, p. 680.

Selected Bibliography

Books and Collections of Essays by Solzhenitsyn

Solzhenitsyn, Alexander. *Arkhipelag Gulag: Parts I–VII.* Paris: YMCA, 1973, 1974, 1976.

———. *August 1914,* translated by Michael Glenny. New York: Bantam, 1974.

———. *August 1914: The Red Wheel,* translated by H. T. Willets. New York: Noonday Press, 1989.

———. *Avgust Chetyrnadtsatovo.* London: Flegon Press, 1971.

———. *Bodalsya telyonok s dubom.* Paris: YMCA, 1975.

———. *Candle in the Wind,* translated by Keith Armes. New York: Bantam, 1974.

———. *Cancer Ward,* translated by Nicholas Bethell and David Burg. New York: Bantam, 1969.

———. *Détente: Prospects for Democracy and Dictatorship.* New Brunswick, N.J.: Transactions, Inc., 1976.

———. *East and West,* translated by Alexis Klimoff and Hillary Sternberg. New York: Harper & Row, 1980.

———. *The First Circle,* translated by Thomas P. Whitney. New York: Bantam, 1968.

———, Mikhail Agursky, A. B., Evgeny Barabanov, Vadim Borisov, F. Korsakov, and Igor Shafarevich, *From under the Rubble,* translated by A. M. Brock, Milada Haigh, Marita Sapiets, Hilary Sternberg, and Harry Willetts under the direction of Michael Scammell. Boston: Little, Brown, 1975.

———. *The Gulag Archipelago,* translated by Thomas P. Whitney. New York: Harper & Row, 1973.

———. *The Gulag Archipelago II*, translated by Thomas P. Whitney. New York: Harper & Row, 1975.

———. *The Gulag Archipelago III*, translated by Harry Willetts. New York: Harper & Row, 1978.

———. *Iz pod glyb*. Paris: YMCA, 1975.

———. *Lenin in Zurich*, translated by Harry Willetts. New York: Farrar, Straus and Giroux, 1976.

———. *Lenin v Tsyurikhe*. Paris: YMCA, 1975.

———. *Lenten Letter to Pimen, Patriarch of All Russia*, translated by Keith Armes. Minneapolis: Burgess, 1972.

———. *The Love Girl and the Innocent*, translated by Nicholas Bethell and David Burg. New York: Farrar, Straus and Giroux, 1969.

———. *Matrenin dvor*. London: Flegon, 1965.

———. *Mir i Nasilie*. Frankfurt: Possev, 1974.

———. *The Mortal Danger*, translated by Michael Nicholson and Alexis Klimoff. New York: Harper & Row, 1980.

———. *The Oak and the Calf*, translated by Harry Willetts. New York: Harper and Row, 1979.

———. *One Day in the Life of Ivan Denisovich*, translated by Max Hayward and Ronald Hingley. New York: Bantam, 1963.

———. *Pismo Vozhdyam Sovetskovo Soyuza*. Paris: YMCA, 1974.

———. *Prussian Nights*, translated by Robert Conquest. New York: Farrar, Straus and Giroux, 1977.

———. *Sobranie Sochinevii*, 6 vols. Frankfurt: Possev, 1970.

———. *Stories and Prose Poems*, translated by Michael Glenny. New York: Bantam, 1972.

———. *Warning to the West*, translated by Harris Coulter, Nataly Martin, and Alexis Klimoff. New York: Farrar, Straus and Giroux, 1976.

———. *We Never Make Mistakes*, translated by Paul W. Blackstone. New York: W. W. Norton, 1963.

Articles and Interviews by Solzhenitsyn

Solzhenitsyn, Alexander. "The Artist as Witness," translated by Michael Glenny. *Times Literary Supplement*, 23 May 1975, pp. 561–62.

———. "Brezhnev Cannot Look a Priest in the Eye." *Christianity Today* 24 (6 June 1980): 13.

———. "Communism at the End of the Brezhnev Era," translated by Alexis Klimoff. *National Review*, 21 January 1983, pp. 28–34.

———. "Live Not by Lies." *Washington Post*, 18 February 1974, pp. A26.

———. "Prayer." *Time*, 3 April 1972, p. 31.

———. "Our Pluralists." *Survey* 29, no. 2 (Summer 1985): 1–28.

———. "Sakharov i kritika 'Pisma vozhdyam.'" *Kontinent* 2 (1975): 350–59.

———. "Schlesinger and Kissinger," translated by Raymond H. Anderson. *New York Times*, 1 December 1975, p. 31.

———. "Solzhenitsyn on Communism," translated by Alexis Klimoff. *Time*, 18 February 1980, pp. 48–49.

———. "Solzhenitsyn Speaks Out," translated by Albert and Tayna Schmidt. *National Review* 27 (6 June 1975): 603–9.

———. "Solzhenitsyn Speaks Out on Poland." *Cleveland Plain Dealer*, 24 January 1982, pp. 2AA, 7AA.

———. "The Third World War Has Ended." *National Review* 27 (20 June 1975): 652.

———. "Those Who Would Disarm." *Washington Post*, 28 June 1983, p. A15.

———. "Three Key Moments in Modern Japanese History," translated by Michael Nicholson and Alexis Klimoff. *National Review* 81 (9 December 1983): 1536–46.

Books and Commentary about Solzhenitsyn

Allaback, Stephen. *Alexander Solzhenitsyn*. New York: Taplinger Publishing, 1978.

Barker, Francis. *Solzhenitsyn: Politics and Form*. London: Macmillan, 1971.

Beglov, S., et al. *The Last Circle*. Moscow: Novosti, 1971.

Berman, Ronald, ed. *Solzhenitsyn at Harvard*. Washington, D.C.: Ethics and Public Policy Center, 1980.

Bjorkegren, Hans. *Alexander Solzhenitsyn: A Biography*, translated by Kaarina Eneberg. New York: Joseph Okpalu, 1972.

Bosquet, Alain. *Pas d'accord Soljenitsyne!* Paris: Filipacchi, 1974.

Burg, David, and George Feifer. *Solzhenitsyn*. New York: Stein and Day, 1972.

Carlisle, Olga. *Solzhenitsyn and the Secret Circle*. New York: Holt, Rinehart, and Winston, 1978.

Carpovich, Vera V. *Solzhenitsyn's Peculiar Vocabulary: Russian-English Dictionary*. New York: Technical Dictionary Co., 1976.

Carter, Stephen. *The Politics of Solzhenitsyn*. New York: Holmes and Meier, 1977.

Clardy, Jesse V. *The Superfluous Man of Russian Letters*. Washington, D.C.: University Press of America, 1980.

Clement, Oliver. *The Spirit of Solzhenitsyn*, translated by Sarah Fawcett and Paul Burns. London: Search Press Ltd., 1976.

Curtis, James M. *Solzhenitsyn's Traditional Imagination*. Athens: University of Georgia Press, 1984.

Daix, Pierre. *Ce Que Je Sais de Soljenitsyn*. Paris: Editions du Seuil, 1973.

Dunlop, John, Richard Haugh, and Alexis Klimoff, eds. *Alexander Solzhenitsyn: Critical Essays and Documentary Materials*. Belmont, Mass.: Nordland, 1975.

Dunlop, John, Richard Haugh, and Michael Nicholson, eds. *Solzhenitsyn in Ex-*

ile: Critical Essays and Documentary Materials. Stanford, Calif.: Hoover Institution Press, 1985.

Ericson, Edward E., Jr. *Solzhenitsyn: The Moral Vision.* Grand Rapids, Mich.: William B. Eerdmans, 1980.

Feuer, Kathryn, ed. *Solzhenitsyn: A Collection of Critical Essays.* Englewood Cliffs, N.J.: Prentice Hall, 1976.

Freeborn, Richard, Georgette Donchin, and N. J. Anning. *Russian Literary Attitudes from Pushkin to Solzhenitsyn.* New York: Barnes & Noble, 1976.

Galler, Meyer. *Soviet Prison Camp Speech: A Survivor's Glossary.* Supplemented by terms from the works of A. I. Solzhenitsyn. Madison: University of Wisconsin Press, 1972.

Grazzini, Giovanni. *Solzhenitsyn,* translated by Eric Mosbacher. London: Michael Joseph, 1973.

Kelley, Donald R. *The Solzhenitsyn-Sakharov Dialogue.* Westport, Conn.: Greenwood Press, 1982.

Kodjak, Andrej. *Alexander Solzhenitsyn.* Boston: G. K. Hall and Co., 1978.

Kovaly Pavel. *Rehumanization or Dehumanization?* Boston: Branden Press, 1974.

Krasnov, Vladislav. *Solzhenitsyn and Dostoevsky: A Study of the Polyphonic Novel.* Athens: University of Georgia Press, 1980.

Labedz, Leopold, ed. *Solzhenitsyn: A Documentary Record.* London: Penguin Press, 1970.

Lefort, Claude. *Un Homme en Trop: Reflexions sur "L'archipel du Goulag."* Paris: Editions du Seuil, 1976.

Lukàcs, Georg. *Solzhenitsyn,* translated by William D. Graf. London: Merlin Press, 1969.

Medvedev, Zhores A. *Ten Years after Ivan Denisovich,* translated by Hilary Sternberg. New York: Random House, 1974.

Nielson, Niels C., Jr. *Solzhenitsyn's Religion.* Nashville: Thomas Nelson, 1975.

Panachas, George, ed. *The Politics of Twentieth-Century Novelists.* New York: T. Y. Crowell, 1974.

Pomorska, Krystyna, ed. *Fifty Years of Russian Prose: From Pasternak to Solzhenitsyn.* Cambridge: MIT, 1971.

Reshetovskaya, Natalya A. *Sanya: My Life with Alexander Solzhenitsyn,* translated by Elena Ivanoff. Indianapolis: Bobbs-Merrill, 1975.

Rothberg, Abraham. *Alexander Solzhenitsyn: The Major Novels.* Ithaca, N.Y.: Cornell University Press, 1971.

Rzhevsky, Leonid. *Solzhenitsyn: Creator of Heroic Deeds.* University, Ala.: University of Alabama Press, 1978.

Scammell, Michael. *Solzhenitsyn: A Biography.* New York: W. W. Norton, 1984.

Ulam, Adam B. *Ideologies and Illusions: Revolutionary Thought from Herzen to Solzhenitsyn.* Cambridge: Harvard University Press, 1976.

Weerakoon, R. *Alexander Solzhenitsyn: Soldier, Prisoner, Writer.* Colombo, Ceylon: Gunaratne & Co., 1972.

Yakovlev, N. *Solzhenitsyn's Archipelago of Lies.* Moscow: Novosti, 1974.

Articles and Commentary about Solzhenitsyn

Allen, James. "Solzhenitsyn's Vision of the Reconstruction of East and West." B.A. honors thesis, Kenyon College, 1982.

Aron, Raymond. "Alexander Solzhenitsyn and European 'Leftism.'" *Survey* 22, no. 3 / 4 (Summer / Autumn, 1976): 233–41.

Aurich, P. "Solzhenitsyn's Political Philosophy." *Nation* 219 (October 1974): 273–74.

Buckley, William F., Jr. "Continuing Presence of Solzhenitsyn." *National Review* 28 (15 October 1976): 1140–41.

———. "Estrangement of Solzhenitsyn." *National Review* 30 (21 July 1978): 913.

———. "Solzhenitsyn v. Kissinger." *National Review* 28 (23 October 1976): 53.

Burnham, James. "The Logic of Détente." *National Review* 27 (15 August 1975): 873.

Casillo, Robert. "Techne and Logos in Solzhenitsyn." *Soundings* 70, no. 3–4 (Fall-Winter 1987): 519–37.

Clardy, Jesse V., and Betty Clardy. "Solzhenitsyn's Ideas of the Ultimate Reality." *Ultimate Reality and Meaning* 1 (1978): 202–22.

Davies, R. W., and S. G. Wheatcraft. "Steven Rosefielde's *Kliukua.*" *Slavic Review* 39 (December 1980): 593–602.

Diakin, Nadia Odette. "Solzhenitsyn's *First Circle.*" *Explicator* 42 (Fall 1983): 59–61.

Donald, Roy H. "Solzhenitsyn's Religious Teaching." *Faith and Reason* 7 (Winter 1981): 305–19.

Dunlop, John. "Solzhenitsyn in Exile." *Survey* 21 (Summer 1975): 133–53.

———. "The Almost Rehabilitation and Re-Anathematization of Alexandr Solzhenitsyn." Working paper, Hoover Institution, Stanford University, February 1989.

Fairlie, Henry. "Mother Russia's Prodigal Son." *New Republic,* 29 July 1978, pp. 18–20.

Feifer, George. "The Dark Side of Solzhenitsyn." *Harpers* 260 (May 1980): 48–51.

Gleason, Abbott. "Solzhenitsyn and the Slavophiles." *Yale Review* 65 (Autumn 1975): 61–70.

Grey, Paul. "Russia's Prophet in Exile." *Time,* 24 July 1989, pp. 56–60.

Hallet, Richard. "Beneath the Closed Visor: Dimitry Panin and the Two Faces of Sologdin in Solzhenitsyn's *First Circle.*" *Modern Language Review* 78 (April 1983): 365–74.

Halperin, David M. "Solzhenitsyn, Epicures, and the Ethics of Stalinism." *Critical Inquiry* 7 (Spring 1981): 475–97.

Heller, Michael. "The Gulag Archipelago and Its Inhabitants." *Survey* 20 (Summer 1974): 211–27.

———. "*The Gulag Archipelago* vol. 2: Life and Death in the Camps." *Survey* 20 (Autumn 1974): 152–66.

———. "Lenin, Parvus, and Solzhenitsyn." *Survey* 21 (Autumn 1975): 188–94.

———. "Survivors from Utopia." *Survey* 23 (Autumn 1977): 155–65.

———. "Yesterday and Today in Solzhenitsyn's *The Red Wheel*." *Survey* 29 (Summer 1985): 29–45.

Hook, Sidney. "Solzhenitsyn and Secular Humanism: A Response." *Humanist* 38 (November / December 1978): 4–6.

Howe, Irving. "Open Letter to Solzhenitsyn." *New Republic* 182 (3 May 1980): 18–19.

Hunter, Holland. "The Economic Cost of the *Gulag Archipelago*." *Slavic Review* 39 (December 1980): 588–92.

Jatras, James George. "Solzhenitsyn and the Liberals." *Modern Age* 28 (Spring 1985): 143–52.

Jones, Jack. "Solzhenitsyn's Warning: A Secular Reinterpretation." *Chicago Review* 32 (Winter 1981): 141–64.

Johnson, Paul. "Solzhenitsyn: Hero of Our Time." *Washington Post Book World*, 2 September 1984, pp. 1, 11.

Kennan, George. "Between Heaven and Hell." *New York Review of Books*, 21 March 1974, pp. 3–7.

Kerns, Gary. "Solzhenitsyn's Portrait of Stalin." *Slavic Review* 33 (Autumn 1974): 1–22.

Kraft, Joseph. "Solzhenitsyn's Message." *Washington Post*, 3 July 1975, p. A23.

Kramer, Hilton. "Solzhenitsyn in Vermont." *New York Times Review of Books*, 11 May 1980, pp. 3, 30–32.

Krasnov, Vladislav. "The Social Vision of Alexandr Solzhenitsyn." *Modern Age* 28 (Spring-Summer 1984): 215–21.

———. "Wrestling with Lev Tolstoi: War, Peace, and Revolution in Alexandr Solzhenitsyn's New *Avgust Chetyrnadtsatovo*." *Slavic Review* 45 (Winter 1986): 707–19.

Kuhn, Harold. "Solzhenitsyn and Some Spiritual Implications." *Christianity Today* 23 (3 November 1978): 55–56.

Laber, Jeri. "The Real Solzhenitsyn." *Commentary* 37 (May 1974): 32–35.

Lukacs, John. "What Solzhenitsyn Means." *Commonweal* 102 (1 August 1975): 269–300.

Medvedev, Roy. "Solzhenitsyn's *Gulag Archipelago II*," translated by Georg Saunders. *Dissent* 23–24 (Summer 1974): 155–63.

Mills, Richard, and Judith Mills. "Solzhenitsyn's Cry to the Soviet Leaders." *Commonweal* 100 (9 August 1974): 433–36.

Morganthau, Hans. "What Solzhenitsyn Doesn't Understand." *New Leader* 61 (3 July 1978): 12–13.

Morris, Roger. "Solzhenitsyn with a Grain of Salt." *New Republic* 173 (16 August 1975): 310–12.

Mudrich, Marvin. "Solzhenitsyn versus the Last Revolutionary." *The Hudson Review* 34 (Summer 1981): 195–217.

Muggeridge, John. Review of *Solzhenitsyn: A Biography* by Michael Scammell. *American Spectator*, 8 August 1985, p. 31.

Niemeyer, Gerhardt. "The Eternal Meaning of Solzhenitsyn." *National Review* 25 (19 January 1973): 83–86.

Oja, Matt F. "Shamalov, Solzhenitsyn, and the Mission of Memory." *Survey* 29 (Summer 1985): 62–69.

Perlinski, Jerome. "Solzhenitsyn's Spirituality." *Christian Century* 95 (27 September 1978): 901–2.

Podhoretz, Norman. "The Terrible Question of Alexandr Solzhenitsyn." *Commentary* (February 1985): 17–24.

Purcell, Brendan. "Solzhenitsyn's Struggle for Personal, Social, and Historical Anamnesis." *Philosophic Studies* 28 (n.d.): 62–82.

Rancour-Laferriere, Daniel. "The Deranged Birthday Boy: Solzhenitsyn's Portrait of Stalin." *Mosaic* 18 (Summer 1985): 61–72.

Remnick, David. "'Ivan Denisovich' Returns." *Washington Post,* 21 November 1989, p. D1.

———. "Solzhenitsyn—A New Day in the Life." *Washington Post,* 7 January 1990, p. B3.

———. "Solzhenitsyn Denies Talking with Soviets." *Washington Post,* 28 June 1988, p. A10.

———. "Soviet Journal to Publish Solzhenitsyn." *Washington Post,* 21 April 1989, pp. C1, C9.

———. "Witness to the Gulag." *Washington Post,* 9 July 1989, p. B7.

Rosefielde, Steven. "The First 'Great Leap Forward' Reconsidered: Lessons of the *Gulag Archipelago.*" *Slavic Review* 39 (December 1980): 559–87.

Shin, Un-chol. "Conscience, Lie, and Suffering in Solzhenitsyn's *The First Circle.*" *Modern Age* 29 (Fall 1985): 344–52.

Siegal, Paul N. "Solzhenitsyn's Portrait of Lenin." *CLIO* 14 (Fall 1984): 1–13.

Trueheart, Charles. "Solzhenitsyn and His Message of Silence." *Washington Post,* 24 November 1987, pp. D1, D4.

Wilson, Raymond J., III. "Solzhenitsyn's *August 1914* and *Lenin in Zurich*: A Question of Historical Determinism." *CLIO* 14, no. 1 (Fall 1984): 15–36.

Winthrop, Delba. "Solzhenitsyn: Emerging from under the Rubble." Paper presented at the annual meeting of the American Political Science Association, New York, August 1978.

———. "Solzhenitsyn: Emerging from under the Rubble." *Independent Journal of Philosophy* 4 (1983): 91–101.

———. "Solzhenitsyn Reconsidered II." *American Spectator* 13 (December 1980): 14–16.

Wood, Alan. "Solzhenitsyn on the Tsarist Exile System: A Historical Comment." *Journal of Russian Studies* 42 (1981): 39–43.

Yarup, Robert L. "Solzhenitsyn's *One Day in the Life of Ivan Denisovich.*" *Explicator* 40 (Spring 1982): 61–63.

General Bibliography

Allen, James. *No Citation.* London: Angus & Robertson, 1955.

Alliluyeva, Svetlana. *Twenty Letters to a Friend.* New York: Harper & Row, 1967.

Amalrik, Andrei. *Notes of a Revolutionary,* translated by Guy Daniels. New York: Alfred Knopf, 1982.

———. *Will the Soviet Union Survive until 1984?* translated by Peter Reddaway. London: Pelican Books, 1980.

Andies, Helmut. *Rule of Terror,* translated by A. Lieven. New York: Holt, Rinehart & Winston, 1969.

Arendt, Hannah. *The Origins of Totalitarianism.* New York: Harcourt, Brace & World, 1968.

Aristophanes. *Clouds,* translated by Thomas G. West and Stacy Starry West. Ithaca, N.Y.: Cornell University Press, 1984.

Aristotle. *Nichmachean Ethics,* translated by J. A. K. Thompson. Middlesex, England: Penguin Books, 1955.

———. *Politics,* translated by Carnes Lord. Chicago: University of Chicago Press, 1984.

Aron, Raymond. *Marxism and the Existentialists,* translated by Helen Weaver, Robert Addis, and John Weightman. New York: Simon and Schuster, 1970.

Avineri, Shlomo. *The Social and Political Thought of Karl Marx.* Cambridge: Cambridge University Press, 1968.

Balabanoff, Angelica. *Impressions of Lenin.* Ann Arbor: University of Michigan Press, 1968.

Beck, R., and W. Godin. *Russian Purge.* London: Hurst & Balckett, 1951.

Berdyaev, Nicholas. *The Origins of Russian Communism.* Ann Arbor: University of Michigan Press, 1972.

Billington, James. *The Icon and the Axe.* New York: Vintage Books, 1970.

Braudel, Fernand. *Les Structures du Quotidien: Le Possible et L'Impossible.* Paris: Librairie Armand Colin, 1979.

Brown, Edward. *Russian Literature since the Revolution.* New York: Collier Books, 1969.

Brzezinski, Zbigniew. *The Permanent Purge.* Cambridge: Harvard University Press, 1956.

Bukovsky, Vladimir. *To Build a Castle,* translated by Michael Scammell. New York: Viking Press, 1978.

Burke, Edmund. *Reflections on the Revolution in France.* New Rochelle, N.Y.: Arlington House, 1966.

Carr, Edward H. *The Bolshevik Revolution: 1917–1923.* New York: Macmillan, 1951.

Ceaser, James W. *Presidential Selection: Theory and Development.* Princeton: Princeton University Press, 1979.

Cherniavsky, Michael. *Tsar and People: Studies in Russian Myth.* New York: Random House, 1969.

Conquest, Robert. *The Great Terror.* New York: Macmillan, 1968.

———. *Kolyma: The Arctic Death*. New York: Viking Press, 1976.

———. *Power and Policy in the U.S.S.R.* New York: Harper and Row, 1967.

Cracraft, James, ed. *The Soviet Union Today*. Chicago: University of Chicago Press, 1987.

Cropsey, Joseph. *Political Philosophy and the Issues of Politics*. Chicago: University of Chicago Press, 1977.

Dallin, Alexander, and W. Breslauer. *Political Terror in Communist Systems*. Stanford, Calif.: Stanford University Press, 1970.

Dallin, Alexander, and Alan Westin. *Politics in the Soviet Union*. New York: Harcourt, Brace & World, 1966.

Dante. *The Divine Comedy,* translated by Dorothy Sayers, New York: Penguin, 1949.

Deutscher, Isaac. *The Unfinished Revolution: Russia, 1917–1967*. Oxford: Oxford University Press, 1975.

Dostoevsky, Fydor. *The Devils,* translated by David Magarshack. New York: Penguin, 1953.

———. *The House of the Dead,* translated by Constance Garnett. New York: Dell, 1959.

Easton, Lloyd, and Kurt Guddat, eds. and trans. *Writings of the Young Marx on Philosophy and History*. Garden City, N.Y.: Doubleday, 1976.

Etkind, Efim. *Notes of a Non-conspirator,* translated by Peter France. Oxford: Oxford University Press, 1978.

Fainsod, Merle. *Smolensk under Soviet Rule*. New York: Vintage Books, 1958.

Fanon Frantz. *Wretched of the Earth,* translated by Constance Farrington. New York: Grove Press, 1968.

Fleron, Frederick, ed. *Communist Studies and the Social Sciences*. Chicago: Rand McNally, 1969.

Fremantle, Anne, ed. *Mao Tse-tung: An Anthology of His Writings*. New York: New American Library, 1962.

Friedrich, Carl, and Zbigniew Brzezinski. *Totalitarian Dictatorship and Autocracy*. Cambridge: Harvard University Press, 1956.

Fromm, Erich. *Marx's Concept of Man*. New York: Ungar, 1961.

Germino, Dante. *Beyond Ideology*. Chicago: University of Chicago Press, 1976.

———. *Machiavelli to Marx*. Chicago: University of Chicago Press, 1979.

Ginzburg, Euginia. *Journey into the Whirlwind*. New York: Harcourt, Brace & World, 1967.

Goldman, Marshall. *Gorbachev's Challenge*. New York: W. W. Norton, 1987.

Gorbachev, Michail S. *Perestrioka: New Thinking for Our Country and the World*. New York: Harper & Row, 1987.

Hamilton, Alexander, John Jay, and James Madison. *The Federalist Papers*. New York: Modern Library, n.d. Hamison, Leopold. *The Russian Marxists and the Origin of Bolshevism*. Boston, Beacon Press, 1955.

Hayward, Max, ed. *On Trial*. New York: Harper & Row, 1967.

Heller, Mikhail, and Alexandr Nekrich. *Utopia in Power: The History of the Soviet Union from 1917 to the Present*. New York: Summit, 1987.

Hobbes, Thomas. *Leviathan*. Cleveland: Meridian Books, 1963.

Hough, Jerry. *Russia and the West: Gorbachev and the Politics of Reform.* New York: Simon and Schuster, 1988.

——. *Soviet Leadership in Transition.* Washington, D.C.: Brookings, 1980.

Hyde, Montgomery. *Stalin.* London: Rupert, Hart & Davis, 1971.

Inkles, Alex, and Raymond Bauer. *The Soviet Citizen.* New York: Atheneum, 1968.

Johnson, Chalmers. *Change in Communist Systems.* Stanford, Calif.: Stanford University Press, 1970.

——. *Revolutionary Change.* Boston: Little, Brown, 1966.

Kanet, Roger E. "Soviet Foreign Policy and the End of the Postwar Era." *PS: Political Science and Politics* (June 1989): 225–31.

Kant, Immanuel. *Critique of Pure Reason,* translated by F. Max Mueller. New York: Macmillan, 1957.

——. *Fundamental Principles of the Metaphysics of Morals,* translated by Thomas K. Abbott. New York: Liberal Arts Press, 1940.

Karklins, Rasma. "Perestroika and Ethnopolitics in the USSR." *PS: Political Science and Politics* 21 (June 1989): 208–14.

Kissinger, Henry. *The White House Years.* Boston: Little, Brown, 1979.

——. *Years of Upheaval.* Boston: Little, Brown, 1982.

Koestler, Arthur. *Darkness at Noon,* translated by Daphne Hardy. New York: Bantam, 1966.

Kuznetsov, Edward. *Prison Diaries,* translated by Howard Spier. New York: Stein & Day, 1975.

Lapenna, Ivo. *Soviet Penal Policy.* London: Bodley Head, 1968.

Laue, Theodore H. Von. *Why Lenin? Why Stalin? A Reappraisal of the Russian Revolution, 1900–1930.* New York: J. B. Lippincott, 1971.

Lenin, Vladimir I. *Collected Works.* 45 vols. London: Lawrence & Wisehart, 1960.

Lincoln, Bruce W. *Passage through Armageddon: The Russians in War, 1914–1918.* New York: Simon and Schuster, 1987.

Linden, Carl A. *Khrushchev and the Soviet Leadership.* Baltimore: Johns Hopkins, 1966.

Machiavelli, Niccolo. *The Prince and the Discourses.* New York: Random House, 1950.

Mandelstam, Nadezhda. *Hope against Hope,* translated by Max Hayward. New York: Antheneum, 1983.

Marchenko, Anatoly. *My Testimony,* translated by Michael Scammell. New York: E. P. Dutton, 1969. Marcuse, Herbert. *Eros and Civilization.* New York: Vintage Books, 1962.

——. *Reason and Revolution.* Boston: Beacon Press, 1969.

Marx, Karl. *Capital.* New York: Modern Library, n.d.

——. *Capital III.* Moscow: Progress Press, 1976.

——. *Collected Works.* 25 vols. to date. New York: International Publishers, 1975.

——. *Critique of Political Economy.* Moscow: Progress Press, 1976.

————. *The German Ideology,* ed. R. Pascal. New York: International Publishers, 1933.

————. *The Poverty of Philosophy.* Moscow: International Publishers, n.d.

Medvedev, Roy. *Let History Judge,* translated by Colleen Taylor. London: Macmillan, 1971.

Mendel, Arthur, ed. *Essential Works of Marxism.* New York: Bantam, 1965.

Merleau-Ponty, Maurice. *Humanism and Terror,* translated by John O'Neill. Boston: Beacon Press, 1969.

Mickiewicz, Ellen. "Mobilization and Reform: Communication Policy under Gorbachev." *PS: Political Science and Politics* 21 (June 1989): 199–207.

Milosz, Czeslaw. *The Captive Mind,* translated by Jane Zielonko. New York: Vintage Books, 1953.

Moore, Barrington, Jr. *Social Origins of Dictatorship and Democracy.* Boston: Beacon Press, 1966.

Nobokov, Vladimir. *The Provisional Government.* New York: John Wiley, 1970.

Odom, William E. "*Glasnost, Perestroika, and Novoye Myshleniye*: Reform in the Soviet Union and Eastern Europe." *PS: Political Science and Politics* 21 (June 1989): 193–98.

Oliva, Jay L. *Russia and the West from Peter the Great to Khrushchev.* Boston: D. C. Heath, 1965.

Pasternak, Boris. *Doctor Zhivago,* translated Max Haywood. New York: Pantheon Books, 1958.

Payne, R. *The Life and Death of Lenin.* New York: Pan, 1964.

Pipes, Richard. *Russia under the Old Regime.* New York: Charles Scribner's Sons, 1974.

————. *The Russian Intelligentsia.* New York: Columbia University Press, 1961.

Plato. *Republic,* translated by Allan Bloom. New York: Basic Books, 1968.

Podhoretz, Norman. "Why Can't You Call a Communist a Communist?" *Washington Post,* 16 March 1986, p. D8.

Remnick, David. "Corrupt Soviet Uzbekistan Learns about 'Our Rotten History.'" *Washington Post,* 7 October 1988, pp. A1, 27.

————. "Lenin's Errors Aired in Pages of *Pravda.*" *Washington Post,* 30 December 1989, p. A12.

Riasanovsky, Nicholas. *A History of Russia.* London: Oxford University Press, 1969.

Rigby, T. H., ed. *The Stalin Dictatorship.* Sydney: Sydney University Press, 1960.

Rubenstein, Joshua. *Soviet Dissidents.* Boston: Beacon Press, 1980.

Sakharov, Andrei. *Progress, Coexistence, and Intellectual Freedom,* translated by *The New York Times.* New York: W. W. Norton, 1968.

Santoli, Al. "Why the Viet Cong Flee." *Washington Post, Parade* section, 11 July 1982, pp. 1–6.

Schapiro, Leonard. *The Communist Party of the Soviet Union.* New York: Vintage Books, 1960.

Seton-Watson, Hugh. *The Decline of Imperial Russia: 1855–1914.* New York: Praeger, 1962.

Shalamov, Varlam. *Kolyma Tales*, translated by John Glad. New York: W. W. Norton, 1980.

Simms, James Y. "The Crisis in Russian Agriculture at the End of the Nineteenth Century: A Different View," *Slavic Review* 36, no. 3 (September 1977): 377–93.

Stalin, Joseph. *Leninism*, translated by Eden and Geden Paul. New York: International Publishers, 1933.

Stevenson, Adlai. *Friends and Enemies*. New York: Harper & Brothers, 1959.

Strauss, Leo. *On Tyranny*. Ithaca, N.Y.: Cornell University Press, 1968.

———, and Joseph Cropsey, eds. *History of Political Philosophy*. New York: Rand McNally, 1972.

Talbott, Strobe, ed. *Khrushchev Remembers*. Boston: Little, Brown, 1971.

Tatu, Michel. *Power in the Kremlin: From Khrushchev to Kosygin*, translated by Helen Katel. New York: Viking Press, 1972.

Tocqueville, Alexis de. *Democracy in America*, translated by George Lawrence. Garden City, N.Y.: Doubleday, 1969.

Tolstoy, Leo. *War and Peace*, translated by Louise and Aylmer Maude. New York: W. W. Norton, 1964.

———. *What Men Live By*, translated by Louise and Aylmer Maude. New York: Pantheon Books, n.d.

Tucker, Robert C., ed. *The Marx-Engels Reader*. New York: W. W. Norton, 1978.

———. *The Marxian Revolutionary Idea*. New York: W. W. Norton, 1970.

———. "Stalin, the Last Bolshevik." *New York Times*, 21 December 1979, p. 35.

———, and S. Cohen, eds. *The Great Purge Trials*. New York: Grosset and Dunlap, 1965.

Ulam, Adam. *A History of the Soviet Russia*. New York: Praeger, 1976.

———. *The Bolsheviks*. New York: Collier Books, 1965.

———. *Lenin and the Bolsheviks*. New York: Fontana, 1966.

Valladares, Armando. *Against All Hope*. New York: Alfred Knopf, 1985.

Voegelin, Eric. *From Enlightenment to Revolution*. Durham: University of North Carolina Press, 1975.

Weisskopf, Michael. "Spring in Peking Is Birdless, Shrubless." *Washington Post*, 26 April 1982, p. A24.

Witten, Thaddeus. *Commissar: The Life and Death of Beria*. New York: Macmillan, 1972.

Wolfe, B. *Three Who Made a Revolution*. New York: Pelican, 1966.

Yanov, Alexander. *The Russian Challenge and the Year 2000*, translated by Iden Rosenthal. Oxford: Basil Blackwell, 1987.

Index